INSIDE FOOTBALL

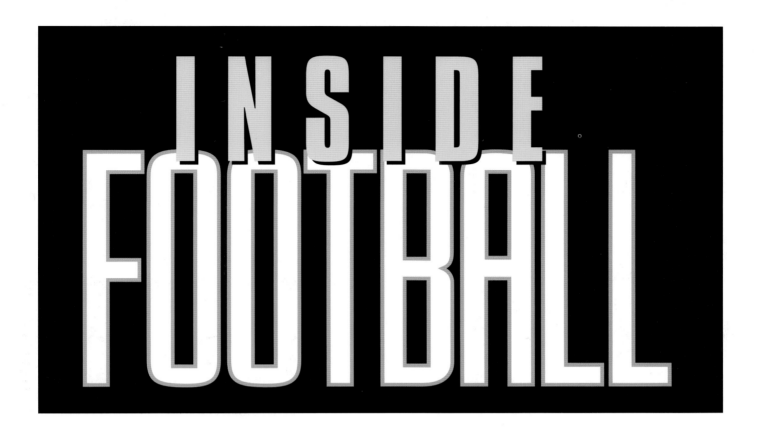

GREG GARBER

MetroBooks

MetroBooks

An Imprint of Friedman/Fairfax Publishers

©1998 by Michael Friedman Publishing Group, Inc.

Library of Congress Cataloging-in-Publication Data

Garber, Greg
    Inside football / by Greg Garber.
        p.   cm.
    Includes bibliographical references and index.
    ISBN 1-56799-420-2
    1. Football—United States—History. I. Title.
    GV950.G37   1998
    796.332—dc21   98-19595

Editors: Nathaniel Marunas and Steve Slaybaugh
Art Director: Kevin Ullrich
Design: Robert Beards Design, Inc.
Photography Editor: Amy Talluto
Photography Researcher: Simone Katz
Production Manager: Susan Kowal

Color separations by HK Scanner Arts Int'l Ltd.
Printed in China by Leefung-Asco Printers Ltd.

10 9 8 7 6 5 4 3 2 1

For bulk purchases and special sales, please contact:
Friedman/Fairfax Publishers
Attention: Sales Department
15 West 26th Street
New York, NY 10010
212/685-6610 FAX 212/685-1307

Visit our website:
http://www.metrobooks.com

ENDPAPERS: Quarterbacks, running backs, and wide receivers get the big money and the headlines, but the game of football, distilled to its essence, can be found in the mayhem of the trenches.

PAGE 2: With Dallas quarterback Troy Aikman under center, the Cowboys were under control all the way in a 30–13 Super Bowl XXVIII victory over Buffalo.

CONTENTS PAGE: Defensive coaches are always asking the players to "get a few hats on that guy." "Hats," in football parlance, are helmets. Here, the New England Patriots, playing the role of Mad Hatters, bury a Miami Dolphins running back.

Dedication

For my family—Gerry, Emily, and Christopher—who patiently wait for me
to return from Dallas or Miami or Buffalo each week of the football season.

Acknowledgments

Thanks are due to numerous people and institutions: the global resources of ESPN, the leader in sports programming; the *Hartford Courant*, which pays me to write about football; the players of the NFL, many of whom shared their secrets and opinions; the league's public relations arm, which facilitates access; the Pro Football Hall of Fame, keeper of treasures and the eternal flame; and my editor, Nathaniel Marunas.

CONTENTS

BEGINNINGS

The scene at Chicago's O'Hare Hilton was chaotic. The National Football League's owners were flying in from all over the country for a special meeting on February 8 and 9, 1996. The Dallas Cowboys had defeated the Pittsburgh Steelers in Super Bowl XXX less than two weeks before, but attention was now focused on the virus infecting one of the most stable organizations in professional sports.

Jerry Jones, the Dallas Cowboys' bombastic owner, drew his usual circle of reporters in a corner of the room at the Hilton. Curiously, though, the infamous star of the session was one Arthur B. Modell. Three months earlier, team owner Modell had stunned the football world by announcing that he was uprooting his Cleveland Browns, a storied and cherished franchise, and taking the team to Baltimore, of all places.

The city of Cleveland, predictably, responded with a venomous lawsuit on behalf of the loyal fans who had filled Cleveland Stadium for so long. The NFL was compelled to negotiate with Mayor Michael White, and on the second day of that winter meeting the bitter terms were announced: Modell could take his team to Baltimore, a city that had lost its beloved Colts to Indianapolis before the 1984 season. But the proud Browns name and the team colors belonged to Cleveland. For dropping the lawsuit, Cleveland received more than $11 million from Modell in damages and lease fees. The NFL in turn promised to lend the city as much as $48 million to build a new stadium and produce another team by 1999—probably a team from another city.

OPPOSITE: Back in the 1920s, Harold "Red" Grange was about as big as a celebrity could be in the United States. When he joined the National Football League in 1925, he brought the fledgling league instant recognition.

After all the press conferences, no one sounded happy. Modell said he would have stayed in Cleveland if the NFL had helped finance a new stadium there. The city was bracing itself for three seasons without football. At the same time, many of the league's owners had resigned themselves to the uncomfortable fact that the NFL was entering a new era, where loyalty and continuity finish second to bottom-line profits.

What began in 1982 when the Oakland Raiders relocated to Los Angeles and continued with the Colts' move two years later had become a full-scale problem by the mid-1990s. The Raiders moved back to Oakland for financial reasons in 1995, the same year the Rams jumped from Los Angeles to St. Louis, which had been vacated by the Cardinals after the 1987 season. Suddenly Los Angeles, a huge metropolis, was without an NFL franchise.

That same season, the Houston Oilers consummated a deal that would land them in Nashville, Tennessee. The Seattle Seahawks, meanwhile, eyed the lucrative Los Angeles market. And then there were Tampa Bay, Cincinnati, and the New England Patriots all casting around for better stadium arrangements.

"It's crazy," conceded Jones after the Cleveland settlement was announced. "But the cost of doing business in the NFL has gone up dramatically. Some of these teams feel they have little choice."

Jones, who made a fortune in the oil and gas business, is actually part of the NFL's prob-

When Cleveland Browns owner Art Modell, seen here circa 1968, moved his franchise to Baltimore in 1996, it left fans bitter.

lem. The original ownership of teams going back to the 1920s is more an exception today than the norm. Jones went against league rules in 1995 and signed an independent marketing deal worth millions with the Nike sports apparel company.

As the NFL celebrated its seventy-fifth birthday, the gap between the NFL's haves and have-nots was widening into a chasm. That wasn't the prevailing philosophy when the league was created in 1920.

A Galloping Success

As the nineteenth century turned into the twentieth, professional football was not exactly a big deal. There were no sold-out seven-

ty-thousand-seat stadiums, no record television ratings, no $5 million player contracts.

In fact, while baseball was inaugurating its World Series in 1903, the Franklin (Pennsylvania) Athletic Club won the second (and last) World Series of professional football over the Oreos A.C. of Asbury Park, New Jersey, the Watertown Red and Blacks, and the Orange Athletic Club. Pro football was in its infancy; the first athlete to openly play for money was John Brallier, who accepted $10 (plus expenses) to play for the Latrobe (Pennsylvania) YMCA in 1895.

The professional game was a rough-and-tumble affair concentrated in parts of Ohio and Pennsylvania. Massillon and Canton were the two powers in the Ohio League. In 1915, Canton signed Olympian Jim Thorpe to star as running back for $250 per game. In 1916, Canton went 9–0–1 and won the Ohio League championship.

In 1920, there was a watershed meeting at the Jordan and Hupmobile auto showroom in Canton on August 20. Management for the Akron Pros, Canton Bulldogs, Cleveland Indians, and Dayton Triangles wrestled with the dire problems facing their sport: escalating player salaries, the use of college players while they were still in school, and the helter-skelter manner in which players jumped from team to team. On that day, the American Professional Football Conference was born. The name was changed a month later to the American Professional Football Association, and Thorpe was elected president. Here was the roster for the league that would become the National Football League two years later: Akron, Canton, Cleveland, and Dayton from Ohio; the Hammond Pros and Muncie Flyers from Indiana; the Rochester Jeffersons from New York; and the Rock Island Independents, Decatur Staleys, and Racine Cardinals from Wisconcin.

The NFL was modestly successful, but the hearts of American sports fans in those days belonged to college football. That all changed in 1925 when Red Grange, "the Galloping Ghost," gave the league instant credibility.

He was a three-time All-America halfback at the University of Illinois, and in his team's November finale he rushed for 192 yards,

Red Grange physically and figuratively carried the ball for the young NFL: when Grange was in the Chicago Bears lineup, big crowds almost always materialized.

completed a touchdown pass, and intercepted a pass to insure a hard-fought 14–9 victory over Ohio State. At that time, he was viewed as the finest college football player in history, on a par with the great athletes of the time, baseball's Babe Ruth and boxing's Jack Dempsey.

"Pro football was pretty questionable in those days," Grange said years later. "Most of the college coaches and the sportswriters were very down on it."

Even Grange's college coach, Bob Zuppke, didn't want him to ruin his reputation by going professional.

"You get paid for coaching, Zup," Grange told him. "Why should it be so wrong for me to get paid for playing? I'll play football, because that's what I do best."

Grange's agent, C.C. ("Cash and Carry") Pyle, saw enormous possibilities. On November 22, Grange signed a contract with the Chicago Bears (née Decatur Staleys) that called for $3,000 per game and a percentage of the gate. He watched from the bench that day as the Bears defeated Green Bay, but four days later, on Thanksgiving Day, he was in the lineup for a game against the Chicago Cardinals. Even though it was snowing, there were an NFL-record thirty-six thousand people in the seats at Wrigley Field. The two teams played to a scoreless tie, largely because the Cardinals repeatedly punted the ball away from Grange. He managed to field only 3 punts, breaking 1 return for 20 yards. Grange gained only 36 yards on the ground and threw 6 incomplete passes, but his postgame receipts were phenomenal: he netted an impressive (for the time) $12,000.

Seeing the potential, the Bears quickly arranged a barnstorming tour that featured eight games in twelve days in St. Louis, Philadelphia, New York, Washington, Boston, Pittsburgh, Detroit, and Chicago. At the first stop, St. Louis, Grange scored 4 touchdowns. In New York on December 6, seventy-three thousand fans filled the Polo Grounds in a game credited with saving football in the nation's largest city. Grange met Babe Ruth and President Calvin Coolidge. When it was over, Grange had an injured arm, but he split $100,000 with Pyle. A second tour that swung through the West netted another $100,000. While in Los Angeles, Pyle arranged for Grange to star in a movie, *One Minute to Play.*

Grange's success launched professional football as a major enterprise, but a year later he defected to the newly created American Football League. Although he never equaled the commercial success of that first NFL season, his athletic style and personality changed the game forever. Now, if the NFL could take advantage of the spark Grange provided . . .

Achieving Stability

The 1930s were a pivotal period for the NFL. It was during this decade that the league took the shape that we recognize today; two divisions were created, a championship was instituted, and in 1936, the NFL held its first college draft. Rivalries between teams, like the Packers and Bears and the Giants and Redskins, began to evolve. Players named Bronko Nagurski, Sid Luckman, and Sammy Baugh graced the NFL's fields.

Before the 1933 season, the NFL made a radical move. Breaking away from the college rules that the league had followed for years, the forward pass was legalized from anywhere behind the line of scrimmage. The Chicago Bears' Bronko Nagurski, one of

history's most feared runners, faked a dive into the line in the 1933 championship game, the league's first formal title game, and feathered a perfect 8-yard pass to Bill Karr. The winning touchdown against the New York Giants came when Nagurski again pretended to run the ball but passed it to teammate Bill Hewitt, who lateraled to Karr, who went 14 yards for the winning score.

The football, which to this point had been a swollen, zeppelin-like affair, was slimmed down in 1934. It was mandated that the axis had to be between $21\frac{1}{4}$ and $21\frac{1}{2}$ inches (54 and 55cm). While this rule diminished the role of the dropkick in the game, it helped the development of the forward pass.

A year later, Green Bay receiver Don Hutson raised pass receiving to an art form. He first came to national attention playing college ball at Alabama, where he caught the well-timed passes of quarterback Dixie Howell. Hutson, at six feet one inch (185cm) and 180 pounds (82kg), had a sprinter's body and speed to go with it.

"You can be as fast as the wind, but it doesn't mean anything if you can't catch the ball," Hutson said. "That's what I prided myself on. At Alabama, we passed twelve, maybe fifteen times a game, which was a lot by those standards. Now, they fling it every chance they get."

Howell and Hutson discovered that they had a decided advantage over opposing defensive backs because the duo knew where the ball was going even before the play started. The Packers took notice and signed Hutson in 1935, matching him with quarterback Arnie Herber. Together, Hutson and Herber made a shambles of the receiving record book. In Hutson's professional debut, they provided the only touchdown, an 83-yard scoring play, on the Packers' first play from scrimmage. When he retired after the 1945 season, Hutson had 488 catches, nearly 300 more than Jim Benton, who was then second on the all-time list.

It was Sammy Baugh, however, who put the new passing game over the top, so to speak. He was a star at Texas Christian University and his versatile style left opposing defenses wondering what was coming. Would Baugh run the ball himself or quick-kick it? Would he pass the ball to a receiver or pitch it back to one of his running backs? It was precisely this kind of uncertainty that appealed to Washington Redskins owner George Preston Marshall, who had moved his team from Boston after the 1936 season.

Baugh, who led the college all-stars to a stunning 6–0 victory over the NFL champion Green Bay Packers in the then-traditional game against the NFL champions, was the Redskins' first draft choice in 1937 and was signed to a $5,000 contract. After much publicity, Baugh proved he was worthy of his press clippings. In his debut, Baugh completed 11 of 16 passes in a 13–3 victory over the

LEFT: Green Bay wide receiver Don Hutson virtually invented the pass route in the 1930s.

OPPOSITE: Chicago T-formation quarterback Sid Luckman helped usher the NFL into a new era: the air era.

New York Giants. When the Redskins reached the championship game, Baugh did not look like a rookie. He passed for 335 yards and 3 touchdowns, carrying the Redskins to a 28–21 win.

The Single Wing, featuring an unbalanced line, two deep running backs, a blocking quarterback, and a wingback set outside, was embraced as the formation of the future. Though he often ran the ball, Baugh managed to lead the league in passing three of his eight seasons as a single-wing tailback.

By 1944, however, change was in the air—literally. The Wing-T formation removed many of the running responsibilities from a gifted passer. Washington coach Dudley DeGroot installed Baugh as his quarterback in the new system, and Baugh earned three more NFL passing titles. In 1939, Sid Luckman joined the Chicago Bears and became the greatest T-formation quarterback of his time. Thanks to Hutson, Baugh, and Luckman, the game would never be the same.

A Level Playing Field

The 1940s opened for the NFL in inauspicious fashion. Baugh's Washington Redskins somehow lost to the Chicago Bears 73–0 in the league's championship game. Worse, it was the first football game ever carried by network radio. Sportscaster Red Barber called the one-sided action for the 120-station Mutual Broadcasting System.

There were three NFL games under way when the Japanese attacked Pearl Harbor on December 7, 1941, and the league spent a decade trying to regain the momentum it had produced in the 1930s. More than six hundred people involved with the league gave their time to the war effort. Attendance dropped dramatically as a nation focused on more important matters.

Fifty years before Cleveland Browns owner Art Modell created enormous turmoil by moving his team to Baltimore, another move by the Cleveland franchise changed the look of the league. The Cleveland Rams had won the NFL title in 1945 with a compelling 15–14 victory over the Redskins, but twenty-seven days later owner Dan Reeves moved his champions to Los Angeles. While the move stunned league observers, it eventually worked out well for both cities.

The Rams prospered, drawing nearly forty thousand fans to each of their games. Cleveland, meanwhile, embraced an entry in the fledgling All-America Football Conference. The team was called the Browns, after their coach, Paul Brown, and they won the first AAFC championship, defeating the New York Yankees, 14–9.

Very quietly, the Rams made another first in March 1946 when they signed UCLA running back Kenny Washington to a contract. Washington was black. There had been black men in professional football before, but never on a major league team. And while Jackie Robinson is credited with breaking the color barrier in professional sports, consider that Washington arrived a year earlier. In an

"Slingin'" Sammy Baugh was the first and the best of the single-wing tailbacks.

incredible coincidence, Washington and Robinson actually played together in the UCLA backfield in 1939.

"He was the greatest football player I have ever seen," Robinson said of Washington. "He had everything needed for greatness—size, speed, and tremendous strength. I'm sure that he had a deep hurt over the fact that he had never become a national figure. It would be a shame if he were to be forgotten."

From 1937 to 1939 Washington broke UCLA's running and passing records and managed to outhit Robinson by 200 points in baseball. When Reeves moved his Rams to Los Angeles, he pursued the Los Angeles Coliseum as the team's home. One of the lease stipulations: a tryout for Washington, a favorite son. And although the NFL had an unwritten policy against black players, Reeves signed Washington and UCLA teammate Woody Strode. History was made.

By the time he reached the NFL, Washington was twenty-eight years old and had two banged-up knees. Two years later, after gaining a modest 859 yards, his knees forced him to retire. Also in

THE BALTIMORE RAVENS

On a gray, chilly March afternoon, exactly twelve years to the day after the Colts left Baltimore behind, the city named its new National Football League team the Ravens.

The team's players and management were still very much the Cleveland Browns, but the name and the team's rich history were left behind in Cleveland; actually, the cartons of artifacts were stored under lock and key at the Pro Football Hall of Fame in Canton, Ohio. It was part of an early 1996 settlement with Cleveland when owner Art Modell left the city for a better financial deal in Baltimore.

The fans themselves made the choice; of 33,288 fans voting in the *Baltimore Sun*'s phone-in poll, 21,108 chose the "Ravens." The "Americans" (5,597) and "Marauders" (5,583) were distant runners-up. It was Edgar Allan Poe, one of Baltimore's most famous sons, who immortalized the dark and sinister bird in his poem "The Raven."

"It gives us a strong nickname that is not common to teams at any level, and it gives us one that means something his-torically to this community," Modell said on the day the winning nickname was announced. "This is a new beginning and a new era for us, and it will be for you, too. Our job now is to reward you with a winning team, and we're going to."

1946, the Cleveland Browns signed two black players, guard Bill Willis and fullback Marion Motley, who both went on to long and productive careers.

After World War II ended, the NFL enjoyed unprecedented popularity. The NFL and the rival AAFC drew fans in record numbers. The question on most people's minds: how would the Browns, who won all four AAFC championships from 1946 to 1949 and produced an amazing record of 51–4–3, stack up against the more established NFL teams? The 1950 season would hold the answer.

A New Frontier

Paul Brown's Cleveland team was easily the best of the upstart league; the Browns signed forty of the 1946 college all-star team's players and welcomed more than a hundred former NFL players into the AAFC fold. In 1950 the NFL, with the steady hand of commissioner Bert Bell, acknowledged the strength of the AAFC by absorbing its better components.

The franchises in Cleveland, Baltimore, and San Francisco joined the NFL, and the league's thirteen teams drafted the remaining players from the disbanded AAFC. Bell, capitalizing on the interest in the league's new dynamic, immediately brought the debate to the playing field. In the first game of the season, reigning AAFC champion Cleveland met the defending NFL champion, Philadelphia. The Eagles were favored by 6 points in what newspapers called "the most talked-about game in NFL history."

The Browns throttled the Eagles, 35–10. The championship game that year was far less one-sided. Cleveland went 10–2 during the regular season and, after dispatching the Giants in the playoffs, met the Los Angeles Rams in the championship game. The Rams were winning, 28–27, but Cleveland placekicker Lou Groza converted a 16-yard field goal with twenty-eight seconds left to give the Browns the title, 30–28. Cleveland went on to appear in the next four championship games.

Three new teams, the adoption of the free substitution rule, and better-schooled players all combined to make the game more popular. Perhaps the greatest fan-friendly development involved television. The Rams had become the first NFL team to televise all of its games, both home and away, in 1950 but the new technology had a disastrous effect at the Los Angeles Coliseum: attendance was cut nearly in half. After 1950, the Rams televised only away

Signed off the sandlots, the Baltimore Colts' Johnny Unitas blossomed into one of the NFL's great all-time quarterbacks.

games, a policy that to this day has helped the league entrench itself with the nation's fans.

Nothing boosted the game, however, more than the combination of television and the marvelous 1958 championship game. In retrospect, it was the sport's breakthrough game. The powerful Cleveland Browns might have been the best match for the Baltimore Colts, the Western Conference champions, but the New York Giants beat them in back-to-back games to reach the final.

The Giants took a 3–0 lead on a field goal by placekicker Pat Summerall, who had been the difference in a 24–21 regular-season victory. A Frank Gifford fumble, however, gave Baltimore the ball on the Giants' 20-yard line and quarterback Johnny Unitas handed off the ball six straight times, the last from 2 yards out to full-back Alan Ameche to give the Colts a 7–3 second-quarter lead. A pass from Unitas to Raymond Berry made it 14–3.

Baltimore seemed to have the game in hand early in the third quarter, but three straight running plays from the Giants' 3-yard line failed to yield a touchdown. On fourth-and-goal, Unitas sent Ameche wide to exploit the Giants' packed-in defense. The Giants,

however, saw the play coming and stuffed Ameche for a 4-yard loss. Mel Triplett's 1-yard touchdown dive narrowed the score to 14–10 and Charlie Conerly's 15-yard pass to Gifford gave the Giants a 17–14 lead. Beginning with 1:56 left, Unitas rallied the Colts down the field and a 20-yard field goal by Steve Myrha tied the game at 17 with seven seconds left; the game went into overtime.

Never before had a championship game been decided in sudden death; the crowd at Yankee Stadium and a nation watching at home on television were captivated. The Giants were forced to punt on the first possession and Baltimore started a drive from its own 20-yard line. Unitas engineered a drive that brought the ball to the Giants' 1-yard line. There, Ameche took a handoff from Unitas and slipped behind a block from halfback Lenny Moore off right tackle. Ameche scored standing up, and 8:15 into overtime the greatest game in NFL history ended with a 23–17 Colts victory.

A Different League

The 1960s in America were a decade marked by turbulence. In football, it was no different.

The NFL had seen a handful of new leagues try to capitalize on the game it popularized, but never was there a greater threat than the American Football League. Lamar Hunt, an oil man from Texas, put the AFL together in 1959 and, with investors secured, asked NFL commissioner Bert Bell if he would preside over both leagues. When Bell died in October 1959, so did the last chance for a peaceful coexistence.

Originally, Hunt's new league had six franchises: Dallas, Denver, Houston, Los Angeles, Minneapolis, and New York. But when the NFL countered by offering Minnesota an expansion franchise, the AFL placed teams in Oakland, Buffalo, and Boston. The competition for talent quickly escalated.

Los Angeles Rams general manager Pete Rozelle actually signed 1959 Heisman Trophy winner Billy Cannon to an undated contract during his final season at Louisiana State University. The terms—a $10,000 signing bonus and a $10,000 first-year salary followed by two years at $15,000 each—were exorbitant at the time.

But the Houston Oilers signed Cannon after his final game to a staggering three-year contract that guaranteed him $110,000. The Rams went to court, but a judge ruled the Oilers' contract valid and the first round went to the AFL.

The Oilers won the first AFL championship over the Los Angeles Chargers, 24–16. And though the young league supplemented its rosters with NFL players clearly past their prime, the AFL would ultimately change the face of football.

It didn't receive much attention at the time, but on January 26, 1960, Rozelle was elected the NFL's new commissioner. The Rams executive was a compromise choice—finally selected on the twenty-third ballot—but his twenty-nine-year rule would turn the NFL into the most prominent international professional sports league. Rozelle had a hand in bringing the NFL and AFL together in 1966, a merger that strengthened the league enormously.

While retaining separate schedules through the 1969 season, the two leagues agreed to play a championship game. That first

Pittsburgh running back Franco Harris ran past the Raiders and every other team on his way to enshrinement in the Pro Football Hall of Fame in Canton, Ohio.

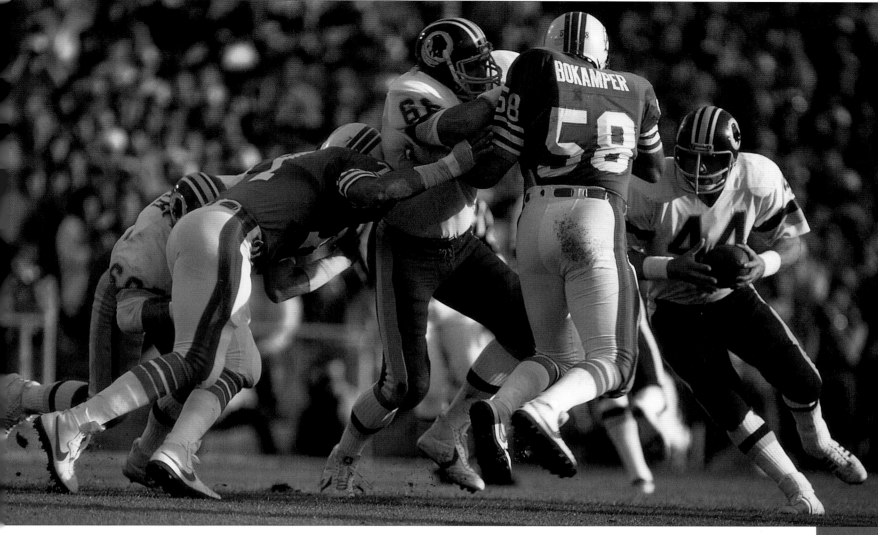

Washington Redskins running back John Riggins, whose career began in the watershed 1970s, turns upfield.

meeting was hardly superb, but the Kansas City Chiefs and the Green Bay Packers made history when they met on January 15, 1967. Vince Lombardi's Packers defeated the Chiefs, 35–10, before 61,946 spectators at the Los Angeles Coliseum.

The Packers won again the following year, beating the Oakland Raiders, 33–14, but the third Super Bowl produced an astonishing result. Led by brash quarterback Joe Namath, the New York Jets stunned the Baltimore Colts, 16–7, in a game that lent credibility to the AFL and the coming merger.

Best and Brightest

In many ways, the 1970s represented the game of professional football at its zenith. When the NFL celebrated its seventy-fifth anniversary in 1995, a blue-ribbon selection committee was commissioned to determine the greatest players of all time. Twenty-nine of the forty-eight players chosen were active for some part of the 1970s—far and away more than any other decade. When a Pro Football Hall of Fame committee selected the league's forty greatest games, fourteen were played in the 1970s.

Some highlights:

- New Orleans placekicker Tom Dempsey, who was born with only a partial kicking foot, boots a record 63-yard field goal against Detroit on November 8, 1970.
- Pittsburgh running back Franco Harris makes "the Immaculate Reception" to defeat the Oakland Raiders in the 1972 playoffs.

- The 1972 Miami Dolphins make history by winning all of their games, including the American Football Conference final against the Steelers. The 17–0 Dolphins set the record with a 14–7 victory over Washington in Super Bowl VII.
- Buffalo running back Orenthal James Simpson runs for 200 yards in the regular-season finale against the New York Jets on December 16, 1973. Simpson finishes the year with an awesome total of 2,003 rushing yards, a new record.
- The Pittsburgh Steelers defeat the Dallas Cowboys in Super Bowl XIII, 35–31, to become the first team ever to win three Super Bowls. The television audience is estimated at ninety-six million.

In 1970, the NFL went to the conference configuration we know today. Three teams—the Baltimore Colts, Cleveland Browns, and Pittsburgh Steelers—agreed to play in the AFC for a hefty $3 million relocation fee. The league was then divided into six divisions.

ABC's Monday Night Football was also born in 1970. There were three men in the broadcasting booth: play-by-play announcer Keith Jackson, former Dallas Cowboys quarterback Don Meredith, and the acerbic Howard Cosell. Frank Gifford replaced Jackson after the first season and America had a new cultural phenomenon.

From the beginning, NFL action buoyed what might otherwise be dull Sundays. Here, the New York Giants and Philadelphia Eagles tear it up.

A Moving Decade

All those good games and great players translated to the NFL's monstrous appeal in the 1980s. The 1980 regular-season attendance total of nearly 13.4 million was a record for the third year in a row. The average paid attendance for the 224-game schedule was 59,787, the highest in the league's sixty-one-year history. Television ratings that season were the second-highest in history, not far behind the network numbers posted in 1976.

Still, there was a restless quality to the game, especially in the West. The Rams moved from the Los Angeles Coliseum, their home since 1946, to Anaheim Stadium in Orange County. The Raiders moved to Los Angeles under more difficult circumstances.

When the NFL blocked owner Al Davis' move from Oakland to Los Angeles in 1980, Davis went to court, joining the Los Angeles Coliseum suit that contended the league's policy violated antitrust laws. On May 7, 1982, a Los Angeles federal court agreed with Davis and the Coliseum. And so the Raiders, who defeated the Philadelphia Eagles, 27–10, in Super Bowl XV on January 25, 1981, were permitted to move to Los Angeles for the 1982 season.

On the field, there were some dramatic moves as well.

When the Dallas Cowboys met the San Francisco 49ers on January 10, 1982, the Cowboys were bidding for their sixth Super Bowl appearance in twelve years. The 49ers, of course, hadn't yet been in one. Not surprisingly, the Cowboys led, 27–21, with just under five minutes left in the National Football Conference championship game. Somehow, San Francisco drove 83 yards, all the way to the Dallas 6-yard line. There were fifty-eight seconds left when Joe Montana, in his first year as starting quarterback, dropped back to pass. The play, sprint-option right, was designed

to go to wide receiver Freddie Solomon, but he was covered. Seeing Montana in trouble, Dwight Clark, the other 49ers wide receiver, ran along the back of the end zone toward the right corner. Throwing off his back foot, Montana heaved the ball in Clark's direction. The lithe wideout elevated and managed to come down with the ball, and "the Catch," as it became known in the Bay Area, put the 49ers on the map. It would lead to San Francisco's 26–21 victory over the Cincinnati Bengals in Super Bowl XVI, the first championship for the franchise in its thirty-two NFL seasons.

The 49ers would win three more Super Bowls in the 1980s; the Cowboys would never get there in that decade.

In 1982, the pull and tug seen across the nation between management and employees spilled into the NFL. At midnight on September 20, minutes after the Monday Night Football game between the Green Bay Packers and New York Giants, the players walked off the job. For fifty-seven days, in the heart of autumn, there was no professional football. In the end, the players came back, armed with minimum salary schedules, better training camp and postseason compensation, and improved medical insurance and retirement benefits. That left time for only seven more regular-season games and an unsettling Super Bowl tournament. Two teams with losing records—Detroit and Cleveland—made it into the field but the two best teams reached the final game. The Redskins prevailed over the Dolphins, 27–17, after Washington's John Riggins' 38 carries gave him a Super Bowl–record 166 yards. It was the Redskins' first title in forty seasons.

Officiating football games is, at best, an imperfect science; seven men attempt to patrol nearly half a million cubic feet (14,000 cu m) of airspace. On March 11, 1986, the NFL's owners approved the limited use of instant replay for the first time in history. When

THE JFK ASSASSINATION

On November 22, 1963, the Dallas Cowboys were practicing at their training complex when President John F. Kennedy was shot five miles (8km) away at Dealey Plaza.

"I remember we were right in the middle of practice," says Hall of Fame coach Tom Landry. "Someone came out and said, 'The President has been shot.'"

Hall of Fame defensive tackle Bob Lilly says, "We were sick, basically. We were just nauseous. It was just sickening. It just killed practice."

Two days later, after NFL commissioner Pete Rozelle made the agonizing and controversial decision to play the NFL's full Sunday schedule, the Cowboys played the Browns in Cleveland. When they arrived, the porters at the airport and the bellhops at the team's hotel wouldn't touch any of the Cowboys' luggage, nor the crates with the footballs, uniforms, and equipment.

People screamed, "Kennedy killers! Kennedy killers!"

The Browns organization postponed "Ray Renfro Day" and assigned extra police to protect the Dallas ownership group in the stands and the players on the bench.

The Cowboys' George Andrie was concerned for his personal safety. Word had come to the teams before the game that Jack Ruby had shot Kennedy's killer, Lee Harvey Oswald.

"We were told to keep our helmets on before the game and at halftime because they didn't know what was going to happen," Andrie says. "I think from the back of my mind, I was always wondering if there was a guy in the upper deck with a rifle or something, taking a bead on me."

Dallas' Don Perkins said, "We went out for the pre-game warmup and it was like a morgue. You didn't feel the enthusiasm. The Browns were lethargic on their side of the field, too."

The flag was at half-mast. The players and fifty-five thousand fans stood at attention for taps and the national anthem. And then there was a moment of silent prayer for the slain president.

"The game was played in entire silence," remembers Cleveland owner Art Modell. "There was no emotion, no cheering, nothing. It was like playing in a studio."

Lilly says it was the only game in his career that he didn't want to play.

"It looked kind of like zombies [playing]," he says. "I mean, we all had our capes on on the sidelines because the weather was dreary. Nobody was jumping up and down; everyone had a long face."

There was no television coverage and the Oswald shooting preempted the radio coverage. The Browns won, 27–17, and moved into first place. Cowboys quarterback Don Meredith threw 4 interceptions and the Browns' Frank Ryan threw 3.

And though the Cowboys would later become known as "America's Team," for several years following the assassination, the players were reminded by fans around the league of what happened in Dallas that November day.

"'Murderers, you murdered John Kennedy,' they yelled at us," says the Cowboys' Lee Roy Jordan. "If you were close enough to be at the sidelines, it was you who did it, not the guy who actually pulled the trigger."

Cleveland running back Jim Brown rambles for 10 yards against the Cowboys.

CHARACTERS OF THE GAME

In the old, raucous days of the National Football League, players' salaries equaled those of school teachers, off-season conditioning was an oxymoron, and everyone, it seemed, was a character.

Today's NFL is a little more buttoned-down. When the league cracked down on excessive end zone celebrations a few years ago, the players called it the "No Fun League." Sure, "Neon" Deion Sanders is an interesting personality, but he is essentially a global marketing phenomenon. Today, very rarely do players eat raw meat for laughs.

Listen to Al LoCasale, executive assistant to Oakland Raiders owner Al Davis: "In the old days with the Raiders squads, with the Marv Hubbards, the Phil Villapianos, people like that, if somebody

from the commissioner's office came into the locker room before the game and said, 'TV just went out of business, there's no more contract, we're playing for $100 a man but the team that loses goes out and buys the beer,' they would all get dressed up and go out and play. That's not the way it would be today."

Joe Browne, the NFL's senior vice president for communications and government affairs, disagrees.

"I think there's a perception that cars aren't made as well as they used to be, that people aren't as friendly as they used to be, and that players aren't as colorful as they used to be," Browne says. "And I don't believe that."

Browne refers to two Raiders players now retired, Howie Long and Bob Golic, as characters of the game.

"It's hard to be a character and a little bit of a thug when you're making $800,000 and you're getting your clothes dry-cleaned," responded Long, now a Fox television analyst.

Salaries, which have escalated dramatically in recent years, have tended to restrain players from straying too far from the norm. And then there are the actual rules. For example, Rule 5, Section 3, Article 6 states: "Towels are limited to a maximum of 12 inches [30.5cm] in length and must be tucked into the front of the pant[s]."

"Just about every week," Golic says, "we get the notice from the league, talking about guys whose uniforms don't conform. And for me, it's like, 'Hey, close enough.' Black, silver—what else do you want?"

The Raiders' Howie Long, "a little bit of a thug," breaks through the Chargers' line.

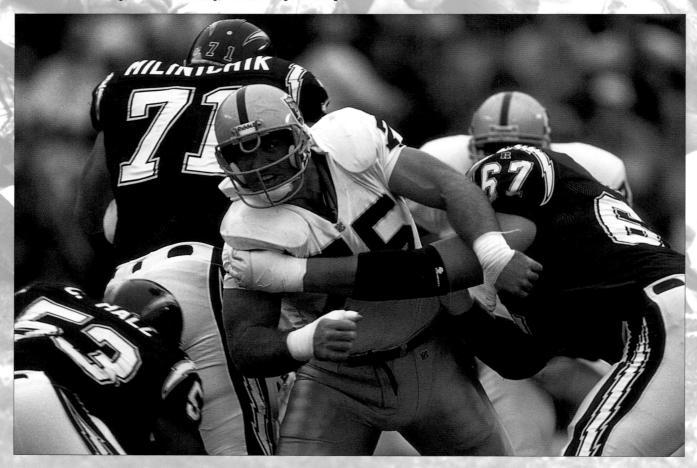

The Buffalo Bills always managed to fall short of superb in the NFL's ultimate game.

the dust settled, the league's officials were vindicated. Of the 374 plays that were scrutinized by the review process, only 38 were reversed. If only the Buffalo Bills could have reversed the result in one or two of their Super Bowl games in the coming decade.

Toward the Millennium

On January 30, 1994, the Buffalo Bills made some uneasy history in Super Bowl XXVIII: they became the first team to appear in the NFL's ultimate game four years in a row. The fact that the Bills lost to the Dallas Cowboys, 30–13, and, incredibly, lost all four games by a combined score of 139–73 makes the Bills' indomitable spirit even more remarkable.

"What are we going to do, stop trying to get to the game because we lost a few?" asked Buffalo quarterback Jim Kelly at the team's 1994 training camp. "In football, you try to win every time out. That's what we'll do this year, too."

The Bills lost their edge that season, winning only seven games, but the NFL has always been about change. Sixty years after Art Rooney picked up the Pittsburgh Steelers for some loose change ($2,500), the NFL commanded a price tag of $140 million for each of its two new expansion franchises, Carolina and Jacksonville, in 1993. The league's roster had climbed to thirty teams and television rights had soared well past the $1 billion mark. The new network on the block was Fox, which outspent longtime NFL supporter CBS for the National Conference package. Fox bid an amazing $1.6 billion for the rights to televise four seasons' worth of games.

The NFL made a concentrated effort in the 1990s to establish football beyond the continental United States. After five years of American Bowl games in such locales as London, Tokyo, Montreal, and Berlin, the NFL launched the World League in 1991. It was jointly a developmental league for young players and a way for football to find fans around the globe. The London Monarchs defeated the Barcelona Dragons, 21–0, in World Bowl 1991.

While the Dallas Cowboys and head coach Jimmy Johnson drew most of the attention in the 1990s for winning back-to-back

Super Bowls to crown the 1992 and 1993 seasons, Miami Dolphins coach Don Shula was making history that almost certainly will never be repeated.

Shula took over for Baltimore head coach Weeb Ewbank in 1963. Shula was just thirty-three years old, making him the youngest coach in NFL history. In seven seasons with the Colts, Shula was 73–26–4. He joined the Dolphins in 1970 and continued to have unprecedented success. He had the NFL's first undefeated team in 1972 and piled up six Super Bowl appearances.

On November 14, 1993, Shula broke the record for coaching victories when the Dolphins defeated the Philadelphia Eagles, 19–14. It was his 325th coaching win, surpassing the record of George Halas.

"I'm proud of that record because it primarily represents team success over a long period of time," Shula said. "I've always felt that if you prepared as hard as you possibly can each and every week and then played well on Sunday, the numbers would take care of themselves."

After the 1995 season, following his thirty-third NFL season and 347 victories (balanced by only 172 defeats), Shula stepped down as coach of the Dolphins. H. Wayne Huizenga, who had bought the team two years earlier, had eyes for Johnson, who had broken with Cowboys owner Jerry Jones after the 1993 season.

In 1995, an ABC News poll taken during the NFL off-season revealed that American sports fans embraced football as their favorite spectator sport. The final tally was more than a 2-to-1 margin over basketball and baseball (35 percent vs. 16 and 12, respectively). Heading into the 1998 season, the NFL was on unprecedented footing after signing a series of contracts with the television networks worth $17.6 billion over the course of eight seasons. Additionally, there were whispers that the next two expansion franchises might command figures approaching $500 million each.

And so, the NFL was solidly entrenched as an American tradition as the millennium approached. Red Grange would have been extremely proud.

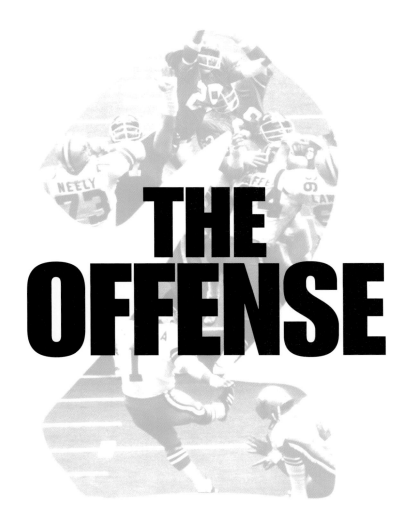

THE OFFENSE

If you think about it, offense versus defense is not exactly a fair fight in the modern era. That's why you don't see too many 0–0 games these days.

Bart Oates, the former center who won three Super Bowl rings in his career with the New York Giants and San Francisco 49ers, has a pretty good handle on offenses.

"We're in the huddle and the quarterback is getting the play relayed to him from the sidelines,"

Oates says. "The quarterback makes the call and we're all there listening, thinking about what our responsibilities are going to be. We know where we're going, exactly what we're going to do. The defense? They have no clue."

Offense is organization and clinical efficiency, as opposed to facing the void of the unknown. Brains versus brawn is clearly an unfair generalization, but offensive players, as a rule, are a pretty sensitive, well-mannered group. Why, some offenses even hold hands in the huddle—demonstrating a very '90s sort of solidarity. Defenses wouldn't get caught dead holding hands.

Look at the Giants offensive line that won Super Bowl XXI against the Denver Broncos. By today's standards, those five players were undersize, averaging about 270 pounds (123kg) each. What they lacked in girth they made up in guile.

Left tackle Brad Benson was an overachieving finesse player who today owns one of the country's most successful Jaguar dealerships. Left guard Billy Ard is a stockbroker in New Jersey. The right guard was Chris Godfrey, a genteel fellow who could discuss psychology even in the heat of the locker room. Right tackle Karl Nelson had a wonderful nickname from taciturn coach Bill Parcells: "Cinnamon,"

OPPOSITE: Wide receiver Jerry Rice, the ultimate San Francisco treat, rises to the occasion over Dallas cornerback Deion Sanders.

The Giants' offensive line in Super Bowl XXI was relatively undersized, but the five starters intelligently dissected the Denver defense.

after the cinnamon rolls he used to bring from home. Nelson's second career was financial services. And what of Oates? Even while he was finishing up his career in San Francisco, Oates passed the New Jersey bar and practiced as a lawyer. Not bad for a bunch of hurly-burly football knuckleheads, eh?

So, if you are offered input into the future son-in-law decision process, think offense versus defense. Who would you rather have supporting your daughter into old age, Jerry Rice or, say, Jack Lambert? Troy Aikman or Lawrence Taylor?

As former Giants general manager George Young likes to say, football is not exactly a sport for the well adjusted. It's just that offensive players are a little more in step with the real world.

Offense has another advantage. Offense sells—always has.

In football's infancy, touchdowns were not fully recognized as the monumental and inspirational achievements they are today; they were worth only 4 points. Then, as football's brain trust began to see the marketing possibilities, the touchdown became worth 5 points in 1898 and, finally, the present-day 6 points in 1912. The mundane field goal dropped from 5 points to 4 to 3 in that same period of time.

In 1933, the first year they kept track of points in standings, the Chicago Bears won the league title with a record of 10–2–1. They scored a dizzying total of 133 points, or an average of just over 10 per game. The 1985 Bears, a team noted for its wild-and-woolly defense, scored an amazing 456 points in winning 15 of their 16

regular-season games. That works out to 28.5 points each time out—a total that might have pained founding father George "Papa Bear" Halas, a purist who, by the way, grew up playing on the offensive side of the ball.

The NFL, recognizing that a beautifully coordinated 38-yard touchdown pass is far more compelling than a 1-yard gain off tackle has always aided and abetted the offensive side. Was it a coincidence that after the 1932 championship game—a gruesomely dull 9–0 affair won by the Bears—the forward pass was legalized? The only spark of excitement in that game was a touchdown pass, a nifty little a piece of heresy, from fullback Bronko Nagurski to Red Grange.

Every season, it seems, brings new advantages for offensive players, whether it's liberalized blocking rules, stricter pass defense measures, or protection of the quarterback to almost ridiculous proportions. In 1994, the NFL went even further. It adopted college's 2-point conversion rule. The combination of better placekickers and stagnant offenses had reduced the touchdowns-to-field-goals ratio to 4-to-3, and the league attempted to make the traditional 6-point score more appealing. The net effect was only marginal; teams went for 2 points after touchdowns only in limited situations. Still, the intent was there.

Quick! When you think of NFL stars, who comes to mind? Aeneas Williams or Terry McDaniel? Merton Hanks or Eric Turner? Perhaps not. Those were the starters in the 1995 Pro Bowl

If you are a quarterback, one of your worst nightmares is Green Bay Packers defensive end Reggie White blowing through the back door and sacking you from behind.

at right cornerback and free safety, respectively. These are as opposed to the starting quarterbacks, Steve Young and John Elway, whose name recognition rivals Bill Clinton's. This sort of bias can be seen even in the Pro Football Hall of Fame. For example, there are seven cornerbacks enshrined in Canton, Ohio, but there are twenty-three quarterbacks. What a difference three or four letters can make.

Over the years, offenses have evolved to the point that having a major in quantum physics does not guarantee an understanding of the schemes employed today. There are a myriad of complicated offensive plays, including the No-Huddle offense, the Run-and-Shoot, the five-wide receiver set, etc., etc.

"Pretty soon," muses Oates, "it's going to take a law degree to understand what's going on out there." When the time comes, Oates will be ready—he's already making a living in his second career as a lawyer in New Jersey.

The Quarterback

The next time the quarterback for your favorite professional team spins to avoid a violent pass rush, scrambles to his right, and sends a pass whistling over the head of an open receiver, do not rise from your armchair and curse. Think back to those high school days, perhaps those sandlot afternoons in the fall when you took a giddy turn under center. Remember the general feeling of hysteria when the pass rusher closed in and forced you to throw the ball away? And you never had to face a charging Reggie White in ill humor, either.

On the surface, anyway, the quarterback's job is a glamorous one. He gets the big contract and all the media attention, and he always gets the girl. There is a downside, however. Two or three times a game, someone like Bryce Paup or Leslie O'Neal is going to drill you. And for every official sack there is a handful of whacks and smacks and some exceedingly annoying behavior that interferes with the concentration needed to properly execute the position.

The quarterback gets credit for victory, but he also is the most convenient scapegoat when the team loses. The pressure on a quarterback is almost unnatural; he has the ball in his hand, but he is truly at the mercy of the twenty-one other players on the field.

"The quarterback position is different from any other position," says Dallas quarterback Troy Aikman, who had already led the Cowboys to three Super Bowl victories before he reached the age of thirty. "I have to know the calls, the reads, what the receivers are doing on routes, what our [blocking] protection is. The other guys just have to know what they're doing, and that's it."

Style and Substance

Although quarterbacks won the Most Valuable Player Award in sixteen of the first thirty Super Bowls, there are times when they rise above the other players on the field—times when they transcend the sport. The booming success of the league, in some ways, can be traced to two quarterbacks: Johnny Unitas and Joe Namath. They are both enshrined in the Pro Football Hall of Fame, but Unitas and Namath resided at opposite ends of the style spectrum, from their heads to their toes.

Unitas almost missed out on the NFL—or was it vice versa? He was a walk-on at the University of Louisville, and the Pittsburgh Steelers took the 145-pounder (66kg) in the ninth round of the 1955 draft. He hadn't had the opportunity to throw a pass in the regular season when the Steelers cut him loose. The Bloomfield Rams, the local semiprofessional team, were happy to have Unitas calling their signals. The Rams paid him $6 a game for his considerable services. A tip from a Bloomfield fan prompted a call from Baltimore Colts coach Weeb Ewbank. Years later, Ewbank liked to say that Unitas cost the Colts 80¢, the cost of a phone call from Baltimore to Pittsburgh. Ewbank was impressed with Unitas and offered him a $17,000 contract. The rest, as they say, is history.

Unitas, in his black high-top cleats and razor-sharp crew cut, was from the old school. He wasn't flashy, just effective. Many football experts believe, with all due respect to Joe Montana, that Unitas is the greatest quarterback in history. He played in ten Pro Bowls and won the NFL's MVP Award three times. On three occasions he directed the Colts to the league championship.

In his signature game, the 1958 championship, Unitas helped football win over an entire nation. Television had just recently focused its cameras on the NFL, and in 1958 the Colts and New

Jets quarterback Joe Namath was the perfect player to cement the young alliance between the AFL and NFL: overwhelming substance in a stylish package.

Quarterback Joe Montana, under pressure from Denver, leaves his San Francisco office rather abruptly.

York Giants authored a marvelous and dramatic game. With two minutes left, the Giants led, 17–14, but Unitas guided the Colts to a game-tying field goal at the end of regulation. And so, the NFL had its first sudden-death championship. It was Unitas who drove the Colts 80 yards. His final handoff, to Alan Ameche, resulted in the winning score 8:15 into overtime, the precise time America began to notice professional football.

Everything the old-school Unitas was, Namath wasn't. He had long hair and flashy white shoes. He was not afraid to speak his mind, even if it meant offending opponents. Seven years after the Colts and Giants raised the game to a new level, the University of Alabama quarterback was the object of a heated bidding war. The New York Jets of the upstart American Football League offered the college star a staggering $400,000, the fattest contract in professional football history. Namath, cocky as ever, thought he was worth it; he spurned the NFL and signed with the AFL.

In retrospect, Namath was worth every cent, not just to the Jets but to the entire AFL. Eighteen months after Namath bucked tradition, the NFL and AFL merged. And just when the skeptics wondered why in the world the NFL would weaken its talent pool, Namath had an answer: Super Bowl III.

"I guarantee we are going to win the Super Bowl," Namath told anyone who would listen, leading up to the January 1969 contest between the Colts and the Jets. The Las Vegas experts rated the Jets as 17-point underdogs, but Namath carried the Jets past the

15–1 Colts. The Jets were actually leading, 16–0, in the fourth quarter when Unitas finally got Baltimore into the end zone. Namath completed 17 of 28 passes for 206 yards and the Jets won, 16–7.

While Namath and Unitas were contrasts in style, their fundamental skills were actually quite similar. It doesn't take much to succeed at quarterback: only dazzling physical skills, enormous cunning and courage, and the ability to lead a team to victory. The oldest sports cliché in the book is that the quarterback is a field general. Like most clichés, this one is true, except that no general ever had to play in the pocket.

Eye of the Storm

The quarterback's office is a little piece of real estate called the pocket. Like snowflakes, no two pockets are ever alike. Each pocket is created and destroyed in a single play. Standing in the pocket, a loose collection of blockers fending off opposition pass rushers, can be a surreal experience, yet it is painfully real and volatile, oddly tranquil and at once comforting and terrifying.

"You can look at this game film and you can look at that game film," says New York Jets quarterback Neil O'Donnell, who led the Pittsburgh Steelers to Super Bowl XXX. "But it's nothing like it ever is when you're out there in the pocket. It's totally different." Minnesota quarterback Warren Moon, the first professional quarterback to reach 60,000 passing yards, says, "It's like being in the middle of a gang fight, but you're not the guy who's fighting."

No less an authority than Joe Montana says trying to stay in the pocket is like waiting to make a left-hand turn into heavy traffic. While literally a ton of humanity teems around you, the quarterback must look past the chaos of the trenches, tune out the screams, and target the outstretched arms of the teammate who is scheduled to advance the ball toward the goal posts.

Washington Redskins coach Norv Turner, who is credited with polishing the skills of Troy Aikman when he was the Dallas Cowboys' offensive coordinator, explains the phenomenon of the rush. "The biggest key is when you're blinded for that quick instant at the snap of the ball," Turner says. "The thing is not to look down and find the rush. You have to remember that whatever's blinding you is going to keep moving. Your vision is going to come back and you're going to be able to see up the field."

Turner is not one of those fellows who subscribes to the those-who-can't-do-teach school. He knows of what he speaks, having played three seasons as a quarterback at the University of Oregon. He understands, like all quarterbacks, that mastering the pocket is an intuitive skill.

"You have to have a sense of the pocket, a feel for where you have to move and how much time you have to throw the ball," says Dan Marino, the Miami Dolphins quarterback who has thrown for more yards in the NFL than any other quarterback. "You have a clock in your head and it tells you when it's time to let go."

Boomer Esiason, who played quarterback for the Cincinnati Bengals, New York Jets, and Phoenix Cardinals, asks a compelling question: "How do you develop poise in the pocket?"

Jim Kelly of the Buffalo Bills has the answer: "Maybe your offensive tackle yelling, 'Look out'? Seriously, I think all quarterbacks thrive on being able to step up in the pocket and have a guy miss him before throwing it right before he's going to hit you."

Captain Courageous

Certainly Jim Kelly's view of the world is a little skewed or maybe it's just that he doesn't have to deal with the wrath of teammate Bruce Smith, who has terrorized the other quarterbacks in the league for years. Still, most of the great quarterbacks have an uncommon measure of courage.

ART SCHLICHTER

He was the greatest passer in the history of the Ohio State University football program, and he was destined to become one of the great quarterbacks in National Football League history. But it never happened for young quarterback Art Schlichter. Instead of joining contemporaries like Dan Marino, John Elway, Jim Kelly, and Steve Young, Schlichter wasn't setting records in 1995. He wasn't even setting an example; he was thirty-five years old and doing time in the Hamilton County Jail in Noblesville, Indiana, for a variety of offenses related to his one, ultimately fatal vice: gambling.

Football, both professional and college, has always feared gambling above all other dangers. More than anything, the cloud of fixed games threatens the integrity of the game.

Sensing his weakness early in life, Schlichter attended his first Gamblers Anonymous meeting at the age of twenty-two, after he had lost, by his count, more than a million dollars and been bounced by the NFL. After that, he says, it was all downhill.

"As I look back," he told *Inside Sports* magazine in 1995, "I know that some of the emotional problems I had growing up fed the disease later. I had always struggled trying to figure out who I was. Gambling killed the pain for me. But it also became a compulsion, and from there a disease that took control of my life. The more I gambled, the more I lost. The more I lost, the more inferior I felt. The more inferior I felt, the more I gambled to kill the pain caused by what I was doing. I finally ran into a wall going 150 miles an hour and found myself face down in jail. It took that crash to save my life.

"I think if I had gone to jail earlier in my life it would have made a difference. But I don't know if I would have stopped gambling forever. I don't even want to think about that. And I don't have to. All I have to do is not gamble today. My choice is recovery, admitting my guilt, and taking responsibility for what I have done. When I look around I realize that's my only choice."

In 1995, Brett Favre demonstrated he had more than most. The Green Bay Packers' signal caller had a history of playing hurt. Favre, who came to Green Bay in 1992 from Atlanta in exchange for a first-round draft choice, produced three straight 9–7 seasons for coach Mike Holmgren, two of them resulting in playoff berths.

In the tenth game of the 1995 season against Chicago, Favre probably shouldn't have played. His swollen, sprained left ankle had not permitted him to practice all week. Though virtually immobile, he played against the Bears and beat them. He threw for 5 touchdowns and no interceptions.

"There's no better way to earn respect in this league than to play hurt," Favre said afterward. "Even if I hadn't played that great, the guys would have said, 'Heck, what a tough quarterback.'"

But Favre played a nearly perfect game, which was typical of his breakthrough season. When it was all over, Green Bay was 11–5 and Favre was the league's Most Valuable Player. He completed 63 percent of his passes for a league-high 4,413 yards and 38 touchdowns. The statistic he was most proud of: he had played in 61 consecutive games as the Packers' starting quarterback, 18 more than anyone else.

The streak almost died in its infancy, however, seven games into 1992. Future teammate Reggie White, playing for Philadelphia, crashed into Favre and separated the quarterback's shoulder. Favre, who saw backup Don Majkowski warming up on the sidelines, considered coming out for about two seconds.

"I was laying down there and thinking, 'How hurt am I? Am I hurt enough to possibly lose my job?' I'm thinking, 'If he goes in, he may take my spot, just like I did his.' So I played with half a shoulder that day, and the next week, too." Favre won his second consecutive MVP award in 1996, leading the Packers to a 13–3 record. And then in 1997, Favre won the MVP yet again, completing an unprecedented trifecta in league history.

Phil Simms, the former Giants quarterback who was the Most Valuable Player in Super Bowl XXI, says courage and leadership are synonymous. "Players feed off results and facts," says Simms, now an announcer for CBS. "If you show them you'll hang in there for them, take a hit, they'll listen to what you have to say. If you want to be a leader, you've got to be a player on the field. Once you're a player and you have that possibility of taking the team down the field, then you can exert yourself, use your influence off the field."

Best and Brightest

Historians believe that Sammy Baugh and Johnny Unitas are two of the greatest quarterbacks the game has ever seen. Joe Montana and Otto Graham are the others usually mentioned on the same, very short list.

Montana retired after the 1994 season, but his numbers rate with the very best of his profession. Flip through the NFL record book and you will find Montana's name written all over it. And they are not merely quantitative statistics of longevity, but quality:

- The second-highest career passer rating in history, 92.3, in thirteen seasons with the San Francisco 49ers and two more with the Kansas City Chiefs. The NFL's complicated passer rating, based on five different categories, rewards efficiency and accuracy.
- The second-highest passer rating for a single season, 112.4, in 1989.
- The second-highest career completion percentage, 63.24.
- Four Super Bowl rings and three Super Bowl Most Valuable Player Awards.

That final statistic, of course, is the one that Montana is most proud of. It underlines the success he brought to his team, the 49ers.

"He has all the intangibles you could want," says Bill Walsh, his Hall of Fame coach. "When the game is on the line, he is the man you want to have the ball."

Montana, at six feet two inches (188cm) and 195 pounds (89kg), was not exactly the strapping prototypical quarterback like, for example, Dan Marino or Troy Aikman. His arm strength, according to scouts, was merely mediocre. In fact, in 1979, he was lucky to be drafted in the third round by the 49ers. They actually had eyes for Phil Simms of Morehead State, but the New York Giants drafted him in the first round. Walsh and the 49ers eventually settled for the spindly quarterback from Notre Dame. Simms, Jack Thompson, and Steve Fuller were all drafted ahead of Montana, but Walsh had a hunch. He liked Montana's cool hand under pressure, the poise he demonstrated in driving his team down the field.

Montana completed only 13 passes in his rookie season because Walsh wanted to bring him along slowly. By 1981, Montana was the starter, and he carried the 49ers to a 13–3 record. He completed 14 of 22 passes for 157 yards in Super Bowl XVI, a 26–21 victory over the Cincinnati Bengals. Three years later, Montana was the MVP of Super Bowl XIX; he completed 24 of 35 passes for a Super Bowl–record 331 yards and 3 touchdowns as the 49ers defeated the Miami Dolphins, 38–16.

Montana's finest moment came in Super Bowl XXIII, when he led the 49ers to another victory over Cincinnati, this one perilously close to the end. The Bengals led 16–13 at Joe Robbie Stadium in Miami with 3:20 remaining. Montana stepped under center on his own 8-yard line and proceeded to bring San Francisco down the field in 10 plays to the Bengals' 10-yard line. Then, with thirty-four seconds left in the game, he found wide receiver John Taylor marginally open on a slant pattern. The touchdown gave the 49ers the 20–16 lead they would take to the final gun. And though teammate Jerry Rice, who caught 11 passes for a Super

OPPOSITE: Miami quarterback Dan Marino is the most prolific quarterback in the history of the NFL.

CHAPTER 2: THE OFFENSE

Bowl–record 215 yards, won the MVP, it was Montana who delivered every ball. The following year, Montana was the MVP in Super Bowl XXIV when the 49ers dismantled the Denver Broncos, 55–10. Montana completed 22 of 29 passes for 297 yards and a Super Bowl–record 5 touchdowns.

Consider Montana's four breathtaking performances in football's ultimate game: an off-the-charts passer rating of 127.8, 83 completed passes for 1,142 yards, and 11 touchdowns—Super Bowl records all.

Although today's younger football fans might not believe it, in many ways, Otto Graham was every bit Montana's equal. But there is a record that, most likely, will never be equaled: in his ten seasons (four in the All-America Football Conference, six in the NFL), Graham led his Cleveland Browns to ten championship games. The Browns won seven of those games, one of them in 1950, their first year in the NFL.

"The test of a quarterback," said Paul Brown, Graham's coach, "is where the team finishes. By that standard, Otto was the best of them all."

It's hard to argue with results like that. By today's pass-happy standards, Graham did not rack up monstrous statistical numbers but he is still one of history's most efficient passers, with a respectable rating, 86.6, that places him high on the list.

Graham made the Northwestern University team as a walk-on; he was discovered lofting parabolic passes in a freshman intramural game. Brown was coaching at Ohio State when Graham led Northwestern to an upset victory over the Buckeyes. When Brown got the chance to build his first professional team, Graham was the first player he went after.

In his first two seasons, Graham led the AAFC with 17 and 25 touchdowns, respectively, compared to a total of only 16 interceptions. In three of his four AAFC seasons, Graham led the league in passing yardage. More importantly, the Browns won all four championships in those seasons. And, against the expectations of cynics, Graham led the Browns to their first NFL title in 1950, throwing 4 touchdown passes in a 30–28 victory over the Los Angeles Rams.

Graham retired at the age of thirty-three, but Brown coaxed one more season out of him in 1955. It was a beauty. Graham led the Browns to the championship and passed for 2 touchdowns and ran for 2 more in a 38–14 victory over the Rams.

Head of the Class

In 1983, no fewer than six quarterbacks were taken in the first round of the NFL's college draft. The last one drafted was Dan Marino of the University of Pittsburgh. Today he stands, far and away, at the head of the class—not just the class of 1983, but among all those quarterbacks who have passed through the NFL.

John Elway, Todd Blackledge, Jim Kelly, Tony Eason, and Ken O'Brien were all drafted earlier, but Marino owns the most cher-

ished records among quarterbacks. Heading into the 1995 season, he was second to Fran Tarkenton in four categories. After the 1996 season, Marino was far ahead with 6,904 attempts, 4,134 completions, 51,636 yards, and 369 touchdowns. It is worth noting that Marino achieved these totals in thirteen seasons, while Tarkenton needed eighteen. And after the 1997 season, Marino's two most impressive all-time totals had risen, touchdown passes to a whopping 385 and passing yards to a mind-boggling 55,419.

Marino's strong arm and lightning-quick release make him, in many ways, the perfect pass thrower. In 1984, he threw an amazing 48 touchdown passes. That's four better than history's second-highest total of 44, which also belongs to Marino. In that marvelous 1984 season, Marino also became the first NFL player to pass for more than 5,000 yards, in this case 5,084.

The one thing that has eluded Marino throughout his career has also cursed the entire class of 1983. Heading into Super Bowl XXXII, not one of those quarterbacks had ever won a Super Bowl. Kelly was 0-4, Elway was 0-3, and Marino and Eason were both 0-1. And then Elway broke through with a dramatic victory over the Green Bay Packers to end the 0-9 streak.

Like Marino, Denver's John Elway is seen as a future Hall of Famer. He has won more games as an NFL quarterback (149, including playoffs) than anyone else. He is strong, possesses an incredibly powerful arm, and has an extraordinary sense of timing. In his career, Elway has engineered no fewer than 41 game-winning drives in the fourth quarter. He is the master of the two-minute drill made famous by Dallas quarterback Roger Staubach. It is one of the few statistics that puts Elway's career in the proper context.

"We were always scrambling to catch up to teams," Elway says. "You sort of get into that two-minute mode, where you've got to get it done. It's something I've gotten used to over the years. Sure, I'm proud of it, but that's the quarterback's job: getting the ball down the field."

The passer rating, which demands efficiency, has never done Elway justice. He has never been surrounded by hugely talented teams and has had to rely largely on himself to win games. Heading into the second decade of his career, he had thrown exactly one more touchdown (158) than interceptions (157).

Elway's watershed game was the 1986 AFC championship game against Cleveland. Elway moved the Broncos 98 yards in 15 plays and hit receiver Mark Jackson with a 5-yard touchdown pass that sent the game into overtime. It became known as "the Drive." Denver ultimately prevailed in overtime, 23–20, and Elway's legend was secure.

Young at Heart

Today, Steve Young is seen as the quarterback's quarterback. He wears three Super Bowl rings and has won all the individual accolades possible. But, as much as anyone, Young has paid his dues.

35

After playing in the enormous shadow cast by Joe Montana, Steve Young (No. 8) had his own turn to celebrate.

He set a National Collegiate Athletic Association record his senior year at Brigham Young University with a completion percentage of .713, but instead of joining the NFL, the left-hander signed a $40 million contract with the rival United States Football League. Two seasons later, he bought his way out of the deal with the Los Angeles Express and signed with the woeful Tampa Bay Buccaneers. In 1987, San Francisco coach Bill Walsh engineered a trade for Young, sending the Bucs second- and fourth-round draft choices. There was only one problem: the 49ers' starting quarterback was a fellow named Montana.

"There were times when I thought it would be better if I left San Francisco because I was so frustrated," Young says. "But in the end, I didn't think I had any control in the matter. If the 49ers wanted to trade me, they'd trade me. If they wanted me to stay, I was going to stay.

"Now I look back and see that I really had the best situation. I was in the best offensive system, I had the best coach in Bill Walsh, and I could learn by watching Joe. Now, I have the chance to do what I can with all the great talent around me. . . . It wasn't easy stepping in as the leader. People have to decide to follow you—

that's what makes you a leader. It wasn't easy because I was following one of the great field leaders of all time."

But the one talent Montana never mastered was staying healthy. He broke his hand in the fourth quarter of the 1990 NFC championship game and his career was effectively over in San Francisco. Montana played part of one game in 1992 before the 49ers traded him to Kansas City before the 1993 season. Young, on the other hand, stepped into the starter's position and flourished.

From 1991 to 1994, Young was the NFL's highest-rated quarterback; previously, no quarterback topped the league in efficiency for more than two years in a row. Only Sammy Baugh, with six NFL passing titles, has more than Young's four. And Young did something else that neither Montana nor any other quarterback in the NFL history ever did: for three straight seasons he posted a passer rating over 100.

In 1994, Young had a career season worthy of his predecessor. He completed 324 of 461 passes for 3,969 yards, 35 touchdowns, and only 10 interceptions. The rating was 112.8, the best single-season mark ever, eclipsing the record of 112.4 set by Montana in 1989. That season also vaulted Young into first place for best career passer rating, 96.8. Montana was second on the list with 92.3, followed by Dan Marino's 88.2.

Although Young had laid to rest all the doubts about his individual ability, there was the small matter of an NFL title. Young lifted the 49ers past Dallas, the two-time defending Super Bowl champions, in the NFC championship game, 38–28. And then, in Super Bowl XXIX at Joe Robbie Stadium in Miami, Young was incandescent. He completed 24 of 36 passes for 325 yards and 6 touchdowns; the old record of 5 belonged to Montana. The 49ers prevailed over the Dolphins, 49–26, and Young had a ring he could call his own.

The NFL never had a full Moon, but after six seasons in Canada, he joined the ultimate professional league and set several records.

Full Moon

While the 1995 season belonged to Miami's Dan Marino as he claimed the NFL records for pass attempts, completions, yards, and touchdowns, Warren Moon very quietly made a piece of history himself.

It happened in Pittsburgh on September 24. The Minnesota Vikings quarterback faked a handoff, rolled out of the pocket, and tossed an 18-yard pass to tight end Adrian Cooper. The Vikings would go on to win, 44–24, at Three Rivers Stadium, but the number of consequence was 60,000. That's how many passing yards the thirty-eight-year-old veteran had amassed in eighteen seasons. Purists will tell you that more than 21,000 yards came in six seasons in the inferior Canadian Football League, which is why you won't find Moon at the top of the NFL record book.

"The biggest thing I remember people saying is they didn't think I could throw the football," Moon says. "I couldn't understand it. Because I didn't run a pro-style at [the University of] Washington, that was the big knock against me. I had to go to Canada to prove I could throw the football.

"I could have been drafted by the NFL and stood around and carried a clipboard for a few years, but I felt I was better than that."

Moon led his Edmonton Eskimos to six consecutive Grey Cup championships, the CFL version of the Super Bowl. In 1984, Moon signed with the Houston Oilers and ran their run-and-shoot offense for a decade. In 1994, he joined the Minnesota Vikings, set single-season records for yards (4,264) and completions (371), and was selected to his eighth consecutive Pro Bowl. It was no fluke. In 1995, Moon finished with 4,228 yards and 377 completions.

Heading into the 1998 season, despite those six seasons in Canada, Moon has worked his way into the NFL record book. You will find him third in yards passing, behind Marino and Elway, and ahead of Joe Montana and Johnny Unitas. What does the record mean to him?

"It means I've been playing a long time," Moon says. "It's something I'm definitely proud of because people didn't give me credit when I first came into the game. It's something I think I've earned."

Buffalo's former quarterback Jim Kelly is another spirited veteran who earned the respect of his peers. Like Steve Young, he passed on the NFL to lend credibility to the USFL. In two seasons with the Houston Gamblers, 1984 and 1985, Kelly threw up some ridiculous numbers: 9,842 yards and 83 touchdowns. The Buffalo Bills, who had drafted him in the first round of the 1983 draft, finally got him into uniform in 1986.

Slowly, the cast of players around Kelly improved and so did the team's record, from 4–12 that first season to 7–8 to 1988's 12–4 record, good for first place in the AFC East. It was a position the Bills would occupy for four straight seasons.

In 1990, Kelly led the Bills to their first Super Bowl in Tampa. Buffalo was probably a better team than the New York Giants, but placekicker Scott Norwood's 47-yard field goal attempt with seconds remaining sailed wide right. The Giants prevailed, 20–19, and in retrospect, it was as close as the Bills would come in a record four consecutive Super Bowl appearances.

The Future

Here is what Troy Aikman had accomplished before his thirtieth birthday:

- Completed 1,704 passes in 2,713 attempts for a completion percentage of 62.8.
- Threw for 19,607 passing yards and 98 touchdowns versus 85 interceptions.
- Won three Super Bowl championships and one Most Valuable Player Award (for Super Bowl XXVII).

Dallas coach Jimmy Johnson saw it coming. He drafted UCLA's quarterback first overall in the 1989 draft, envisioning Aikman as the cornerstone of a dynasty. And that's just about how it worked out.

The six-foot-four-inch (193cm), 216-pound (98kg) Aikman learned the hard way, however. The Cowboys lost fifteen of sixteen games that first season; the only victory came with Aikman catching his breath on the sidelines. He threw twice as many interceptions as touchdowns as a rookie, but his decisions were better in 1990, when the Cowboys managed to win seven games. Their record was 11–5 in 1991 and Aikman's passer rating was actually better than that of Dan Marino and Warren Moon.

The Cowboys reached the Super Bowl at the end of the 1992 season and Aikman took advantage of the opportunity. He completed 22 of 30 passes for 273 yards and 4 touchdowns against the Buffalo Bills, and Dallas won Super Bowl XXVII by the lopsided score of 52–17. Aikman was the youngest quarterback to win the MVP since Joe Montana won it in 1982. Aikman, one of history's most accurate passers, threw eight touchdowns in three postseason

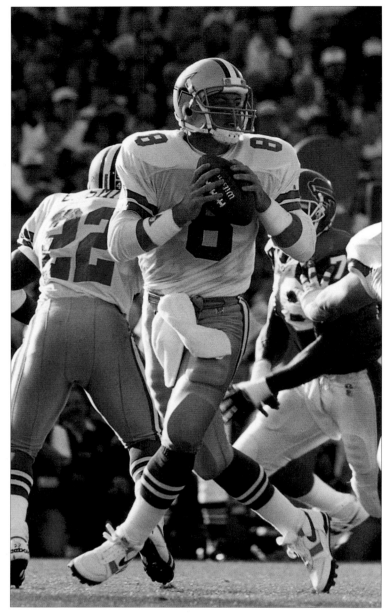

Dallas Cowboys quarterback Troy Aikman is one of the most accurate passers in league history.

games that season, balanced by no interceptions. His passer rating for the playoffs was a blistering 116.7, far better than the previous record of 104.8, held by Green Bay's Bart Starr.

Then Aikman helped the Cowboys win a second consecutive Super Bowl. The Bills were victims again, this time losing, 30–13, in Super Bowl XXVIII. Aikman became only the fourth quarterback to take his team to consecutive Super Bowl victories. (The others were Starr, Pittsburgh's Terry Bradshaw, and Montana.)

When the Cowboys beat the Pittsburgh Steelers in Super Bowl XXX, 27–17, to punctuate the 1995 season, Aikman joined an even more select circle. Bradshaw and Montana were both a perfect 4–0 in Super Bowls. Aikman is now 3–1. With the support of two gifted future Hall of Famers—running back Emmitt Smith and wide receiver Michael Irvin—and one of the best offensive lines ever, Aikman could surpass both Bradshaw and Montana.

History suggests that Aikman is just now coming into his prime. If he can avoid the effects of numerous concussions that have dogged his career, he could finish as one of the all-time greats.

There are some other great quarterbacks on the horizon, too. Green Bay's Brett Favre, if he can stay healthy, promises to put up some historic numbers. The quarterback with the best chance of making a long-term mark, though, is probably New England's Drew Bledsoe.

Patriots coach Bill Parcells, who had inherited the worst team in football, drafted the six-foot-five-inch (196cm), 233-pound (106kg) quarterback with the first pick of the 1993 draft. The results were predictably mediocre. Somehow, Bledsoe threw as many touchdown passes as interceptions (15) and the Patriots came away with five victories, three more than the previous season.

In 1994, the precocious Bledsoe had a breakthrough season. He threw more times (691) and completed more passes (400) for more yards (4,555) than any other quarterback that year. His 691 passes placed him fourth in the league behind Steve Young, Brett Favre,

and Dan Marino. In a memorable game against Minnesota, Bledsoe rallied the Patriots from a 20–0 deficit by completing 45 of a record 70 attempts for 421 yards.

After the 1994 season, the Patriots signed Bledsoe to a $42.5 million, seven-year contract, another NFL record. Then in 1995, Bledsoe and the Patriots stumbled badly. New England, which went 10–6 and made the playoffs in 1994, slipped to 6–10. Bledsoe, who threw 20 interceptions and only 13 touchdowns, finished as the AFC's lowest-rated passer with a mark of 63.7.

Still, Bledsoe has one of the brightest futures in the NFL. In February 1995 he became the youngest player (twenty-two years old) to ever play in the Pro Bowl. During the 1995 season, Bledsoe managed to throw for 3,507 yards, allowing him at the age of twenty-three to become the youngest quarterback to pass for 10,000 yards. In 1996, Bledsoe led the Patriots to Super Bowl XXXI. In 1997, he had his best statistical year ever, completing more than 60 percent of his passes, for 3,706 yards, 28 touchdowns, and just 15 interceptions.

The Tight End

The tight end is all things to all people.

He is typically a six-foot-four-inch (193cm), 250-pound (114kg) athlete with a frightening combination of speed and power. He must have the muscle to clear outside linebackers from the path of his running back and, sometimes on the same play, have the soft hands capable of gathering in a speeding bullet from his quarterback.

"It's the nature of the position," says speedy Ben Coates, the New England Patriots tight end. "We do a little bit of everything."

Coates is viewed by many as the best tight end in the game today. At six feet five inches (196cm) and 245 pounds (111kg), he is of prototypical size. He also has enough speed to elude the safeties who try to cover him.

Drew Bledsoe, of the New England Patriots, is the quarterback with the best chance of eventually catching Miami's Dan Marino in the record books.

40 The Jets' Kyle Brady is built like a prototypical tight end. That is to say, he is built like a tank.

In 1993, Bledsoe's first season, Coates become a larger force in the Patriots offense. He caught the first touchdown pass of Bledsoe's career and finished the year with 53 catches for 659 yards and 8 touchdowns. At the same time, he was a punishing blocker—something Parcells prized as much as his results as a receiver.

Coates made the Pro Bowl two seasons in a row, in 1994 and 1995, but he struggled for much of the 1995 season on a severely sprained ankle. With teams often devoting two and three players to cover him, Coates' output was limited to 84 catches, 915 yards, and only 6 touchdowns. At the same time, however, Patriots rookie running back Curtis Martin rushed for 1,487 yards, the league's third-highest total. There are no statistics to prove it, but Ben Coates was clearly one of the big factors in Martin's success.

In 1994, Coates caught a staggering 96 passes, the all-time single-season record for tight ends. He was the most reliable target for Drew Bledsoe as the Patriots won ten games and made the playoffs under coach Bill Parcells. Coates broke the record of Todd Christensen, who caught 95 passes for the Raiders in 1986. Christensen also caught 92 passes in 1983, good for third on the all-time list. San Diego's Kellen Winslow (1980) and Cleveland's Ozzie Newsome (1983 and 1984) each recorded 89 catches. Twice, in 1981 and 1983, Winslow finished with 88 catches.

It's a pretty short list, underlining how truly rare great tight ends are. In fact, with the exception of the nose tackle, the tight end is probably the most difficult position to stock through the college draft. Consider the case of Coates.

Coates played football for only one season at Greenwood High School in South Carolina, then persevered in anonymity at Livingstone College in Salisbury, North Carolina. He was the team's best player as a freshman and a sophomore, but went out for basketball and track as a junior. He went back to football as a senior and caught 36 passes, worth 504 yards and 9 touchdowns, and drew modest national attention. The Patriots studied his résumé—103 catches, 1,228 yards, and 18 touchdowns in three seasons—and selected him in the fifth round of the 1991 draft. Coates, the 124th player taken, seemed to justify the hesitation by teams to select him in his first two seasons. He started in only four games and caught a total of 30 passes for 266 yards and 4 touchdowns.

The Brady Bunch?

The next generation of tight ends is best represented by Kyle Brady of the New York Jets. The Jets made the versatile Penn State athlete the ninth overall selection of the 1995 draft and the league's highest-drafted tight end in more than a decade. Brady, at six feet six inches (198cm) and 260 pounds (118kg), has a classic build and pliable hands to go with it. He also has the get-down-and-dirty attitude shared by the great tight ends.

"The nice thing about him is that he can do the little things that are important," explained quarterback Boomer Esiason during Brady's rookie season. "He doesn't have to worry about how many catches or how many yards he has."

Blocking is neither fun nor particularly easy, but Brady relishes it.

"If you've got a great running back, he's not going to be a great one if he doesn't have people who can open holes," Brady says. "After blocking for five years, you learn to accept those responsibilities and learn to take pride in whatever you're asked to do.

"Just putting on the uniform sort of starts the transformation towards aggressiveness for me. I guess it's like Pavlov's dog. Putting on the uniform is like the bell sounding so you can relieve all your frustrations."

Spoken like a true tight end.

One of the people who helped Brady understand the position's responsibilities was the St. Louis Rams' Troy Drayton. It was

New England's Ben Coates set a record for tight ends with 96 catches in 1994.

Jay Novacek, the Dallas Cowboys' hard-working tight end, was the most anonymous star among Troy Aikman's celebrated targets.

Drayton who took Brady's starting job at Penn State as a walk-on in 1992, prompting Brady to leave school for a few days of contemplation. Eventually, Brady returned and became an All-American. Drayton matriculated to the NFL, where he was drafted in the second round of the 1993 draft. Drayton's reception totals have improved each season, from 27 as a rookie to 32 in 1994 and 47 in 1995.

In recent years, two NFL tight ends have perhaps stood out more than others because they play for the two best teams: Dallas' Jay Novacek and San Francisco's Brent Jones. Both have suffered the lot of most tight ends: underappreciation.

Indeed, when you think of the Cowboys' potent offense, you think immediately of quarterback Troy Aikman or running back Emmitt Smith or wide receiver Michael Irvin. Novacek, who played college ball for Wyoming and came to Dallas as a free agent in 1990, is not exactly a marquee name. Yet the argument can be made that without Novacek all of those marvelous players would be diminished. And would the Cowboys have won three Super Bowls without Novacek in the lineup?

His numbers in six seasons have been admirably consistent: more than 56 catches to go along with nearly 600 yards and 4 touchdowns per season.

Likewise, Jones has toiled in the shadow of history's two greatest quarterbacks in technical terms, Joe Montana and Steve Young, and perhaps the best wide receiver ever, Jerry Rice.

Jones played for a Division II school, Santa Clara, and in 1986 was waived by the Steelers. The 49ers signed him as a free agent, and slowly Jones grew into the position. He caught 40 passes in 1989, the year the 49ers won their second straight Super Bowl. In 1993, at the age of thirty, Jones made the first of three consecutive Pro Bowl appearances, then retired after the 1997 season.

Lunch-Pail Attitude

If the tight end has a snarling face, the quintessential attitude belongs to Mike Ditka.

This is the man who grew up hard in a steel town in Pennsylvania, the man who once broke his hand pounding a locker in frustration after a loss. Most people know Ditka as the hard-hitting analyst for NBC Sports or as the brash coach of the 1985 Super Bowl champion Chicago Bears. Now, just imagine all six feet three inches (191cm) and 230 pounds (104kg) of that attitude harnessed into a football uniform.

While today's tight end is hardly appreciated for his skill and valor, before Ditka people had never even heard of the position. Ron Kramer of the Green Bay Packers made the transition from third tackle to tight end in the early 1960s, but Ditka revolutionized the position.

After a career at the University of Pittsburgh, Ditka joined the Chicago Bears, a blue-collar team in a blue-collar city that perfectly suited his lunch-pail personality. Ditka was a receiver first and a blocker second. As a rookie in 1961, Ditka caught 56 passes, 12 of them for touchdowns—amazing totals at the time. Moreover, he gained 1,076 yards, an average of 19.2 yards per catch. Ditka had the speed to get behind defensive backs, something tight ends had never done.

Ditka caught 58 passes in 1962, 59 in 1963, and then 75 in 1964. That last was a record for tight ends that would endure for sixteen years. Like famed teammate Dick Butkus, a linebacker with an appetite for violence, Ditka liked to throw blocks with authority. When he had the ball he was almost as dangerous; his straight-arm was a weapon feared by defenders.

Ditka is one of only four tight ends enshrined in the Pro Football Hall of Fame. The others, in order of entrance, are John Mackey, Jackie Smith, and Kellen Winslow.

Mackey, who played primarily for the Baltimore Colts, caught 331 passes for 5,236 yards, amassing 38 touchdowns in ten seasons. With the feisty air of a tight end, Mackey was one of the first players to challenge the NFL's free agency system in court.

Smith also had a terrific career. From 1963 to 1978, he caught 480 passes for 7,918 yards and 40 touchdowns. But the one thing Smith is remembered for is the pass he didn't catch. It was Super Bowl XIII at the Orange Bowl in Miami and Smith's Dallas Cowboys were battling the Pittsburgh Steelers. Smith was wide open in the end zone in the third quarter when he inexplicably dropped Roger Staubach's perfect throw. A touchdown would have tied the score at 21–all, but the Cowboys would never catch the Steelers. Pittsburgh won a classic game, 35–31.

Winslow's college career was largely given to blocking. At the University of Missouri he caught only 71 passes in four seasons, but the San Diego Chargers saw past the statistics. In 1979, they used the draft's twelfth overall pick on Winslow. At six feet six inches (198cm) and 250 pounds (114kg), Winslow had the size and muscle to play any position along the offensive line and the speed to step in as a wide receiver.

For four seasons, from 1980 to 1983, Winslow was the most dangerous receiver in the NFL. In 1980 and 1981 he led the league with 89 and 88 catches, respectively, good for a total of 2,365 yards and 19 touchdowns.

Quarterback Dan Fouts had a talented group of wide receivers—Charlie Joiner, John Jefferson, and Wes Chandler—but Winslow was his favorite target. In a 1981 game against the Raiders, the defending Super Bowl champions, Fouts found Winslow 13 times, five of those catches resulting in touchdowns to tie an NFL record. No one, before or since, has ever scored 30 points in a single game in a Chargers uniform.

Later that same season, Winslow was the star of one of the greatest games in the history of the NFL. On January 2, 1982, the Chargers visited the Miami Dolphins for an AFC playoff game. After fifteen minutes, the game appeared to be over; San Diego led

24–0. Miami coach Don Shula sent quarterback David Woodley to the bench in favor of backup Don Strock. Somehow, Strock rallied the Dolphins with 17 unanswered points.

The game bounced back and forth, with Miami taking a 38–31 lead on the first play of the fourth quarter. The Chargers tied it when Fouts put together an 82-yard drive and flipped a 9-yard touchdown pass to James Brooks with fifty-eight seconds left in regulation.

Winslow, dehydrated and exhausted, was carried off the field several times by his teammates during the game. But with the game on the line, a few ticks from overtime, Winslow managed to block Miami's 43-yard field goal, which would have won the game for them. Winslow was not a regular part of the Chargers' special teams, but the play demonstrated his versatility and his heart.

The placekickers did their best to prolong the game in overtime; San Diego's Rolf Benirschke missed a 27-yard attempt and Miami's Uwe von Schamann had a 35-yard kick blocked. Ultimately, Fouts found Joiner with a 39-yard pass play and the Chargers were in business on the Miami 10-yard line. Wasting no time, Benirschke immediately kicked the winning 29-yard field goal. The Chargers won, 41–38, in an epic game that required an extra thirteen minutes and fifty-two seconds to play.

And when it was over, Kellen Winslow had caught 13 passes for 166 yards.

The Wide Receiver

There was a time not so many years ago—1983, to be precise—when 100-catch seasons didn't exist in the National Football League. But Art Monk of the Washington Redskins changed all that in 1984 when he caught 106 passes, by all accounts an ethereal number.

That was then; this is now. For a breathtaking perspective, consider the league's leading 1995 regular-season pass receivers:

1. Herman Moore, Detroit: 123 catches
2. Cris Carter, Minnesota: 122 catches
3. Jerry Rice, San Francisco: 122 catches
4. Isaac Bruce, St. Louis: 119 catches
5. Michael Irvin, Dallas: 111 catches
6. Brett Perriman, Detroit: 108 catches

That's right—Monk's monstrous season would have placed him seventh on the list. In today's NFL passes are caught with such frequency that number ten on the list, Cincinnati's Carl Pickens, had 99 catches for 1,234 yards and 17 touchdowns.

"It's not just good receivers we're talking about, either," says Miami Dolphins coach Jimmy Johnson. "These are great receivers. These guys aren't just getting a lot of balls thrown at them. They're making incredible plays. This is the most I've ever seen. I'd hate to try to figure out who the top three or four guys in the league are anymore."

Clearly, these are the times to be a wide receiver. In the old days, wideouts were known merely as ends and they were lucky to find work at all. During the first five seasons they kept records in the NFL (1932–36), the five receiving leaders—Ray Flaherty of the Giants, Brooklyn's John "Shipwreck" Kelly, Philadelphia's Joe Carter, Tod Goodwin of the Giants, and Green Bay's Don Hutson—combined for a total of 119 catches, the same number Bruce produced for the Rams.

Offense sells tickets, and the NFL has altered its rules over the years to make it easier for quarterbacks and receivers to hook up more frequently. Historically, NFL teams used to run the ball more than they passed it, but now many teams throw it more often. The wide receivers, the game's new glamour players, are the chief beneficiaries.

Woody Hayes, the legendary coach at Ohio State, was the quintessential conservative football man. His idea of an innovative offense was two runs up the middle followed by a sweep. He always used to say that three things could happen when you threw the football, and that two of them (an incompletion and an interception) were bad. Maybe so, but Hayes never had Jerry Rice on his team.

The San Francisco Treat

Jerry Rice turned thirty-three during the 1995 season—ancient by NFL standards—but he somehow managed to catch 122 passes for 1,848 yards and 15 touchdowns. The yardage figure was an NFL single-season record. Just as Miami Dolphins quarterback Dan Marino collected most of quarterbacking's cherished records in 1995, Rice wrapped up a number of the all-time career marks wide receivers covet in his eleventh season. Through 1996, the totals were 1,050 catches, 16,377 yards, and 154 touchdowns.

Rice produced his tenth consecutive season with more than 1,000 receiving yards, another record, and his 156 total touchdowns (including scores via the ground) are far and away the most in league history. Jim Brown (126) and Walter Payton (125) will no doubt watch in agony as Rice puts the record out of reach in the coming years. And make no mistake: Rice is likely to put all of his records on a ridiculous level that may not be approached for years. In 1996, for example, Rice merely led the entire NFL with 108 catches, good for 1,254 yards and 8 touchdowns.

"Now, as I get older, people are looking for me to slip," Rice says. "They are waiting for me to lose a step. That hasn't happened and I will get out of it before it does. If anything, I'm faster and better than I have ever been."

How did a six-foot-two-inch (188cm), 195-pound (89kg) athlete who is not blessed with blinding speed put together such a

record of consistent excellence? The answer is a combination of ability and ruthlessly hard work.

Rice's off-season workout regimen borders on torture. Led by longtime trainer Raymond Farris, Rice endures punishing workouts like this one on a July 1995 morning near the 49ers training facility in Santa Clara, California:

After twenty minutes of stretching, Rice ran 100-yard sprints—fourteen of them—the first 20 yards at an accelerating pace, the next 60 yards flat out, and the final 20 at a decelerating pace. There was an hour of exhausting hill work—two or three hills, ranging from one to two miles (1.6 to 3.2km) each—and agility training.

As dangerous a receiver as Jerry Rice is, the San Francisco athlete is even scarier when he runs after the catch.

Then Rice did several sets of pyramids, then a 100-yard sprint, followed by a 90-yard dash, and so on, down to 20 yards, then back up again. Oh, and then he was ready for more than two hours of weight lifting. There was a brisk cooldown on the StairMaster, bringing his workout time to five hours.

Other professional athletes, from Barry Bonds of the San Francisco Giants to Detroit running back Barry Sanders, have joined Rice in these sessions. Not many come back for seconds.

"I think it would blow people away to know how hard Jerry works during the off-season and the week before games," says Brent Jones, the 49ers' Pro Bowl tight end. "And I'm talking about

people on other teams, not the fans. I've heard how others guys at this level, on other teams, take days off whenever they want, when they're not hurt that bad. Jerry runs hard. Every play. Every day."

In his first nine seasons, Rice did not miss a single game because of injury, a remarkable figure for a man who makes his living dodging bullets in opposing secondaries. And then there was his streak of 127 straight games with at least 1 reception.

On the sidelines, before and during games, Rice plays catch with lefty equipment manager Ted Walsh, thereby preparing himself for the peculiar spin of Steve Young's left-handed passes. Rice runs out every pass route—20 yards, 30, 40, 50—whatever it takes.

"Even if we win another Super Bowl I wouldn't retire," Rice says. "I was watching Charles Barkley on television and he was talking about how he would like a championship. When I see a great athlete in that position it makes me work harder and not take what I've accomplished for granted."

Rice, for the record, has four Super Bowl rings and a spot reserved at the Pro Football Hall of Fame in Canton, Ohio. But he never forgets where he came from, a place called Mississippi Valley State.

"I have to fight for everything," he says. "I always have. I have to prepare myself every year. There is always some young guy who thinks he can take me. And then when the day is done, he realizes he can't. Even when I was younger, people were waiting to see if I was a fluke. And I proved time and time again that I wasn't."

It was 49ers coach Bill Walsh who first understood the ability and desire that Rice brought to the football field. Walsh was on a scouting trip in 1984 and just happened to catch a game between two NCAA Division II teams, one of them Mississippi Valley State. Rice caught a handful of touchdowns that day and soon Walsh was on his way to Itta Bena, Mississippi. Rice's statistics (more than 100 catches his senior year, for more than 1,800 yards and 28 touchdowns) were phenomenal, but the cynics wondered about the level of competition and Rice's lack of pure speed.

Walsh, on the other hand, was so taken with Rice—he thought he would be the perfect complement to young quarterback Joe Montana—that he arranged an elaborate Draft Day trade with the New England Patriots. Rice was the third wide receiver taken in the 1985 draft, after Al Toon and Eddie Brown, but he quickly established himself as one of the best wideouts in the game.

His signature pass route is the slant. Rice lines up wide of the line of scrimmage and, after a few moves at the line of scrimmage, streaks at an angle toward the middle of the field. Because of his acceleration and body positioning, it is virtually impossible for a defender to stop a pass if it is thrown reasonably well. Rice has never wowed the scouts with stopwatches, but his separation speed is potent. Many of his touchdowns came on short pass plays and brilliant runs after the catch. And while Rice's incandescent numbers draw attention to his receiving skills, he is said to be one of the best blocking wideouts in the league.

As a rookie, Rice produced impressive numbers, but he never learned quickly enough to meet his own exacting standards. He was inconsolable after dropping a potential touchdown pass against the Kansas City Chiefs in November 1985, but three weeks after the tears, in a highly visible Monday night game, Rice caught 10 passes for 241 yards. In 1987, Rice caught an NFL-record 22 touchdown passes in a strike-shortened, 12-game regular season.

He was the Most Valuable Player in Super Bowl XXIII, with 11 catches and 215 yards. In fact, if Montana hadn't been the quarterback, Rice might have won another MVP trophy. Consider Rice's

record in his three Super Bowl games with the 49ers. He is first in all-time catches (28), total yards (512), and touchdowns (7). The three players in second place—John Stallworth and Lynn Swann from Pittsburgh, and the Raiders' Cliff Branch—are tied with 3 touchdowns.

"I know it's going to come to an end, don't get me wrong," Rice says. "It's time to start thinking about retirement. I know it's coming. But as long as that fire is still there and I'm productive, I'll play."

Rice's 1997 season ended in the first game, when his knee was shredded. He mounted a dramatic comeback at the end of the regular season, but just as he caught a touchdown, he was leveled and suffered a season-ending injury. He vowed almost immediately to return in time for the 1998 season.

The Reverend Ike

Rice is not the only terrific wide receiver in the game who wears No. 80 and comes from an obscure college program. The other's name is Isaac Bruce. Here are some other things the Rams wideout shares with the greatest receiver of all time:

- A hard-working, highly principled approach to the game.
- A father who made his living doing construction work.
- His first NFL game against the Atlanta Falcons.
- A fastidious fashion sense, right down to a new pair of receivers' gloves for every game.
- A breathtaking 1995 season.

While Rice was setting an NFL record in 1995 for yards (1,848) in a single season, Bruce was right behind with 1,781. That is the second-best single-season yardage total—ever. And it was only his second season in the NFL. Even Rice fell short of that mark in his second year.

"Rice has Hall of Fame written all over him," says former Rams coach Rich Brooks. "I think it's really unfair to compare Isaac Bruce with Jerry Rice. Now, I don't want to take anything away from him because I was one of the guys in training camp that felt he was going to become a hell of a player, which he has become.

"But you don't become Jerry Rice in a season or two. You have to do it for a long period of time, consistently, when people are trying to take you out of the game. They're up there busting you in the mouth when you come off the line of scrimmage. Isaac's going to see more of that. How he responds and whether he'll keep making the plays with the consistency he's demonstrated so far, that will be the test."

Bruce, who is almost painfully humble about his abilities, says elements of his game come from watching Rice, on television and film.

"I can't say there's just one true number 80," Bruce says, "but [Rice] is a great player. I think he's the greatest that ever played

Isaac Bruce, the Rams' wide receiver has a model role model: Jerry Rice.

receiver. Some of the things he does I've patterned myself after. It's a great honor to be compared to a great player who's won so many Super Bowls and shown up for every game, but sometimes I try to hide the blushing."

In truth, Bruce is two inches (5cm) and nearly 20 pounds (9kg) smaller than Rice. He doesn't have the natural leverage Rice enjoys when matching up with the league's bigger, stronger defensive backs. Somehow, though, he makes the plays. That was what the Rams were hoping for when they drafted him from Memphis State in the second round of the 1994 draft.

Listen to Bruce's teammates. "You see the speed, you see the quickness, the flashes of brilliance," says Rams wide receiver Todd Kinchen. "Isaac doesn't have the big name yet, but he's got the big talent. Believe me, people are going to be double-teaming him very quickly. If Isaac has the opportunities that Jerry Rice had, he can be that kind of special player. He's still coming into his own, he's still working on his technique, but Isaac Bruce is that good."

Says Jessie Hester, also a Rams receiver, "[Bruce] is very, very quick. We call it suddenness. I mean out of the break, off the line of scrimmage he's quick as a cat."

According to Brooks, Bruce's success comes from his deceptive speed. That's what they said about Rice when he broke into the league.

"He just glides through things," Brooks says. "It isn't the type of thing where you see him just go voooooooommmm, out like a jet. He just kind of floats softly out there and, all of a sudden, he's running away from people.

"I think he just has an innate ability to make the cut at the right time. He knows when the defensive back is thinking he's going to do something different and then, boom, he comes out of it."

Bruce smiles when this description is related to him later. "I have a long stride," he says. "People don't think I'm that fast, so it's sort of deceptive. Once I break their cushion, they don't think I'm going to run by them.

"The whole thing is hard work. It's just competitiveness. I just compete on every play."

Humility is the only way to go when you are the thirteenth of fifteen children. And when you grow up in Fort Lauderdale, Florida, with a Pentecostal minister as a mother, it is mandatory. Bruce plans to follow his mother, K, and two sisters into the ministry, which is

From 1995 to 1997, no one in football had more catches than Herman Moore: a staggering 333.

why some teammates call him Reverend Ike. But for now, he'll save his preaching for the football field, where he is a different person.

"He is a different cat," says quarterback Chris Miller, who provided the arm behind most of Bruce's catches in 1995. "He's a Jekyll-and-Hyde-type guy. You'll be walking down the hallway and you say hello to Isaac and it's like if he just says hello, man, he's having a great day."

Hester adds, "But game time, I mean, like a switch goes off and on. It's like night and day. You hear him talking jive to big linebackers and defensive linemen. The guy just has a lot of fire in him. Where it comes from, I do not know."

Bruce does not disagree with this assessment.

"I guess that's the South Florida coming out in me," he says. "They sort of come at me, and once they get to talking I have to do something to shut them up."

If the trend continues, defensive backs will be quiet on the subject of Isaac Bruce for years to come.

Moore and More

For a single season, 1994, Cris Carter owned the NFL record for most catches in a year. He posted 122 receptions, and then as fast as you can say Herman Moore, the record was gone. Not that Carter had an off-season in 1995—far from it. He caught another 122 passes, for more yards and more than twice as many touch-

downs. It's just that Moore managed to come up with one more catch to set a new record: 123.

Like Bruce, Carter does not have Rice's prototypical body, but at five feet eleven inches (180cm) and 181 pounds (82kg) he is as physical as he needs to be. Carter, too, has great acceleration, but his soft hands and the control he exerts over his body in midair allow him to make some incredible catches. Sometimes, you have to watch his highlight plays two or three times to see how he did it. Clearly, genes play a role, too; his older brother, Butch, played seven seasons in the National Basketball Association.

Coming out of Ohio State, the antithesis of schools like the University of Miami that make their mark passing the ball, Carter was only a fourth-round choice of the Philadelphia Eagles in the 1987 supplemental draft. In retrospect, the fact that Carter set single-season marks for touchdowns (11) and yardage (1,127) in a program steeped in running history should have tipped off NFL teams that he was something special. On November 1, 1987, the rest of the NFL found out about Carter when his first league catch was a 22-yard touchdown. He played in nine games and caught only 5 passes as a rookie, but 2 of them were for touchdowns. In 1988, Carter led Eagles receivers with 6 touchdowns to go with 39 catches and 761 yards.

In 1990, after the Eagles inexplicably waived him, the Minnesota Vikings signed Carter and he produced the best seasons of his career. He led the Vikings with 72 catches in 1991, 53 in 1992, and 86 in 1993 before quarterback Warren Moon arrived from Houston in 1994. The results of their collaboration were astonishing and unprecedented: 122 catches, 1,256 yards, and 7 touchdowns. Carter caught at least 9 passes in five different games, including 14 receptions against the Arizona Cardinals.

In 1995, Carter matched his NFL record total and accumulated 1,371 yards and 17 touchdowns, the latter equaled only by Carl Pickens of Cincinnati. In any other year, Carter's catches would have been an NFL record. But 1995 happened to be the year that Moore finally caught fire.

Moore was drafted out of Virginia in the first round of the 1991 draft and the Detroit Lions thought they had a good one. He had world-class speed and size (six feet three inches [191cm] and 210 pounds [95kg]) and a respectable work ethic, but he caught only 11 passes in his rookie season, for a paltry 135 yards and no touchdowns. Gradually, Moore learned to use his size to his advantage against defensive backs. His 1992 totals of 51 catches, 966 yards, and 4 touchdowns were second to Brett Perriman. Improvement was steady, if unspectacular, as Moore's reception total rose to 61 in 1993, then 72 in 1994 to go with 1,173 yards and 11 touchdowns.

With Scott Mitchell gaining confidence in every game, Moore started catching passes in bunches in 1995. One of his favorite (and most effective) pass routes was a simple jaunt into the end zone followed by a leap, as if for a jump ball in basketball. Moore found the end zone fourteen times in 1995, but more importantly, he caught a record 123 passes for 1,686 yards. The yardage total was the fourth-highest total in history. In 1996, Moore's 106 catches were second to Rice's 108; in 1997, Moore tied the Raiders' Tim Brown for the leading total of 104 catches.

One player widely missed in 1995, Sterling Sharpe of the Green Bay Packers, was forced to step away from the game in the prime of his career. He had spinal surgery before the season to correct a serious condition, but when the Packers realized rehabilitation might require the entire 1995 season and, even then, not guarantee a complete recovery, Sharpe was cut from the team. Before it was over, Sharpe had sued the Packers for allegedly misleading him. And although he wound up as a successful analyst at the cable channel ESPN, Sharpe's playing career was over after seven glittering seasons.

He was a first-round draft choice in 1988 out of South Carolina. The six-foot-one-inch (185cm), 205-pound (93kg) receiver had all the tools for greatness and his rookie season confirmed the Packers' suspicions. He caught 55 passes for 791 yards, both team-leading totals. In 1989, Sharpe led the entire league with 90 catches, along with 1,423 yards and 12 touchdowns. When head coach Mike Holmgren moved to Green Bay from San

Francisco, where he had coordinated the offense that featured Joe Montana and Jerry Rice, Sharpe's fortunes were bound to improve.

In 1993, Sharpe caught 108 passes, an NFL record he broke the next season with a 112-catch effort. In doing so, Sterling Sharpe became one of only eight receivers to lead the NFL in three different seasons.

The Groundbreakers

Believe it or not, the passing game has roots in the chilly, swirling air of Green Bay, Wisconsin—for, long before Sterling Sharpe, there was a receiver named Don Hutson who revolutionized the art of passing.

NFL offenses, horizontal from the beginning, have grown more and more vertical in recent years. Rule changes, along with bigger, faster, stronger players, artificial turf, and increased emphasis on the passing game make comparisons of different eras troublesome at best.

Still, when you compare Hutson to his peers, he was more dominant than Jerry Rice, if that is possible. The Packers receiver led the NFL in catches eight different times, including five straight seasons, from 1941 to 1945. Lionel Taylor, of the American Football League's Denver franchise, had five receiving titles, and

Before anyone else, Don Hutson had a handle on receiving the football.

Tom Fears of the Los Angeles Rams led the NFL in receiving for three straight seasons, from 1948 to 1950.

six other players—Tom Fears, Pete Pihos, Billy Wilson, Raymond Berry, Lance Alworth, and Sharpe—all did it three times. (Rice isn't in the record book in that category.)

Hutson caught 499 passes in eleven seasons, from 1935 to 1945, but 99 of them went for touchdowns, meaning that, roughly, 1 of every 5 catches was a score. No one—not even Rice—ever had a percentage that good.

Not only was Hutson fast, but he was one of the first receivers to run disciplined, precise pass routes. He was the standard for all the great receivers that followed him in the NFL.

There is only another handful of receivers whom you will find often in the record book—Raymond Berry is one of them. Not only did he not have the size or speed generally needed to make it in the NFL, he was horribly nearsighted and one of his legs was appreciably shorter than the other. But his hands, his marvelous hands, were supple and soft. Any football that ventured anywhere remotely close to Berry was caught.

Getting open, then, was always the greatest obstacle for Berry, who claims he had eighty-eight different moves on the field toward that end. He practiced them again and again, but even after a career including 33 catches and a touchdown at Southern Methodist University, NFL teams weren't very interested. Who could blame them? The Baltimore Colts made Berry their selection as a future in the twentieth round of the 1954 draft. Berry caught only 13 passes as a rookie in 1955, but by 1958 he was the league's best. Berry and quarterback Johnny Unitas perfected their timing in hours of practice each week. Unitas' habit of releasing the ball before Berry made his cut toward the sideline foreshadowed the timing patterns successfully employed by the San Francisco 49ers under Bill Walsh.

In the 1958 NFL championship game, Berry caught 12 passes, a postseason record that stood for twenty-three seasons. Raymond

Berry retired in 1967 with a total of 631 catches, another league record at the time.

History has not always given Lance Alworth his due; he played nine seasons for the San Diego Chargers of the American Football League and finished his career with two more seasons with the Dallas Cowboys. He was quick, nimble, and tough.

In his nine seasons in San Diego, Alworth averaged 50 catches and 1,000 yards a season. From 1963 to 1969, he produced seven consecutive 1,000-yard seasons. In one stretch, Alworth caught at least 1 touchdown pass in 9 straight games. It was Alworth who broke Hutson's record by catching passes in 96 successive games.

Like most great wideouts, Alworth benefited from a more than passable quarterback (John Hadl) and an innovative coach (Sid Gillman). Alworth averaged nearly 19 yards a catch over his career and remains the NFL record holder with five games with more than 200 yards a game.

Alworth never played with Charlie Joiner, but he would have considered the San Diego star a peer in every way. Joiner started out with Houston of the AFL, but his mark was made in eleven seasons in a Chargers uniform. When he retired after the 1986 season, Joiner had amassed 750 catches—an NFL career record—and 12,146 yards. Ten years later, Joiner was finally enshrined at the Pro Football Hall of Fame.

In terms of the record book, Joiner was a victim of timing, caught in the middle between Hutson and Rice. The same can be said of Steve Largent and Art Monk.

From 1976 to 1989, all Largent did for the Seattle Seahawks was catch everything thrown to him. In fourteen seasons, he caught 819 passes—the league's highest career total when he retired—worth 13,089 yards and 100 touchdowns. Those touchdowns were 1 better than Hutson, breaking a mark that had stood for forty-four years. After the 1995 season, only two receivers—Largent and

Rice—had managed to catch 50 or more passes in a decade of seasons. The guile and guts Steve Largent showed on the gridiron later came into play in his second career as a U.S. congressman from Oklahoma.

It wasn't Rice who broke Largent's receiving record; it was Monk, in 1992. Monk, a powerful wide receiver at six feet three inches (191cm) and 210 pounds (95kg), was rarely wide open, but his strength was fending off defenders with his body while his hands took in the ball. With 6 catches for Philadelphia in 1995, Monk's sixteen-season career total had climbed to 940 catches, 2 fewer than Rice.

The Running Back

In golf there is this charming axiom: drive for show, putt for dough. In football, the corollary is: pass for flash, run for cash.

The game of football is won not so much with scintillating 66-yard bombs that draw fans to their feet, but the quiet, forceful 2-yard runs on third-and-1. The best teams have always known this.

In 1983, the American Football Conference drafted all of the best and brightest college quarterbacks available. And while Dan Marino and John Elway have posted Hall of Fame passing numbers, none of those quarterbacks ever won a Super Bowl. In fact, after the Dallas Cowboys won Super Bowl XXX in January 1996, the National Football Conference had won twelve consecutive Super Bowls. A coincidence? Hardly. All of those NFC teams—the Chicago Bears, the New York Giants, the Washington Redskins, the San Francisco 49ers, and the Dallas Cowboys—understood the value of a sound running game. Even when the 49ers were in the process of winning five Super Bowls with a state-of-the-art passing game, they always had a running attack to fall back on when the going got tough.

Running is a matter of exerting your will. Passing, by definition, moves a team through the air. Running is a far more difficult enter-

BOBBY JOE EDMONDS

First there is the name: Bobby Joe Edmonds, the quintessential football name. His phenomenal story sounds like something out of pulp fiction. But believe it or not, it's true.

When Edmonds, a kickoff returner for the Tampa Bay Buccaneers, took the field in Philadelphia to open the 1995 season, it was his first appearance in a National Football League uniform in nearly six years, the second-longest absence in league history.

"If you can visualize something," Edmonds says, "then it is possible. It is not far-fetched that it can happen. Until it doesn't happen, then it can be true."

Edmonds was talking about making the 1996 Pro Bowl, a goal he ultimately failed to achieve. Still, only two kick returners handled more chances than Edmonds, who averaged 19.8 yards per

return. Considering where he came from, that was amazing.

When Edmonds was a Seattle Seahawks rookie in 1986 he actually did make the Pro Bowl. But even as Edmonds led the AFC in punt returns the following year, a history of alcohol abuse—he started drinking at the age of thirteen, shortly after his mother died in a car crash—was eroding his skills.

"I'd be in my limousine and have a couple of bottles of Dom Perignon on ice, and drink in the club and do my thing until two or three in the morning," Edmonds says. "Then I'd get up and go to meetings and practice."

Midway through the 1989 season, playing with the Detroit Lions, Edmonds broke his leg. Suddenly, he was out of football. A dependence on alcohol began to dominate his life even more. Then, on

New Year's Eve 1992, Edmonds stopped drinking completely. It took him three years to get another shot at the NFL.

He approached Tampa Bay director of personnel Jerry Angelo at the Senior Bowl in Mobile, Alabama. After doggedly extracting the promise of a workout, Edmonds played well on the practice field in Tampa. At the age of thirty-one, against all odds, he won a roster spot.

prise because it involves going around, over, and through human bodies intent on stopping you. Even with five or six blockers trying to clear the way, running the football is a fearsome, brutish business—which is why running backs have the shelf life of, well, a pair of AA batteries.

The legs, they say, are always the first things to go. Well, what else does a running back have? Players at other positions can compensate for ankle, knee, hamstring, and Achilles injuries by playing more sparingly in specialized situations. Running backs have nowhere to hide; you either do it, or you don't.

Of the twenty-eight team-leading rushers in 1994, nineteen of them had five seasons or less of NFL experience. Herschel Walker and Marcus Allen were the only team leaders with ten years of professional service, and the only two older than twenty-eight. Quarterbacks, offensive and defensive linemen, and safeties often reach their prime at that age. In seventy-six years of NFL football, running backs thirty years or older have run for 1,000 yards only seventeen times; John Riggins and Walter Payton both managed it three times, John Henry Johnson and Tony Dorsett twice each.

Running backs, then, are the true heroes of football. The only thing certain when you take the handoff is that you are going to get whacked. Physics experts say a collision between a running back under full steam and a streaking linebacker is roughly equivalent to two cars crashing at twenty miles an hour (32kph)—without the car, of course.

No Alias Required

By running back standards, Emmitt Smith III should already be retired or, at the very least, on his last legs. The Dallas Cowboys halfback was only twenty-eight years old when the 1997 season ended, but consider his dizzyingly high mileage: 2,334 carries for 11,224 yards and 119 touchdowns.

In 1995, Smith had an infinitely satisfying season. He won his third Super Bowl ring in four seasons and led the NFL in rushing for the fourth time, carrying 377 times for 1,773 yards and 25 touchdowns. Here is the short list of running backs who have managed four rushing titles: Jim Brown (eight), Steve Van Buren (four), O.J. Simpson (four), and Eric Dickerson (four). Select company, indeed.

Most people didn't think it would ever happen. Heading into the 1995 season, *Inside Sports* wrote this about Smith: "He has already defied the odds, leaving fans to wonder how much longer he can last. Smith's rushing average had been climbing steadily, from 3.9 yards per carry as a rookie in 1990 to 4.3, 4.6, and a phenomenal 5.3 in 1993. Last year it dropped to 4.0. A pulled hamstring forced him to miss his first NFL game due to injury last Christmas Eve, and in the playoffs Smith wasn't the same workhorse the Cowboys had ridden to the previous two Super Bowls."

All Smith did in 1995 was lead the entire league with his 377 carries and average a robust 4.7 yards per carry, a figure surpassed

Emmitt Smith of the Dallas Cowboys, catching a little air, prepares to leave a defensive back behind him.

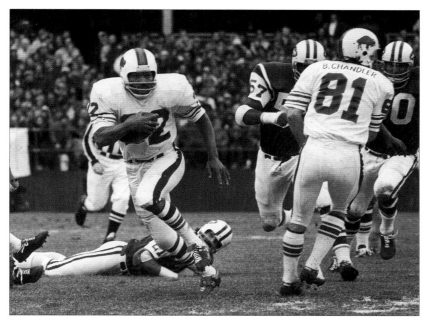

In another, simpler lifetime, Orenthal James Simpson was a pretty terrific running back.

among league leaders only by Detroit's Barry Sanders (4.8). The fact that Smith ran behind one of the best offensive lines in the history of the game did not minimize his accomplishments.

Great running backs want to carry the ball, even when they know every step draws them closer to retirement. "One thing about the Emmitt Smiths is their great competitiveness," says Chicago Bears head coach Dave Wannstedt, formerly the Dallas defensive coordinator. "They want to be in the Hall of Fame. They want to be in the Pro Bowl. They want to be in the Super Bowl. From a coaching standpoint, it's easier said than done to try and not run those guys too much and use them up. They never want to come out of a game."

In many ways, 1993 was Smith's signature season. It defined the five-foot-nine-inch (175cm), 209-pound (95kg) athlete's desire to succeed, individually and from a team standpoint. The Cowboys were coming off their first Super Bowl victory in fifteen seasons, a 52–17 razing of the Buffalo Bills in Super Bowl XXVII, when the consummate team player felt he had to stand up for himself. He had won two league rushing titles and earned three trips to the Pro Bowl in his first three seasons; all he wanted to was to be compensated appropriately, as the league's highest-paid running back. The Cowboys said no.

And so, Smith sat out the first two games. It was agony, especially when the Cowboys lost those games, including an embarrassing loss to Buffalo. Smith was aware that no team ever won a Super Bowl after going 0–2.

A week later the two parties compromised, and Smith signed a four-year, $13.6 million contract. Quickly, things turned around in Dallas. The Cowboys won their next seven games and Smith jumped into the rushing race. In the end, Smith produced seven 100-yard games, including 168 yards in the regular-season finale, to win his third rushing championship with 283 carries for 1,486 yards.

That final regular-season game was one of football's most heroic performances. The Cowboys met the Giants at the Meadowlands with the home-field advantage through the playoffs on the line. With less than two minutes left in the first half, Smith suffered a first-degree separation of his right shoulder. That should have been the end of the game and perhaps the season for Smith, but he told the trainers to tape it tightly.

Smith carried the Cowboys in the second half of a game that they would win, 16–13, in overtime. The Cowboys called on him seventeen times in all, quarterback Troy Aikman putting the ball in Smith's midsection because Smith did not have the effective use of his right arm. After every play, Smith's Dallas teammates helped him to his feet and guided him back to the huddle.

"If there has ever been a time that I've sold my body for my teammates, it was then," Smith says. "I don't think I could ever go through that pain again. The pain was unreal. I've always had a high level of pain tolerance, but that day went far beyond the level of high pain tolerance. I pushed my body and my mind to the limit, to the extreme."

By clinching the home-field advantage, the Cowboys and Smith gave themselves a week off. Playoff victories over Green Bay and San Francisco propelled the Cowboys into their second straight Super Bowl against Buffalo, which, based on the previous year, promised to be a blowout. But with the score tied at 13 in the second half, the Bills hadn't gone anywhere. On the Cowboys' first drive, Smith carried six straight times for 46 yards. After fullback Daryk Johnston caught a pass to move the ball to the Buffalo 15-yard line, Smith blew into the end zone, giving the Cowboys the lead for good.

Dallas won the game, 30–13, and Smith was named the Most Valuable Player of Super Bowl XXVIII. This from a man who would require shoulder surgery after the season.

Smaller Lasts Longer

When Smith won the 1995 rushing title, Barry Sanders was right behind him with an even 1,500 yards. It seems the Detroit Lions running back always is.

Actually, Sanders is a season ahead of Smith, having arrived in the NFL in 1989 as a first-round draft choice from Oklahoma State. The two gifted runners, along with Buffalo's Thurman Thomas, are the best of the 1990s and built along similar lines. Sanders is five feet eight inches (173cm) and 203 pounds (92kg), but don't call him small. His numbers in seven NFL seasons are enormous.

Like Smith, Sanders has the rare ability to make players miss. That is, he eliminates defenders in his path by making a slight, sometimes almost undetectable twitch or flinch that freezes them into leaning the wrong way. This is a physical and mental exercise

OPPOSITE: Buffalo's Thurman Thomas is the quintessential all-purpose running back.

that separates the truly great running backs from those who are merely good. Sanders, in fact, faked out Pittsburgh cornerback Rod Woodson so totally on one play that the future Hall of Famer missed most of the 1995 season with a serious knee injury.

Sanders is quite naturally quick, elusive, and powerful, but his singular style is one of abrupt stops and starts. His stuttering, herky-jerky runs can be breathtaking. Sometimes only slow-motion replays do him justice.

In 1997, Sanders had a career season. He carried 335 times for 2,053 yards (an average of 6.1 yards per carry) and 11 touchdowns. It was the second-highest total ever, and only the third time anyone cleared the 2,000-yard mark.

The first time Sanders won an NFL rushing title, in 1994, he carried 331 times for 1,883 yards and a gaudy average of 5.7 yards per carry. For much of the season he flirted with the hallowed 2,000-yard mark. Through nine seasons, Sanders was the NFC's leading active rusher, with 13,778 yards, which works out to an average of 1,531 yards per season. With his breakthrough season in 1997, Sanders pulled to within striking distance of Walter Payton's all-time rushing mark of 16,726 yards. Heading into 1998, Sanders was less than 3,000 yards—just two routine seasons for him—from passing Payton. Marcus Allen is second on the active list, with 12,243 yards in sixteen seasons.

Third on the active list is Thurman Thomas, whose 643 yards in 1997 gave him a total of 11,405 in ten seasons. He played ahead of Sanders at Oklahoma State and was drafted by the Buffalo Bills in the second round of the 1988 draft. And while Smith and Sanders are likely to surpass his rushing totals, they cannot approach his well-rounded game.

Thomas set a record in 1992 by leading the league in all-purpose yardage for the fourth consecutive year. He carried 312 times for 1,487 yards and caught 58 passes for another 626 yards. That works out to 370 touches of the ball and 2,113 yards, or nearly 6 yards each time the Bills called Thomas' number.

If Buffalo placekicker Scott Norwood had made a 47-yard field goal against the Giants in Super Bowl XXV in Tampa, Thomas would have been the runaway choice for Most Valuable Player. He carried 15 times for 135 yards and caught 5 passes, but the Bills lost and Thomas' effort was reduced to a mere footnote.

Smith, Sanders, and Thomas have all lasted longer than the typical football player, whose average time in the league is just over three seasons. These running backs have something in common beyond greatness: their compact size. All three believe their durability is based, at least in part, on their ability to escape the direct impact of would-be tacklers.

A Historic Gamble

Bill Polian, who drafted Thomas in Buffalo, is now the general manager of the Indianapolis Colts. In 1995, when he had the same

job with the Carolina Panthers, he had the option of taking Penn State running back Ki-Jana Carter, by consensus the best player available. Polian, acutely aware of the learning curve facing the Panthers, passed. He traded the draft's first pick to the Cincinnati Bengals, who used it for Carter, who signed a $19.2 million contract, featuring a signing bonus of $7.1 million. After he suffered a knee injury in the preseason, Carter was lost for the entire year, underlining the fragility of running backs.

Carolina, meanwhile, used the Bengals' fifth overall pick for Carter's Penn State teammate, quarterback Kerry Collins. Polian knew that quarterbacks develop more slowly and last longer than running backs.

"Once we're ready to win, the career of a running back is at an end or approaching it," Polian says. "I look at it from the four-year point of view. The actuarial tables tell you after that, running backs' careers are either over or begin to decline. They tend to contribute early, and they tend to be gambles because one injury can end their career. Would the money we'd have had to pay Ki-Jana Carter as the first player have materially contributed to winning right off the bat? I don't think so."

In retrospect, Polian looked like a genius. Not only did he save his team more than $4 million in salary, but the Panthers won an expansion-record seven games. Collins, for his part, completed 49.4 percent of his passes for 2,717 yards and a respectable touchdowns-to-interceptions ratio of 14-to-19.

In many ways, 1995 was a season of redemption for Ricky Watters of the Philadelphia Eagles. He was a star for the San Francisco 49ers in Super Bowl XXIX against the San Diego Chargers, scoring 3 touchdowns, but the 49ers let him go because they were too close to the salary cap limit. The Eagles signed the former Notre Dame star to a three-year contract that could be worth more than $7 million.

Watters was drafted in 1991, behind backs like Nick Bell, Leonard Russell, and Harvey Williams, and gained more than 1,000 yards in his first active season. But playing in the 49ers' pass-heavy offense, Watters never got the carries and the respect he felt he deserved. In 1995, he got it all in Philadelphia. Watters carried 337 times for 1,273 yards and 11 touchdowns. He also caught 62 passes for 434 yards.

It will be quite some time, if ever, before Watters catches Herschel Walker literally and figuratively. At the age of thirty-three, Walker finished 1995 by going over the 8,000-yard mark for rushing, and that doesn't include the 5,562 rushing yards he amassed in three seasons for the New Jersey Generals of the defunct United States Football League.

Playing in Giants Stadium, the same stadium he graced as a USFL star, Walker defied the odds in a Giants uniform. Like receiver Jerry Rice, he has an impossibly difficult off-season workout schedule that involves six-hour days, seven days a week. Sit-ups, in sets of three hundred to five hundred, are his specialty. Walker has never formally lifted weights, but teams have allowed him to continue his unique regimen because his strength scores have always been off the chart.

"As soon as the season is over, I'm ready to go back," Walker says. "I train myself like the military. Any time they call I'm ready to go. That's the way I am . . . . I work out like a madman."

Heading into the 1995 season, Curtis Martin's prospects did not look good. He had an up-and-down career at the University of Pittsburgh, where he nonetheless gained 2,643 yards in thirty games. Martin, five feet eleven inches (180cm) and 203 pounds (92kg), suffered a season-ending ankle injury in the second game of his senior season. On paper, he had the ability of a first-round draft choice, but the injury left NFL teams leery. He was drafted in the third round by the New England Patriots, who made him the seventy-fourth overall player taken.

In training camp, even in the face of two grueling practices per day, Martin told anyone who would listen that he was happy just to be there.

"I'm blessed with this opportunity," said the extemely grateful Martin, a deeply religious man. "I'm going to try to do the most I can with it."

Even Martin and the Patriots couldn't have dreamed of what came to pass. Playing for coach Bill Parcells—who never met a rookie he really liked—and functioning in quarterback Drew Bledsoe's offensive system, which had broken NFL passing records the season before, Martin became one of the league's most unstoppable forces. He carried 368 times for 1,487 yards and 14 touchdowns. Only Emmitt Smith and Barry Sanders gained more yards. Only Smith carried more times. Martin also had the single busiest day for a running back in 1995, carrying the ball thirty-six times against the Buffalo Bills on October 23.

One of the NFL's most productive running backs ever, Herschel Walker soars over the New York Giants' defensive line for his first-ever NFL touchdown.

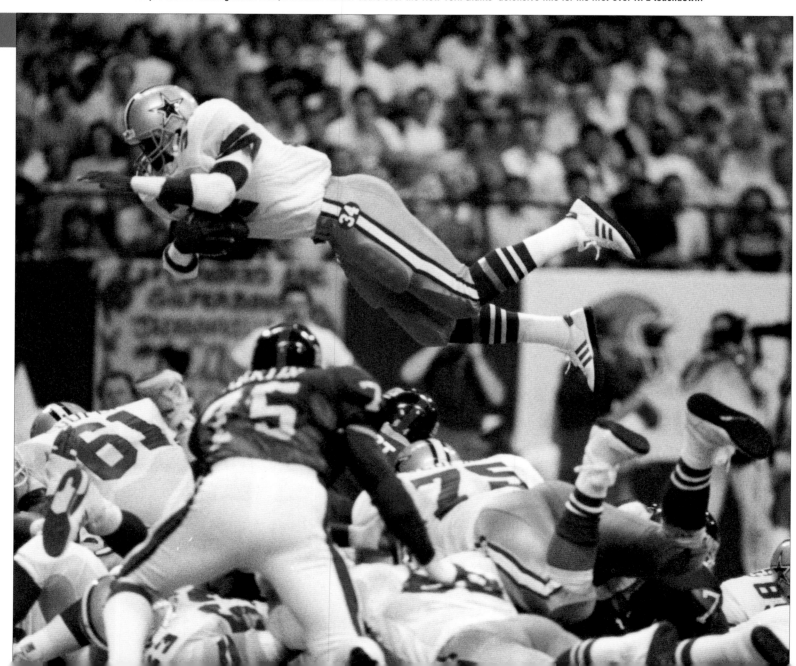

Following the 1997 season, Patriots running back Curtis Martin signed a controversial free agent contract with his former coach, Bill Parcells, who had preceded him to the New York Jets.

Martin's 1,487 yards broke the Patriots' record of 1,458, set by Jim Nance in 1966. That was Nance's second season, which reinforces the idea that running backs, like certain wines from the Tuscany region of Italy, are better when young and fresh. Consider that Martin's effort fell well short of the NFL rookie record. The top three marks belong to Eric Dickerson (1,808 in 1983), George Rogers (1,674 in 1981), and Ottis Anderson (1,605 in 1979).

Rushing into History

To this day, one running back stands above all others. His name is Jim Brown.

Consult the NFL record book and you will find running backs with more yards, many more than his 12,312. But in terms of sheer quality, no one was better than Brown, not even close. Look at the categories that cut across eras:

- Average per carry. Brown gained 5.2 yards every time he ran the ball, making him first on the all-time list, ahead of Mercury Morris (5.14) and the great Gale Sayers (5.0).
- Seasons leading the league. Brown did it eight times in

the nine seasons he played, including five in a row, an incredible mark of consistent excellence and twice as many as any other runner in history.

- Pro Bowls. His peers voted him to the postseason game in each of his nine seasons.
- Scoring. Brown finished with 106 rushing touchdowns, second to the 110 posted by Walter Payton, who played 16-game seasons instead of 12- and 14-game seasons and needed four more seasons to score 4 more touchdowns. Brown led the NFL in touchdowns five times, another record.

He was a phenomenal athlete who, at six feet two inches (188cm) and 232 pounds (105kg), was a fullback with the speed to outrun the swiftest defensive backs and the power to knock out linebackers. Brown was drafted by the Cleveland Browns in the first round of the 1957 draft. Toughness might have been his best quality; he was an All-American in lacrosse at Syracuse University and he never missed a game in the NFL.

He failed to reach 1,000 yards in only two seasons—his first two. In 1963, Brown carried the ball 291 times for a then-record

OPPOSITE: Barry Sanders of the Detroit Lions, perhaps the most elusive running back in NFL history. ABOVE: By contrast, Cleveland's Jim Brown went through defenders (for example, the Los Angeles Rams, seen here) on his way to an NFL record—5.2 yards per carry.

1,863 yards, averaging 6.4 yards per attempt. Two years later, after the 1965 season, Brown, only twenty-nine, was out of the league.

Brown stunned the NFL by leaving for Hollywood and the lucrative movie business. He starred in a number of motion pictures, including *The Dirty Dozen*, but the critics were less than kind. Let's just say his football legacy was never threatened.

Choosing the best of all time is a delicate business, but when the NFL celebrated its seventy-fifth anniversary in 1995, a celebrated panel of experts insisted on including Bronko Nagurski as one of seven honored running backs.

Nagurski was only six feet two inches (188cm) and 225 pounds (102kg), but he was a giant-size legend; his size 19^1/$_2$ championship ring is a popular feature at the Pro Football Hall of Fame.

His given name, Bronislau, was the gift of Ukrainian immigrant parents, but a teacher shortened it to a more recognizable Bronko and soon the NFL had a bruising fullback with a perfect handle. He is credited with 4,301 rushing yards in nine seasons, with an average per carry of 4.9 yards, but statistics of the day are suspect. In the eight seasons from 1930 to 1937, Nagurski helped the Chicago Bears to two championships and made six Pro Bowls. After retiring for five years to concentrate on professional wrestling, Nagurski returned to lead the WWII-depleted Bears to another championship in 1943. Nagurski scored the first touchdown in a 41–21 victory over Washington. He was thirty-five years old.

One name that doesn't roll off the tongue with the readiness of Nagurski or Brown is Steve Van Buren. It should, because he belongs among a small class of running greats.

From 1947 to 1950, the 215-pound (98kg) back led the NFL in rushing, something that had never been done at the time. In all, he led his league peers in four different seasons, something only five other men have accomplished. In addition, Van Buren played defensive back, returned kickoffs and punts, punted, and even kicked some extra points for his Philadelphia Eagles.

If any former player could give Barry Sanders a run for his money in terms of elegant style, it would be Gale Sayers. His career was cut short by knee injuries; he played in only 68 NFL games, but in seven magnificent seasons, from 1965 to 1971, he made a lasting impression.

Sayers' running had an airy, gazellelike quality, and the six-foot (183cm), 200-pound (91kg) halfback had a flair for the dramatic. He broke into the league by scoring an NFL-record 22 touchdowns, 6 of which came in a single game against the San Francisco 49ers, tying an NFL record that stands today. He won NFL rushing titles in 1966 and 1969. In 1967, Sayers returned a punt and 3 kickoffs for touchdowns. He was the Most Valuable Player in three Pro Bowls.

A single statistic captures Sayers' explosiveness: his career average of 30.56 yards per carry for kickoff returns is the NFL's best ever. He averaged a touchdown for every fifteen times he touched the ball.

These days, the name Orenthal James Simpson has a darker, more ominous connotation, but in the context of football, his career was brilliant across the board.

For eleven seasons, from 1969 to 1979, O.J. Simpson was nearly untouchable. He arrived in Buffalo after a career at the University of Southern California, where he won the Heisman Trophy and led the Trojans to back-to-back Rose Bowls. His first three seasons, under coaches John Rauch and Harvey Johnson, were mildly disappointing. Then Lou Saban came in and built the offense around Simpson.

The results were immediate. In 1972, Simpson carried nearly as much as he had in the two previous years and finished with an NFL-high 1,251 yards. In 1973, "Juice" went off the chart. First he broke Brown's single-season record of 1,863 yards; then he cleared the 2,000-yard mark, long thought to be unattainable. Simpson gained an even 200 yards in the regular-season finale against the New York Jets, giving him 2,003 for the year.

Simpson achieved the record in fourteen games, a fact that became relevant when Eric Dickerson broke his record in 1984 with 2,105 yards in sixteen games. Dickerson averaged about half a yard less than Simpson did in his record-breaking campaign.

Walter Payton did not have the raw power of Nagurski or the blinding speed of Simpson, but he outlasted all the running backs in the history of the NFL. Yes, the man they called "Sweetness" survived beautifully, carrying 3,838 times for 16,726 yards in thirteen seasons, both all-time records. Many of those yards came when Payton played for a dreary Chicago Bears team with no apparent offensive line.

Payton ran with a splay-legged abandon that was a joy to behold—unless you were trying to tackle him. His hands were historically underrated, for Payton finished his career with 492 catches, a record for running backs when he retired.

Earl Campbell played only seven seasons with the Oilers, from 1978 to 1984, and two more in New Orleans, but the bruising 233-pound (106kg) back produced 9,407 yards and 74 touchdowns. He led the league in rushing his first three seasons, but never again. He gained 1,934 yards in 1980, including four games with at least 200 yards.

Although Eric Dickerson never won any personality prizes, his running ability was undeniable. He led the NFL in rushing four different times, with the Los Angeles Rams in 1983, 1984, and 1986 and with the Indianapolis Colts in 1988. In 1984, Dickerson ran for 2,105 yards, the best single-season total in history.

And while Dickerson lost his career rushing yardage title to Payton, there was one record he still had a piece of after the 1995 season. Until then, no other runner had ever put together seven consecutive 1,000-yard seasons—not Brown, Payton, Simpson, or Dorsett. When both Barry Sanders and Thurman Thomas cleared 1,000 yards, Dickerson was forced to share his record. Still, considering the company, his career was elevated by their presence.

The Offensive Line

The center adjusts his grip on the football and, on the count of two, thrusts it back to the quarterback, who is already backpedaling. That's it. For about a second, maybe, just maybe, the eyes focus on the middle member of the offensive line, and then it's a matter of following the quarterback's movements. Who will he give the ball to? The running back approaching from behind? The wide receiver slanting across the middle? The tight end lumbering down the sideline?

We are a nation of ball watchers, and so we miss some of football's best action in the trenches, as offensive linemen wrestle with oncoming missiles known as defensive ends, tackles, and linebackers. The only other time offensive linemen are scrutinized is when the yellow penalty flag suggests they are guilty of holding or offsides. For offensive linemen, life really isn't fair. It is the tackles, the guards, and the centers who allow the higher-paid (and better-looking) quarterbacks, running backs, and wide receivers the freedom to function. Basically, the offensive linemen clean up after the elephants.

Men in the Mirror

In many ways, offensive linemen are mirrors of the men they must block. When the New England Patriots play their AFC East rival,

the Buffalo Bills, it's easy to confuse Bruce Armstrong and Bruce Smith. In addition to their first names and an unnatural way with words, they have these things in common:

Number: 78.

Height: six feet four inches (193cm).

Résumé: All-Pro.

They have been locking up—Armstrong, the Patriots' left offensive tackle, and Smith, the Bills' right defensive end—since Armstrong came into the league in 1987. Smith, who arrived in 1985, is one of the most fearsome pass rushers in the history of the NFL, but even in the beginning Armstrong was his match.

"[Smith] had already been a Pro Bowler before I got to my first one [in 1990]," says Armstrong, sitting in the living room of his Massachusetts home. "He was already his team leader, in essence, and that was one of the things I wanted to become. You would sit in a meeting room and they'd say, 'Well, we have to account for this guy. We have to put another guy on him.' That used to burn me up, because I would think, 'Yeah, this guy's a good football player. But so am I.'"

Soon, the Patriots stopped giving Armstrong double-team blocking help. Very quickly, Armstrong learned that Smith, like most great pass rushers, only has a handful of moves—three or four, actually. But Smith's speed (for a man who weighs 273 pounds [124kg], he is faster than light) puts pressure on a lineman and forces him to react quickly, sometimes too quickly, to a feint or false step. Smith's three basic moves are the outside speed rush, the spin and inside rush, and the head-on bull rush. Using these three moves like a pitcher uses a fastball, curveball, and change-up, Smith usually manages to keep the blocker guessing. If he succeeds in fooling him, say, twice and sacks the quarterback, he has done his job for the game. If he doesn't, the lineman wins.

"If the physical skills are a wash," Armstrong says, "then it's like, well, 'Who's going to make the mistake? Who's going to make that first mistake?'"

The answer to that critical question, after nine seasons and hundreds of plays, is, neither one.

After the 1996 season, Smith was second on the all-time list, with 154 sacks. Only Green Bay's Reggie White (176.5 sacks) had recorded more since the league started tracking the statistic in the 1982 season.

And yet, heading into the 1997 season, Smith had only sacked Armstrong's quarterback two or three times. One of the reasons for Armstrong's ability to handle Smith is that he takes his job title, offensive lineman, literally. His name, "Armstrong," captures his essence as he often takes the offensive against Smith and other pass rushers.

"This is the infamous and famous stab that Bruce does better than any tackle in the league," says Smith, running a coaching film over and over in the Bills training headquarters in Orchard Park,

Many of today's guys have big guts. Nate Newton of Dallas is the best example.

the running game because their trapping maneuvers can spring a running back for long gains up the middle.

Centers never have to go far to find the ball because every play starts in their hands. As a result, centers last longer. They are generally cerebral because they often call the blocking schemes at the line of scrimmage, based on the formation a defense is showing.

Offensive linemen practice an exact science that at once demands intelligence, balance, and finesse. Failure is literally painfully obvious in the form of a prone quarterback. The sack is the bane of an offensive lineman's existence. Usually, though, only a few people know whether an offensive lineman has done a merely adequate job or been phenomenal.

After a tough game, offensive linemen dread coming to work on Monday morning. That's when the grades, courtesy of the offensive line coach, who has been up all night studying film of the game, are handed out. The debriefing session that follows can be torturous, but at least the results are not public information.

When you think about it, sacks are the lineman's only official statistic. No one beyond the assistant coaches tracks the times the quarterback remains standing or the times a defensive player is backed up or actually "pancaked" on his back, the lineman's equivalent of a home run.

Bigger Is Better

Less is more, except along the offensive line, where more is almost always more. As football players in general have grown bigger, faster, and stronger over the years, so too have offensive linemen. In fact, the bulk they bring to the table today eclipses the relatively diminutive blockers of earlier eras.

A quick look at several of the great offensive lines in recent history underlines this evolution. The 1966 Green Bay Packers, winners of the first Super Bowl, had an offensive line that would be small by Division II college standards today. The tackles, Hall of Famer Forrest Gregg and Bob Skoronski, both weighed 250 pounds (114kg). Center Bill Curry was a mere reed at 235 pounds (107kg).

Six years later, the 1972 Miami Dolphins went a perfect 17–0 with a similar group, lightweight only in terms of sheer pounds. Left tackle Wayne Moore and right guard Larry Little checked in at 265 pounds (120kg), but the other three starters all weighed 250 pounds (114kg) or less. The average was 255 pounds (116kg).

The big breakthrough came in 1983, when the Washington Redskins put five offensive linemen on the field who weighed more than 1,300 pounds (590kg), a robust average of 274 pounds (124kg). Six-foot-seven-inch (201cm) Joe Jacoby, the hulking left tackle, weighed an even 300 pounds (136kg). Left guard Russ Grimm weighed in at 275 pounds (125kg). The fans at RFK Stadium called them "the Hogs" because they were hardworking, anonymous players who had enormous pride in their work.

New York. "He's aiming for the chest plate or the inside number, but he doesn't always get it there. He slips up every now and then and catches the face mask. If he catches your head, that nullifies your forward momentum."

Smith smiles. He has just thought of another weapon Armstrong uses to his advantage.

"The most important asset he has is his . . . big butt," Smith says. "That center of gravity makes it hard to knock him off balance. It guides him, gives him the balance to pretty much stop any type of rush that anybody can present to him. I guess that's what reminded me of myself so much, because I feel I have a big rear end as well."

The three positions along the line have very different responsibilities, depending on the scheme employed by the particular offense. There is a pecking order even within this universe of the overlooked, and the tackle is the star. In fact, when free agency flowered in the NFL in the early 1990s, big-time tackles were almost as rare as big-time quarterbacks. And it's no coincidence.

If the quarterback is the most valuable (read: highest-paid) player on the field, who then is the second most valuable? Scouts will tell you that the left tackle is not too far behind. That's because the left tackle protects the blind side of the typically right-handed quarterback. If Bruce Armstrong gets beat, the game—or even, in a worst-case scenario, the season—can be over in a flash.

Tackles are generally the best athletes along the line because, despite their size, they must block the burly 300-pound (136kg) defensive ends as well as the blazing-fast outside linebackers who gun for quarterbacks. Tackles are, as they say in the business, out on an island by themselves since they play at the ends of the line. Usually, when a pass rusher gets around the tackle, there is no support team.

The guards, who play inside the tackles, spend more time caught up in the traffic and the terror of the trenches. They often help the tackles double-team troublesome blockers and are vital to

Whap! New Orleans linebacker Pat Swilling says hello to Atlanta quarterback Chris Miller.

POST-CONCUSSION SYNDROME

In week five of the 1994 season, Chicago running back Merril Hoge received a glancing blow off the helmet, courtesy of Buffalo linebacker Cornelius Bennett's knee. It didn't look like much of a hit—hardly the stuff of the league's typically violent highlights—but Hoge's football career was over. He had suffered his fourth concussion in six weeks.

"They asked me where I was and I told them I was in Tampa Bay," Hoge says, "so the doctor said, 'Well, how do you know?' And I said, 'Well, I can hear the ocean.' And they were like, 'Oh, boy.'"

In fact, Hoge was in Chicago. After taking tests and conferring with his Pittsburgh neurosurgeon, Dr. Joseph Maroon, Hoge was advised to leave football.

"He said, 'You do this to your brain again, and I can't help you,'" Hoge remembers. "'I can't help you. Whatever happens, it's done, it's final, it's finished. I mean, if you drool or you can't speak or you can't function, I can't do anything about that.'"

Maroon says there is no way to determine the brain damage that can come with each concussion, but there is general agreement in medicine that the damage is cumulative. Maroon believes that two to four concussions are sustained in each NFL game, a figure many team trainers do not dispute.

How does a concussion occur?

"The brain is floating in spinal fluid, and it will literally smack up against the inside of the skull when one player hits another, particularly helmet to helmet," Maroon says. "There's a vacuum created and the brain gets sucked back into that vacuum. That's when the damage occurs."

New York Jets wide receiver Al Toon in 1992 was the first NFL player to retire with what is now known as post-concussion syndrome.

"In bed, no lights, no noise, no kids, no conversations—I just couldn't deal with the noise. I couldn't deal with anything," Toon says today. "Suicide crossed my mind, yes. I talked to my wife about it. There were times when I just felt like I wanted to get away from here.

"I still have problems with flickering lights. I have problems with ceiling fans. A carousel, I can't look at them. The animals going up and down and spinning? That still makes me sick."

Hoge's condition and the multitude of media stories prompted the NFL to form a committee in 1995 to investigate post-concussion syndrome. A year later, Hoge was in the national news again when Jets quarterback Boomer Esiason and St. Louis Rams quarterback Chris Miller suffered serious concussions. Esiason played on; Miller mulled retirement.

It was Hoge who had spoken with Miller on the phone before the season about his alarming lack of progress. Hoge told Miller he still didn't trust himself behind the wheel of a car and always carried his home telephone number in his pocket, just in case.

"There's a lot of things that Chris Miller wants to enjoy after football," Hoge says. "Those are the kinds of things we talked about. Sometimes the game of football is life, and becomes larger than life. But, really, there is more to life than football."

63

THE CHOP BLOCK

Former Raiders offensive line coach Joe Bugel says his play, "The Knife," was within the rules.

Hidden in the chaos of the trenches is an insidious weapon defensive players call the chop block.

Dan Saleamua, the Kansas City Chiefs' nose tackle, has seen more than a few chop blocks aimed at his knees, his very livelihood. "Your focus is on the offensive linemen, trying to beat him, beat him up," Saleamua says. "And all of a sudden, some guy comes out of nowhere. He blindsides you right at your knee."

Says Reggie White, the Green Bay Packers' stellar defensive end, "It's really the most dangerous block in the league. I mean, it can tear your knee up."

Back in 1991, the chop block was legal in most cases. The offensive lineman locked up high with the defensive lineman and a second offensive player chopped him with a diving, rolling block low. Offensive linemen used it to take a little aggressiveness out of defensive linemen. But after the New York Jets' Brad Baxter

chopped Detroit nose tackle Jerry Ball in December 1991, snapping the medial collateral ligament in Ball's right knee, the rule was changed in 1992. Presently, it's illegal for passing plays, but still legal for most running plays.

In 1995, a rash of chop blocks broke out in the NFL because of a gray area in the rule book. The San Francisco 49ers, working at the margins of the rules for a decade, were the team most closely associated with the chop block. The Oakland Raiders changed all that. In week ten, the Cincinnati Bengals' John Copeland was cut down by the Raiders' Dan Turk.

"The Knife" play was devised by offensive line coach Joe Bugel and it was, technically, within the rules. The Bengals objected on moral and ethical grounds.

"The guard made the call. He said 'Knife,'" Copeland said after the game. "He was being a coward. That's not how a man plays football."

The NFL agreed and Turk was fined $7,500. Copeland escaped with a bruised knee. There were other chop blocks, too, and the league circulated a memo to teams asking them to cease and desist.

According to NFL Rule 12, Section 2, Article 14, a pass rusher cannot be chopped if he is "physically engaged" with another player. Like Bugel, most coaches and players believe engaged means touching. Any separation, they insist, is legal. Intent is not part of the rule, at least on paper. Yet former referee Jerry Seeman, the NFL's director of officiating, instructed officials to call a penalty if there is an "intent to engage" a player, whether the players are touching or not.

Despite talk of re-examining the rule after the 1995 season, the rule went unchanged during the league's off-season meetings.

To the end, Bugel defended "the Knife" as a legal play.

"I swear on the Bible I would never teach something illegal because I'm not in business to ruin a guy's career," Bugel said. "I wasn't worried about hurting anybody because we practiced so hard on it."

But wasn't the block straddling a kind of moral edge?

"Almost doesn't count," Bugel said. "If it was illegal, it's illegal. If it's almost, it's not illegal."

While the 1993 Dallas Cowboys had some of the best skill-position players in the history of the game—quarterback Troy Aikman, running back Emmitt Smith, and wide receiver Michael Irvin—it is possible that the offensive line rivaled its better half in terms of skill. Before it was dismantled to satisfy free agency, advocates called it one of history's best lines.

The Super Bowl XXVIII champions started Erik Williams (325 pounds [148kg]) at right tackle and Kevin Gogan (330 pounds [150kg]) beside him at right guard. The left side wasn't much smaller, with Nate "the Kitchen" Newton (325 pounds [148kg]) at left guard and Mark Tuinei (305 pounds [139kg]) at left tackle. Only John Gesek, a meek six feet five inches (196cm) and 285 pounds (129kg), failed to tip the scales at 300 pounds (136kg). It all added up to more than three-quarters of a ton (681kg) and a staggering average of 314 pounds (143kg).

Some of today's linemen, it seems, could play guard and tackle on the teams of the 1920s and 1930s. Kansas City's John Alt is six feet eight inches (203cm) and 308 pounds (140kg). Atlanta guard Lincoln Kennedy is listed at 350 pounds (159kg), which means he could be well over 370 pounds (168kg), as teams typically list large players at weights lower than they actually are.

The mind's eye conjures up this prototypical picture of the lineman: a low center of gravity, concentrated in the behind and the gut. And while many linemen fit this description, many of the best are almost lean. The one thing they share is long arms, which gives an offensive lineman an automatic edge in the category he seeks to dominate: leverage.

Jim Hanifan, who joined Washington as the offensive line coach in 1990, has coached NFL players for more than twenty years. It was Dan Dierdorf, who played for Hanifan in St. Louis, who unwittingly put the size issue into perspective for him. Dierdorf, a broadcaster for ABC, stopped by practice one day and was standing by Redskins tackles Jacoby and Jim Lachey, who is six feet six inches (198cm) and 300 pounds (136kg).

In today's NFL, size definitely matters. Consider the weighty matter of the trenches in a game between Green Bay and San Francisco.

"When Dan played, he was one of the biggest men in the league; he stood out," Hanifan says, remembering the six-foot-three-inch (191cm), 288-pound (131kg) player. "But that day at practice I looked over and Dan was standing between Lachey and Jacoby and I thought, 'My God, Dan looks almost small next to those guys.' That's when I realized how much the game had changed."

History's Best

In 1996, Dan Dierdorf was inducted into the Pro Football Hall of Fame. Considering he never scored a touchdown or threw a pass, that's something of an upset. Dierdorf played right tackle for the St. Louis Cardinals from 1971 to 1983. He touched the ball exactly nine times in thirteen seasons: Dierdorf recovered teammates' fumbles seven times, fumbled once himself, and returned a kickoff for no yards.

That said, Dierdorf was a terrific tackle. He played in six Pro Bowls in a seven-year stretch. He became an offensive lineman almost by accident during his sophomore season at the University of Michigan.

"It wasn't my decision," says Dierdorf, who played offense and defense in high school and as a freshman at Michigan. "The starting offensive tackles my freshman year graduated before my sophomore year, but the two defensive tackles were still there. So in spring practice, the coaches worked me at offensive tackle and I just stayed there. It's that simple. I just wanted to play football. If the coaches had told me I was a defensive tackle, that is where I'd be today."

Dierdorf was enshrined in 1996 in Canton, Ohio; in 1973, Jim Parker became the first player elected exclusively as an offensive lineman.

Parker was a two-way player in college. He played both linebacker and offensive guard at Ohio State, where his coach, Woody Hayes, believed defense was his future in the NFL.

The Baltimore Colts, who drafted Parker in the first round of the 1957 draft, weren't so sure. They had drafted wide receiver Raymond Berry three years earlier and added quarterback Johnny Unitas and flanker Lenny Moore, so they placed Parker at tackle to protect Unitas and cement the passing game. All four players wound up in the Hall of Fame.

Parker, six feet three inches (191cm) and 273 pounds (124kg), quickly learned the art of pass blocking, something he never had to do at Ohio State, and helped the Colts win NFL titles in 1958 and 1959. After five seasons of defining the position, he was asked to move to left guard and he never missed a beat. In the end, Parker was voted All-Pro eight years running—four at tackle, three at guard, and one at both positions. He never forgot his place on the Colts' food chain.

"There was the one big rule," Parker says. "Keep them away from John [Unitas]. If I break my arm, I can still play. If he breaks his arm, we're dead. We're just the butter. He is the bread."

Not all offensive linemen are easily identifiable as future stars. In 1953, the New York Giants drafted Roosevelt Brown in the twenty-seventh round of the college draft. That's right. The draft was a thirty-round affair in those days and the Giants had seen Brown's name on the 1952 Black All-America team. They drafted him almost as an afterthought.

Brown had been a wrestler at Morgan State University, but his muscular sprinter's legs and 255 pounds (116kg) suggested he could play football, too. Eventually, the Giants changed their entire offense to take advantage of his peculiar skills. They called him a pulling tackle.

Brown's speed allowed him to sprint out of the tackle position as a blocker for running backs Frank Gifford and Alex Webster. He started thirteen seasons for the Giants at right tackle and was inducted into the Pro Football Hall of Fame in 1975, two years after Parker.

Vince Lombardi, the legendary Green Bay Packers coach, presided over some of the best athletes of his generation: Bart Starr, Paul Hornung, Ray Nitschke, Herb Adderley, Jim Ringo, and Willie Davis. But there was one he prized more than the others, and his name might surprise you: Forrest Gregg.

All of the above found their way to the Pro Football Hall of Fame, but Gregg was indeed something special. At six feet four inches (193cm) and 250 pounds (114kg), he was a monstrous player by the standards of the 1950s and 1960s, but he also had exceptionally nifty footwork.

Although Gregg made his mark at tackle, he filled in for injured guard Jerry Kramer in 1965 and still made All-Pro at season's end. He was that good. In fifteen seasons spanning three decades, Gregg played on six NFL championship teams. The achievement that best revealed his character was the 188 consecutive games in which he appeared, then an NFL record, from his rookie season in 1956 to 1971.

Guards are not blessed with the sometimes spectacular job description enjoyed by tackles. Consequently, you won't find too many of them in the Hall of Fame. John Hannah is an exception.

Like Brown, he was a wrestler in college. Balance and agility were his hallmarks, for at six feet three inches (191cm) and 265 pounds (120kg), Hannah was not an unusually large player. In thirteen seasons, Hannah was voted to eight Pro Bowls by his peers and was named NFL Lineman of the Year five times, including four seasons in a row.

These days, Gene Upshaw is best known as the executive director of the NFL Players Association. There was a time not long ago, from 1967 to 1981, when he was one of the best pulling guards in history.

Paired with left guard Art Shell, Upshaw helped lead the Oakland Raiders to three Super Bowls. He was enshrined in Canton, Ohio, in 1987.

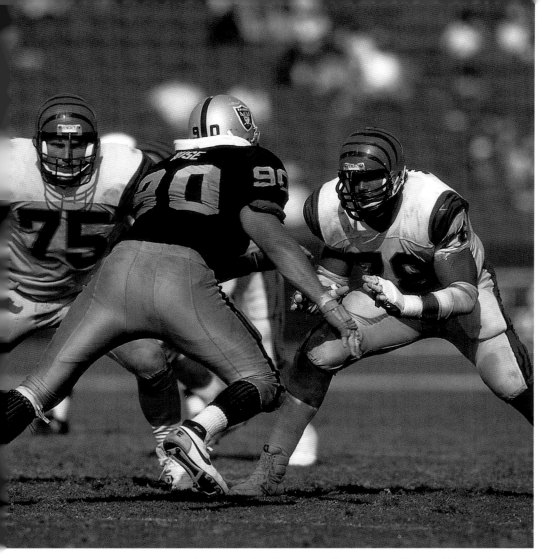

Ushered into the Hall of Fame in 1998, Anthony Munoz is arguably one of history's best offensive linemen.

"That's why kicking is such a mental thing," says Matt Bahr, whose 1996 season was his eighteenth in the NFL. "The pressure can become unbearable if you let it."

Bahr, an exceedingly normal five feet ten inches (178cm) and 175 pounds (79kg), is an interesting fellow. This is, after all, a man who can supply you with the missing "acerbic" in your *New York Times* crossword puzzle. He is also, certifiably, the tenth-leading scorer in the history of the NFL, with 1,422 points.

Bahr, 39, has another place in the NFL record book. His brother, Chris, was also a placekicker and together the two had combined for 2,635 points heading into the 1996 season. Most placekickers came up playing soccer, and the Bahrs were no exception. Their father played on the 1950 U.S. World Cup team that defeated England, 1–0. Matt played professional soccer in 1978, for the Colorado Caribous and the Tulsa Roughnecks of the North American Soccer League.

In 1998, Anthony Munoz joined Upshaw in the Hall of Fame. The Cincinnati Bengals tackle played from 1980 to 1992.

By modern standards, Munoz was not oversize at six feet six inches (198cm) and 290 pounds (132kg), but he was unquestionably an exceptional athlete. Former Cincinnati coach Sam Wyche liked to say that Munoz could have lost 100 pounds (45kg) and played shortstop for fellow Riverfront Stadium tenants the Reds.

Munoz set records for excellence: he made eleven consecutive Pro Bowls and was named NFL Offensive Lineman of the Year seven different times.

The Placekicker

First of all, placekickers are not really football players—at least that's what the big boys in the trenches will tell you. While most of the players are crunching each other in practice, the kicker stands on the sideline, spinning a ball on his finger or talking with the equipment manager. The kicker's entire contribution rests with, on average, a handful of kickoffs per game and maybe a couple of field goal attempts. Imagine—with seven or eight swings of the leg, you've done your job for the week.

Of course, this explains why kickers are more than a little crazy. While most players have dozens of plays on which to redeem themselves after a stinker, kickers have way too much time to dwell on mistakes.

Kicking, as described by Bahr, is all about confidence—to the point that making a kick borders on a study in Zen. Raul Allegre, who shared time with Bahr as the Giants placekicker, used to watch a highlight film of his greatest kicks before every game. He believed visualization of a successful kick increased his odds of making the next one.

Bahr's connect-the-dots career is typical of the talented kicker. He set records at Penn State University for field goals (22) and field goal percentage (.815) in 1978; he was also captain of the soccer team. The Pittsburgh Steelers drafted him and the rookie made an immediate impact. Bahr scored a team rookie record of 104 points, and the Steelers won their fourth Super Bowl.

After two seasons in Pittsburgh and a quick stop in San Francisco, Bahr settled in for nine seasons with the Cleveland Browns. From 1990 to 1992, he kicked for the New York Giants and enjoyed perhaps his greatest game. It was the 1990 NFC championship against the San Francisco 49ers at Candlestick Park. On a day the Giants did not score a touchdown, Bahr provided all the offense with 5 field goals, from 28, 42, 46, 38, and 42 yards. That last kick, which came as time expired, gave the Giants a dramatic 15–13 victory and propelled them toward their win in Super Bowl XXV.

The 1995 season underlined the need for an experienced placekicker. At the venerable age of thirty-five, Norm Johnson of Pittsburgh had a career year. He made 34 of 41 field goals and scored 141 points for the Super Bowl Steelers. Meanwhile, Morten Andersen, also thirty-five years old, made 31 of 37 field goals and

Matt Bahr, formerly of the New England Patriots, says placekicking is a largely mental, not physical, exercise.

scored 122 points for the Atlanta Falcons. Eddie Murray, thirty-nine years old, surfaced in Washington, made 27 of 36 field goals, and scored 114 points. It is worth noting that all three kickers were playing for relatively new teams: Johnson made his mark in Seattle, Andersen was an institution in New Orleans, and Murray kicked for Detroit.

In terms of leading the league, Lou Groza of the Cleveland Browns has no peer. He was the field goal leader five times: in 1950, from 1952 to 1954, and in 1957. Three kickers, Jack Manders, Ward Cuff, and Mark Moseley, managed the feat four times.

Jan Stenerud kicked more field goals than any man in NFL history. His total of 373 was achieved primarily playing for the Kansas City Chiefs from 1967 to 1979, but there were also stints with Green Bay (1980–83) and Minnesota (1984–85). Stenerud is followed in the record book by Nick Lowery (349) and George Blanda (335).

Stenerud's story is a classic that, upon closer inspection, sounds more and more like a Scandinavian fairy tale. He was born in Fetsund, Norway, in 1942, where he became a champion ski jumper. He received a scholarship to Montana State, but football coach Jim Sweeney asked him to try placekicking after he saw Stenerud fooling around one day with a soccer ball.

In 1966, after Stenerud had played football for all of two seasons, he was a third-round pick for the Kansas City Chiefs in the American Football League's red-shirt draft. As a rookie, he scored more than 100 points, his first of a record seven seasons over the century mark. His first field goal, a 48-yarder in Super Bowl IV, helped upset the Minnesota Vikings and set a record that lasted twenty-four years.

George Blanda wasn't the most accurate placekicker, but he had the most longevity by far. In fact, Blanda leads all players at all positions in NFL service with twenty-six seasons. Earl Morrall is a dis-

tant second place with twenty-one seasons. Blanda began with the Chicago Bears in 1949, played with the Baltimore Colts in 1950, returned to Chicago for nine seasons, moved to Houston for seven seasons, and played nine more, from 1967 to 1975, with the Oakland Raiders.

Blanda, who played in 340 games (another record), attempted 637 field goals in his career, 81 more than Stenerud.

Even more improbable than the cases of Blanda and Stenerud is the story of Tom Dempsey. He was, after all, born with only half a kicking foot.

With a special square-toed boot, Dempsey managed to find a place in the NFL. On November 8, 1970, he found a place in NFL history. His New Orleans Saints trailed the Detroit Lions 17–16 with fourteen seconds left in a game that appeared to be over. The Saints returned the ensuing kickoff to their own 28-yard line and quarterback Billy Kilmer completed an innocent 17-yard pass to Al Dodd to move the ball to the Saints' 45. But there were only two seconds left. Nevertheless, coach J.D. Roberts sent in the field goal unit.

Although the long-standing NFL record was 56 yards by Bert Rechichar, Roberts knew Dempsey had a chance; a year earlier, Dempsey had made a field goal from 55 yards out against the Los Angeles Rams. With holder Joe Scarpati setting up a yard deeper than usual to give Dempsey a little extra time to build momentum, the attempt would come from 63 yards away. Dempsey leaned into it and the ball just managed to clear the crossbar.

The Saints won, 19–17.

"There's so much involved in kicking one that long," said Dempsey, whose record still stands. "But I knew I could do it."

Dempsey's unique shoe, and singular achievement, can still be seen today at the Pro Football Hall of Fame.

THE LONG SNAPPER

You are in the den, watching your favorite NFL team playing on Sunday afternoon. At halftime you take your seven-year-old outside to toss the ball around. Instead of playing catch, listen to Larry Peccatiello, the Cincinnati Bengals defensive coordinator.

"Get him a football," Peccatiello says. "Stick it between his legs. And let him throw it back to you."

Meet the long snapper, the quickest ticket to the NFL. It is also the most anonymous position in the NFL. Long snappers—in 1994 there were thirty-five in all for punts and field goals—make half as much as the average player, but they last twice as long.

"I think there's a lot of guys who could do it," says Buffalo's Adam Lingner. "They just don't want to."

Says Bart Oates, formerly of the San Francisco 49ers, "I think it's because guys don't practice it, for the most part, or they're smart enough to realize if they start practicing the coach is going to put them in there."

Only one starting center, Tennessee's Bruce Matthews, snaps for both punts and field goals. "On fourth down, I'm like, 'Wow, I hope I can get it back there.' I'm all sweaty and stuff and hoping the ball doesn't slip out of my hands."

And then there is Greg Truitt, who at age twenty-eight in 1994 was the NFL's oldest rookie in forty-six years. He played at Penn State but pursued a career in hotel management before a series of odd jobs in Nashville, Tennessee. After he ran into two former NFL punters on a high school field, who praised his long-snapping technique, Truitt sent videos to NFL teams. The Bengals, hungry for a quality long snapper, signed him to a contract.

Truitt's job is to deliver the field goal snap to the holder in .35 seconds, a punt snap in .75. Truitt's best effort is a clocking of .59. That works out to a staggering fifty-two miles an hour (84kph).

"My dad told me as a kid growing up, 'If you want to work and learn a trade, you master that trade, then market yourself,'" Greg Truitt says. "'Then, if you become the best, you can get paid for what you love to do.'

"Not everybody is going to be the President of the United States. You know, everybody has a role to play. And this is my role."

Cincinnati's Greg Truitt believed he could play in the NFL, then proved it as a long snapper.

THE DEFENSE

A few years ago, actor Dennis Hopper created a nervous and scruffy referee character who was obsessed with Bruce Smith, the defensive end for the Buffalo Bills. Hopper, who was actually selling shoes for Nike in television commercials, marveled at Smith's athletic talents and cringed (with thinly disguised delight) at the prospect of a collision between Smith and an opposing quarterback. "Bad things happen," Hopper said. "Bad things . . ."

This is a fair overview of the defensive player's place in the game of football. He is, by definition, the enemy. He is charged with ruining the play as conceived by the offense. All teams, college and professional, chart the tackle statistics of their defensive players, but there are only three basic categories in the record book for defenders. All of them are considered "bad things" by the offense.

There are sacks, which occur when the ethereal quarterback is brought to earth. There are interceptions, which come when the wrong man catches the ball. And there are fumbles, which are essentially mistakes by offensive players when they lose their grip on the ball. While offense is all about planning and precision and execution, defense is the art of the execution itself, guillotine-style.

"There's no doubt about it," says Smith, who had leveled quarterbacks exactly 154 times heading into the 1998 season, making him tied for third on the all-time NFL list. "The defense is a bunch of bad cats. Bad cats."

Dallas Cowboys quarterback Troy Aikman is celebrated for delivering the ball accurately and on time. San Francisco 49ers wide receiver Jerry Rice is lauded for getting open and making a catch. Detroit running back Barry Sanders is admired for taking a handoff and

---

OPPOSITE: In 1997, at the age of thirty-four, Buffalo defensive end Bruce Smith recorded 14 sacks on NFL quarterbacks. Here, he lines up Miami's Dan Marino, a longtime foe.

running with it. But, really, do offensive players have to fight through the obstacles a defender faces?

Consider the plight of Smith or another elite player, Reggie White of Green Bay. They are never quite certain where the ball is going, while the offense very clearly is. Smith and White routinely draw two or three opponents with the sole objective of impeding their progress toward the ball. And still they manage to make big plays at critical times.

It takes a certain resilience to play defense. Some would use stronger words.

"You have to be crazy," says Lawrence Taylor, who played linebacker for the New York Giants and is one of three men to play in ten Pro Bowls. "It's not absolutely necessary, but it sure helps."

Listen to Bill Belichick, who was Taylor's defensive coordinator for Super Bowl campaigns in 1986 and 1990 and later head coach of the Cleveland Browns:

"Lawrence had the ability to block out everything when he played," Belichick says. "Pain, injuries, guys coming down on him in the trenches—he blocked out everything and focused on the ball. That's all he cared about. I never saw anyone sell out his body more on every play than Lawrence Taylor.

"The great ones are able to do that."

It takes, well, an unbalanced nature to put the pursuit of the pigskin above bodily harm, but history's gifted defenders were able to pull off that trick.

Listen to Charlie Waters, who played defensive back for the Dallas Cowboys from 1970 to 1981 and went on to coach in Denver:

"Stop and think about it for a minute. Running into guys, big guys, at full speed is not a normal thing to do. In fact, it can be kind of scary at times. You definitely have to psych yourself up to do it, convince yourself that this is something you have to do. The great ones like [Denver safety] Dennis Smith and [San Francisco safety] Ronnie Lott not only do it but they do it with pride and passion."

Linebackers seem to have a disproportionate share of that pride and passion. The Chicago Bears' Dick Butkus comes immediately to mind.

Doug Buffone, who played outside linebacker next to Butkus for eight seasons with the hard-hitting Bears, tells a story that could only be about Butkus, who never met an offensive player he didn't want to deck.

The year was 1973 and Butkus was playing in the second-to-last game of his Hall of Fame career, limping along with thirty seconds left in a hopeless game against Detroit. The Lions were leading, 40–7. Everyone wanted to run out the clock and go home, but Butkus, whose right knee was practically off its hinge, called a time-out. The Lions were amazed; Butkus' teammates were a little upset. Why prolong the agony? Detroit ran another play and Butkus called another time-out.

"I couldn't figure it out," says Buffone. "It was over and he's playing like a madman. Then it dawned on me. He had been having this war with their center, a guy named Ed Flanagan. I watched him after the second time-out and, sure enough, he took a run at him and really drilled him. Then, he called our last time-out and did it again.

"That is how I remember Dick Butkus. His intensity was incredible. If I hit a guy, there was a 99 percent chance he'd get up. If Dick hit a guy, there was a good chance he wouldn't get up."

Mike Ditka, a Hall of Fame tight end, has a healthy admiration for his fearsome former Chicago Bears teammate. "With all due respect," Ditka says of Butkus, "I've got to say that Dick was an animal. He worked himself up to such a competitive pitch that by the day of the game he wouldn't answer a direct question. He'd grunt."

And so, in the finest snarling (and sometimes drooling) tradition of Dick Butkus, Lawrence Taylor, Jack Lambert, and Ray Nitschke, we bring you the defenders of the faith—the men who keep the offense honest, and then some.

The Linebacker

It was fall 1980 when Giants general manager George Young fell in love with Lawrence Taylor. He witnessed the North Carolina linebacker (No.98) beat Clemson virtually by himself.

"I have never seen a guy dominate a game like that," Young says. "I came back to New York and someone asked me if I thought [the University of Pittsburgh's] Hugh Green was the best linebacker in the country. I said, 'Uh, uh.' He asked who was, and I said, 'I'm not telling.'"

When the New Orleans Saints drafted running back George Rogers five months later with the first overall pick, Young finally tipped his hand. The combination of Taylor and a Giants uniform, No. 56, would radically alter the way linebackers were deployed.

Previously, the defensive scheme of choice in the NFL was the 4-3, or four-man front backed by three linebackers. The middle linebacker was the glue that held it all together. Stars of the 1960s and 1970s like Green Bay's Ray Nitschke, Chicago's Dick Butkus, and Pittsburgh's Jack Lambert forced themselves on the game, mostly by stopping the run. But when the rules were changed to open up offenses, running backs and tight ends were employed more and more in the downfield passing game. Defenses were forced to compensate by getting quicker and more flexible off the line of scrimmage.

In the 3-4, as featured by the Giants, one down lineman was turned into a linebacker. Two outside linebackers with the versatility to rush the passer and cover backs and tight ends were bookends to two inside linebackers, whose major task was stopping the run.

ABOVE: The Washington Redskins' Earnest Byner discovers that the Giants' linebacking corps—here represented by Lawrence Taylor (56) and Pepper Johnson (52)—was a major reason the Giants won two Super Bowls, in 1986 and 1990. BELOW: Two of the toughest minds in NFL history: Green Bay linebacker Ray Nitschke and coach Vince Lombardi.

In truth, Taylor was a standup defensive end, but because he could move around at will, teams weren't sure how to block him.

The teams tried tight ends and running backs at first, but they were inadequate—for Taylor, at six feet three inches (191cm) and 243 pounds (110kg), was bigger and, in many cases, just as fast or faster. Eventually, teams tried to block Taylor with hulking offensive tackles in combination with a back or tight end. Sometimes, they double-teamed him with two linemen. As you can imagine, Taylor wreaked havoc with offensive schemes. He was one player that demanded a separate strategy.

"To be honest with you, coming out of college I didn't think there was anything I couldn't do," Taylor says. "Looking back, I guess I was right."

When he retired after the 1993 season, Taylor was the NFL's all-time sack leader, with 132½. He actually had 142 over his thirteen-year career, but sacks did not become an official statistic until 1982, after his rookie season. Taylor was voted to ten Pro Bowls in each of his first ten seasons, another league record. In fact, many football aficionados believe that Taylor is the finest linebacker to ever play the game.

Doing It All

Taylor's unique combination of speed and strength expanded the linebacker's repertoire to include pass rushing in addition to the traditional areas of run defense and the pass coverage of running backs and tight ends. Today's outside linebacker, it can be argued, is the most versatile player on the field. He must be powerful enough to take on 320-pound (145kg) tackles in pass rushing situations and, at the same time, be swift enough to stay with 190-pound (86kg) running backs and occasionally even wide receivers in pass coverage.

Linebacker Ken Norton, Jr., usually takes the shortest route to the quarterback.

The Giants won two Super Bowls, to conclude the 1986 and 1990 seasons, largely because they had two terrific outside linebackers. While Taylor almost exclusively rushed the passer on the right side, Carl Banks held down the left side, wrestling with the opposing tight end. That freed the inside linebackers to concentrate on the run. Many teams' defensive schemes are designed to sacrifice the bigger men up front, leaving the linebackers to make the majority of the tackles.

Pittsburgh's Greg Lloyd is the outside linebacker who today best embodies the spirit of Taylor. Unlike Taylor, Lloyd rarely rushes the passer. He is death against the run and usually drops off into coverage on passing plays. At six feet two inches (188cm) and 226 pounds (103kg), he is smaller but no less intense. Here is how he describes the rage he plays with:

"I always tell the guys when we huddle up, 'You've got to play not only like it's your last battle, but you have to play like somebody broke into your house. Or somebody broke into your car and stole the rims off your wheels and the stereo. And you see him, and you've got to chase him.'

"I understand that the guy on the other side really hasn't done a thing to you. It's just a psych thing. And you've got to get yourself ready for it. Whatever it takes. Like I don't make eye contact with any of the guys on the other side of the ball. I never look at them, except when I'm coming at them on the pass rush."

The rage has a source. He was abandoned by his mother, Nettie, at the age of two.

"Anger," Lloyd says. "I took all the anger and channeled it to positive energy. When parents were screaming for a kid on the other team, it was my job to take that kid out, make sure that kid hurt. My attitude was, 'Okay, scream for him now.' It's kind of sick, but that was my thing.

"It went from grade school right through high school, college, even the NFL. Coming from Fort Valley State [in Georgia], I had to prove I could play NFL ball. I'd hear, 'Where's Fort Valley? Oh, Division II.'"

He was a sixth-round draft choice from that obscure school in 1987 and he has blossomed into a classic linebacker. In 1995, Lloyd led the Steelers to Super Bowl XXX, where they nearly upset the heavily favored Dallas Cowboys. Lloyd was voted to his fifth consecutive Pro Bowl by his peers. He is also a second-degree black belt in the Korean martial art of Tae Kwon Do.

Lloyd, despite his on-field demeanor, is also a devoted citizen of the world. He makes weekly hospital visits, runs an inner-city football league in Pittsburgh, and works tirelessly in the community.

"The things I do with kids are more important than what I do on Sunday," he says. "One of life's basic essentials is to live a life that will outlast your life. What you do with your life is up to you. What your parents did, good or bad, that's their life. Do it yourself, always remembering that complacency is a sin."

San Diego linebacker Junior Seau is also known as "Mr. Intensity."

75

have a lot of money," Seau says. "But we did have a lot of love and I had my dreams."

One of his dreams was to play professional football, something he achieved when the Chargers selected him from the University of Southern California in the first round of the 1990 draft. The other was to establish a foundation to ensure that other unfortunate children had the ability to fulfill their dreams. The Junior Seau Foundation works to combat child abuse and delinquency and to keep kids from falling into drugs and alcohol.

Derrick Thomas has been a force in the community, too. You'll also find him in the record book. He was a six-foot-three-inch (191cm), 247-pound (112kg) terror at Alabama and was a first-round draft choice of the Kansas City Chiefs. Thomas paid immediate dividends with 10 sacks in his rookie season; he made the Pro Bowl that season and each of the next six as well.

In 1990, Thomas was incredible. On November 11, he sacked Seattle Seahawks quarterback Dave Krieg an astounding seven times, breaking Fred Dean's league record of six. In fact, Thomas had Krieg in his grasp for sack number 8, but he broke free and completed a touchdown pass that beat the Chiefs. For the season, only his second as a professional, Thomas produced 20 sacks. Only four other players—Mark Gastineau (22 in 1984), Reggie White (21 in 1987), Chris Doleman (21 in 1989), and Lawrence Taylor (20½ in 1986)—had more.

Thomas, Seau, and Lloyd don't have a single Super Bowl victory among them, but San Francisco linebacker Ken Norton, Jr., won three Super Bowl rings in three seasons—something no other player in NFL history has done.

The son of heavyweight boxer Ken Norton joined the Cowboys in 1988, but a broken thumb all but ended his rookie season. A knee injury prevented the six-foot-two-inch (188cm) 241-pounder (109kg) from playing full-time in 1989. The next year, he broke

Another Dimension

Junior Seau mirrors Lloyd in many ways. In fact, they led their teams to the 1994 season's AFC championship game, won by Seau's San Diego Chargers. Like Lloyd, Seau, a six-foot-three-inch (191cm), 250-pound (114kg) middle linebacker, is relentless. He is also thoughtful and compassionate off the field. He was elected the NFL's Man of the Year in 1994, following fellow linebacker Derrick Thomas.

As a child, Seau's family moved from American Samoa to Oceanside, California. "When I was growing up, my family didn't

Linebacker Dick Butkus had legendary "want-to," as football coaches like to say.

into the starting lineup as the weakside linebacker and led the team in solo tackles. Another breakthrough came in 1991, when he led Dallas with 13 tackles for losses and 17 tackles in two postseason games. As it turned out, Norton was finding himself just as the team was.

In 1992, it all came together. He recorded 120 tackles as outside linebacker, the first time in five seasons a noninside linebacker led the team. In Super Bowl XXVII, Norton was brilliant with a team-high 10 tackles, a fumble recovery, and a subsequent 9-yard run for a touchdown. The Cowboys defeated the Buffalo Bills with ease.

A year later, under great duress, Norton was even better. Playing the season with a painful tear in his right biceps, Norton moved to inside linebacker and made a career-high 159 tackles, the fourth-highest total in Cowboys history. In an almost instant replay, the Cowboys defeated the Bills in Super Bowl XXVIII. Norton was typically terrific with eight tackles.

And then Norton did the unthinkable, as far as Dallas fans were concerned; he made the jump to San Francisco as a free agent to play for the Cowboys' archrivals, the 49ers. Dallas had prevailed in two well-fought NFC championship games, but how would they fare without their man in the middle? The answer came in the season's penultimate game, the third straight NFC championship game featuring Dallas versus San Francisco. Norton, wearing the gold and scarlet of the 49ers, made a game-high 10 tackles against

his former teammates. He added 7 more against the San Diego Chargers in Super Bowl XXIX.

Future and Past

One of Lawrence Taylor's less-celebrated accomplishments was elevating linebacker to one of the glamour positions of the sport. Professional scouts will tell you that little boys who would have grown into tight ends or basketball players in previous generations wanted to be like L.T.

Consider the good fortune of the 1995 University of Illinois football team; not one but two talented athletes played at outside linebacker in Champaign, Illinois. When the NFL drafted college players in 1996, the New York Jets made USC wide receiver Keyshawn Johnson the first overall pick. Incredibly, the next two selections were Illinois teammates. Dick Butkus and Ray Nitschke, two linebackers for the ages, would have been proud. They too played in Champaign.

For the Jacksonville Jaguars, who had an NFL-low 17 sacks in their inaugural season, there was no choice other than Simeon Rice—or was that Kevin Hardy? In the end, it was Hardy, the six-foot-four-inch (193cm), 245-pound (111kg) linebacker the Jags chose second overall. He wasn't as spectacular as Rice, who had posted a school-record 45 career sacks, but while Rice was rushing the passer, Hardy was the versatile player who could cover receivers 40 yards downfield and roam, sideline to sideline, to stop the run.

"We pushed each other to get better," Hardy says. "Certainly, I'd want to go out on the field and outperform [Rice]. He was in the spotlight, because any time you're making big plays, such as sacks, that's what fans want to talk about. Simeon was the sackmaster, so he got all the attention, but it wasn't a big deal to me. I did what the team needed."

In thirty-four career games, Hardy had 221 tackles, 23 behind the line of scrimmage, and 7 sacks.

"Hardy is the best linebacker in the draft," said Dwight Adams, Buffalo's director of player personnel. "He can be an outstanding player in the NFL. He can rush the passer or drop into coverage. He has the ability to play over the end and rush. He was a dominating player in a dominating conference. He has all the intangibles."

The Arizona Cardinals, picking third, took Rice, a six-foot-four-inch (193cm), 254-pound (115kg) quarterback destroyer. He might have been the top pick, but his sack total as a senior dropped to 10 from 16 in 1994. Rice, who is never afraid to speak his mind, wasn't concerned.

"All this year did was make me hungry," he said. "I guarantee you that I'm going to be good at the next level. When it comes down to it, I'm going to be the best of all time."

We shall see, of course. One thing we know for sure: Hardy and Rice represent the future of linebackers, just as Clay Matthews represents the glorious past. Even as Rice was proclaiming himself as the best ever before he had played a single game in the NFL, Matthews could correctly say that no linebacker had ever played more games.

"During the game, people will say stuff to me: 'Hey old man, what are you still doing out here playing?'" Matthews said in 1993, his last season in Cleveland. "The great thing about the game of football is that you enter it at about twenty-two years old and I've never changed since then. My body may have changed a little bit, but my mind-set is still a twenty-two-year-old person."

He was part of the 1978 draft, along with running back Earl Campbell and tight ends Ozzie Newsome and Todd Christensen. In an age of specialization at linebacker, Matthews was a throwback. He played the pass, the run, and special teams.

In 1995 Matthews played his nineteenth season in the league, for the Atlanta Falcons, at the age of forty. He was the oldest active player in the NFL and pushed his record total of games to 278, tied at the time for third on the all-time list. Matthews may well wind up in the Pro Football Hall of Fame.

Matthews, the brother of Houston Oilers Pro Bowl center Bruce Matthews, had a fine career in Cleveland, but the team let him go. He went to five Pro Bowls and produced a Browns record of 76 sacks in his sixteen seasons. He landed in Atlanta and was a force, putting together 115 tackles, the team's third-highest total

and the third-best effort of his career. In 1995, he started all sixteen games and finished with 89 tackles.

"Every Sunday, I look at it as an opportunity to go get this guy, go get the quarterback, go get the running back, make 10 tackles, intercept the ball, be the hero for the day," Matthews says. "That's what it's all about.

"I have five children and I find myself telling them things about commitment, discipline, and so forth. Sometimes you'd like to take one of these younger guys and say, 'Look, it's not that hard. All you've got to do is know what you're supposed to do: prepare, pay attention, do your homework.' It's just not that hard.

"What happens on a given play, when you're a kid, when there is cross-action out there, when there is misdirection—everything is just flying around out there. At my age, it seems real slow. You may not be able to react as quickly with your body, but your mind can make you react much faster; you can actually be there before you could at age twenty-two."

History's Best

Here is all you need to know about linebackers: every year the best linebacker in the country is given an award—the Butkus Award.

He played only nine seasons, half as long as Clay Matthews, but what intensity Dick Butkus poured into those nine seasons. He was born in Chicago and played for the University of Illinois. The Chicago Bears were happy to make the local kid one of their three first-round draft choices in 1965. One of the others was running back Gale Sayers, giving them two future Hall of Fame players in one round.

The Bears had watched Butkus develop in college and won a bidding war with the Denver Broncos for the services of the six-foot-three-inch (191cm), 245-pound (111kg) two-time All-American. In an exhibition game against Cleveland, he made 15 tackles and blocked a field goal. In the season opener against San Francisco, he made 11 unassisted tackles.

Butkus was not blessed with great speed, but he had uncanny intuition, which usually delivered him to the ball on time. Once he got there, his hits were of numbing severity; no man has ever hit harder more consistently than Butkus. And shoulder pads, apparently, weren't always his weapon of choice. One of the many Butkus legends circulating concerns the day in 1973 that the Bears and Baltimore Colts hooked up in a particularly gruesome struggle. The Colts were headed to their airport, the story goes, but stopped suddenly in traffic. Seconds later there was a huge crash; the team bus had been rear-ended by a car. The Baltimore players looked at each other with the same thought: "Butkus!"

He played in eight straight Pro Bowls, recovered 25 fumbles, and made 22 interceptions in nine seasons before a ravaged right knee forced him to quit—something he had never done on the field.

Seven years before Butkus left Illinois, another Illini linebacker, Ray Nitschke, matriculated to the NFL. He was the Green Bay Packers' second pick of the third round. Nitschke had played some fullback at Illinois, but coach Scotter McLean had a feeling he could handle the action at middle linebacker. The Packers went 1–10–1 in Nitschke's first season, but there was an upside; the disaster prompted the hiring of one Vince Lombardi.

Later, Nitschke would credit the legendary coach with calming down his off-field persona and teaching him to use it to his advantage on opposing running backs and quarterbacks. Nitschke was six feet three inches (191cm) and 235 pounds (107kg), and he was a terror in the middle as the Packers rose to greatness and won five NFL championships and the first two Super Bowls. He was strong enough to punish ball carriers and quick enough to stay with receivers.

Surrounded by certifiably great teammates, Nitschke was inexplicably voted to just one Pro Bowl. But when the NFL selected its fiftieth and seventy-fifth anniversary teams, Nitschke was on them. Nine Packers players would ultimately be enshrined in Canton, but Nitschke, appropriately, was the first, in 1978.

Look at the great football dynasties and you are likely to find a linebacker in the middle of it. It was true of the Green Bay Packers, the team of the 1960s. And it was true of the Pittsburgh Steelers, the team of the 1970s.

Steeler Jack Lambert, like Nitschke and Butkus before him, carried the nasty, aggressive mantle of the middle linebacker. At six feet four inches (193cm) and 218 pounds (99kg), he was a little spare for the position, but his attitude was monstrous.

He stepped in as a rookie from Kent State and became a starter in the 1974 preseason. The Steelers, who already had future Hall of Fame defenders in linebacker Jack Ham and defensive tackle "Mean" Joe Greene, became "the Steel Curtain" that year. Pittsburgh won the first of its four Super Bowls with Lambert providing the muscle in the middle. At the same time, he might have been the best of the great middle linebackers in pass coverage. He finished his eleven seasons with 28 regular-season interceptions. His fourth-quarter theft of Rams quarterback Vince Ferragamo helped the Steelers beat the Rams, 31–19, in Super Bowl XIV.

He was the Steelers' defensive captain for his last eight seasons, played in nine consecutive Pro Bowls, and was twice named the Defensive Player of the Year. Finally, in 1984, a dislocated toe forced him to miss most of the season and he was forced to retire.

Because of Lambert's brilliance and the wealth of talent on the Steelers offense—quarterback Terry Bradshaw, running back Franco Harris, receivers Lynn Swann and John Stallworth, and center Mike Webster—Jack Ham was often a forgotten man. Chuck Noll, the coach of those four Super Bowl teams, was one man who understood the contributions of his slight, six-foot-one-inch (185cm), 220-pound (100kg) outside linebacker.

"[Ham] was a quiet guy who didn't like the attention, so no one pushed him as the greatest thing ever," Nolls says. "But, basically, he had no weaknesses. If you wanted to stop the run, there was no one better. If you wanted to stop the pass, there was no one better. If you needed the big defensive play to get you back into a game, there was no one better."

He was a scrawny 185-pound (84kg) high school linebacker who received Penn State's last scholarship in 1967. He played middle linebacker as a senior for the Nittany Lions, but Noll liked the way he ran and saw him as an outside player. Ham finished a twelve-year career with 32 interceptions, eight trips to the Pro Bowl, and the 1975 Defensive Player of the Year Award.

Not surprisingly, there was a linebacker in the middle of the powerful Kansas City Chiefs teams of the late 1960s and early 1970s. Willie Lanier was a solid six feet one inch (185cm) and 245 pounds (111kg) and was the Chiefs' second-round draft choice, from Morgan State, in 1967. They called him "Contact," for obvious reasons. By the fourth game of his rookie season, he was coach Hank Stram's starter.

The Chiefs, who had lost to the Green Bay Packers in the first Super Bowl the year before Lanier arrived, got it right three years later in Super Bowl IV. Lanier led the spirited Kansas City defense to a 13–6 victory over the New York Jets, the defending Super Bowl champions, in the first round of the playoffs. After another stirring defensive effort, a 17–7 shutdown of the Oakland Raiders, the Chiefs found themselves back in the Super Bowl once again. For the third time in three playoff games, the Lanier-led defense held the opponent to 1 touchdown or less. The Kansas City Chiefs defeated the Minnesota Vikings, 23–7, and as usual, Lanier had been in the middle of it.

Ted Hendricks was not exactly the prototypical linebacker. For starters, he was born in Guatemala City, Guatemala, and for another instance, he stood six feet seven inches (201cm) and weighed a lean 235 pounds (107kg). Because of his huge wing span—he wore a size 37 sleeve—he was dubbed "the Mad Stork" at the University of Miami. The Baltimore Colts drafted him in 1969 and he became a versatile force. And although he helped Baltimore win a Super Bowl in 1970 and appeared in the Pro Bowl as a member of the Colts and Green Bay Packers, his true place in the game was with the iconoclastic Raiders.

A free spirit, Hendricks fit in with the Oakland team and was part of three Super Bowl victories. The first, at the conclusion of the 1976 season, was a 32–14 win over Minnesota in Super Bowl XI. Four years later, the Raiders became the first wild-card team to run the table and win a Super Bowl. Hendricks, who finished his career with a record 25 blocked kicks and 4 safeties, did it all for the Raiders in 1980: 9 sacks, 3 interceptions, 2 blocked kicks, and a safety. The final touch was a 27–10 victory over the Philadelphia Eagles in Super Bowl XV. In his final season, 1983, the Raiders—

When Willie Lanier was on the prowl, NFL quarterbacks suddenly found footspeed they didn't know they possessed.

now operating out of Los Angeles—stunned the Washington Redskins, 38–9, in Super Bowl XVIII. Heading into the 1996 season, it was the last time the AFC managed to defeat the NFC in football's ultimate game, a daunting stretch of twelve seasons.

Hendricks produced impressive statistics, including 26 interceptions and 16 fumble recoveries, but here is the most telling number of his fifteen Hall of Fame seasons: he had the tenacity to play in all 215 of his teams' games during his career.

How like a linebacker.

The Defensive Back

The defensive back works directly against the overwhelming tide of sentiment in football. Is there a scenario fans root for more than the scintillating quarterback-to-receiver touchdown pass?

"Everybody wants to see you catch the ball, then spike it, and do your dance," says Darrell Green, the longtime Washington Redskins cornerback. "They don't want to see the little cornerback knock the ball down. America is just that way."

The defensive back, the antihero, defies the odds, too. After all, the quarterback and his receiver have already decided on the play and where it will go. The defensive back can only wonder. Two against one—it's not a fair fight.

"I don't care if you're the best defensive back that ever played this game," says Brian Cox, the outspoken former linebacker for the Miami Dolphins. "If you give a good receiver three, four, five seconds to run a route, I don't care if you're Jesus Christ, you're not going to cover that guy."

Which explains why good defensive backs are so hard to find, and why the great ones are rarer still.

"Life's not fair either," says ex–Pittsburgh cornerback Rod Woodson, one of the great ones. "But that's the challenge as a cornerback or a defensive back."

In this pass-happy era dominated by throwers and catchers, a new star has been born in the NFL. Just as the attacking outside linebacker position, popularized by Lawrence Taylor, grew out of a need to control the passer, the defensive player of the 1990s is the cornerback, or the cover corner. He handles the Jerry Rices and the Herman Moores one-on-one, without help from a safety or a zone defensive scheme.

"Who else can go out in front of ten million people watching on national television and get beat?" Green says. "Everybody saw it, and yet you go home and eat dinner, go to the movies, and so on. Hey, it's what I do."

Meet Woodson and Deion Sanders, the elite of today's cover corners and winners of the NFL's Defensive Player of the Year Awards in 1993 and 1994, respectively. Both of them are able, at times, to dominate games from a position that has always operated out of a, well, defensive posture.

"It took me about four to five years in the NFL to say, 'All right, I'm not nervous covering Jerry Rice anymore. I *want* to go out there and cover him,'" says Woodson, who is destined for the Hall of Fame. "If you can take away Jerry Rice or Michael Irvin, you take away a big part of the 49ers' and Cowboys' offenses. A big part. When you can do that, you're dominating a game."

While Sanders may be better known for playing baseball, selling shoes and pizza, returning kicks, and actually catching passes, he is one of history's great cover corners. Just ask him.

"It's belief," Sanders says. "I believe that I'm better than you on the field. I will outplay you on that field, on that specific play. I think that's the attitude a defensive back must have."

In a defensive scheme, the more talented the back, the less help he gets. Sanders and Woodson are traditionally left alone with the best wide receivers in the game. Most cornerbacks get help, as they say in defensive meeting rooms across the NFL. Here's how it works:

Cornerbacks, as the name implies, are set far away from the hurly-burly of the trenches, opposite the wide receiver. This is appropriate, because there isn't much that separates the players at these positions. Really, the major difference is hands; cornerbacks tend to have hands of stone—otherwise they'd be receivers. These days, receivers tend to be a little taller than defensive backs. Speed is generally a wash. Think about it; defensive backs have to stay even with receivers, and they almost always start out running backward.

The sideline, in this case, is an ally for the corner, since the boundary line acts as a wall. As the corner backpedals at the snap of the ball, he always knows where his help, if there is any, is coming from. It could be the free safety coming over to help with a deep route, or it could be a linebacker or strong safety covering a zone for short or intermediate routes.

In this age of substitution, teams often use more than the standard number of four defensive backs. When an offense finds itself in an obvious passing situation, it will often go to a three-, four-, or five-receiver set. That means one, two, or three linebackers head for the sidelines to be replaced by defensive backs, usually reserve cornerbacks. Teams call a five-back package a "nickel," and six backs are referred to as a "dime." In recent years, some teams have gone to a seven-back scheme to defend five-receiver sets.

In a regular first-down alignment, the left and right corners line up opposite the wideouts, while the strong safety is close to the line of scrimmage, among the linebackers. The free safety, the defense's truest freelancer, is farthest from the line, playing center field. The strong safety, a hybrid linebacker (smaller with more speed), is basically responsible for the run. The free safety, who has sideline-to-sideline responsibilities, is technically the second line of defense for long passes. Sometimes, of course, he is the only line of defense.

"Defensive back is almost impossible to play technically well," says Jerry Angelo, the Tampa Bay Buccaneers' director of player personnel. "Speed and agility are important, but he has to be aware, too. That sixth sense, the ability to anticipate, is really critical. Remember, the further away from the ball you are, the less rehearsed everything is. A lot of times, it's just reacting to a situation you haven't seen or prepared for."

The Island

Clearly, the poet John Donne was not thinking of Deion Sanders when he wrote this in the early seventeenth century:

"No man is an island entire of itself; every man is a piece of the continent, a part of the main; . . . any man's death diminishes me, because I am involved in mankind, and therefore never send to know for whom the bell tolls; it tolls for thee."

In fact, Donne was addressing the divine authority in "Hymn to God My God, in My Sickness." Every cornerback knows he will spend some time during the game on the place they call "the Island." He also knows the bell will toll for him if he doesn't make every play.

"If a defensive lineman makes a mistake, it's a 5-yard gain," says Rams corner Todd Lyght. "If a linebacker makes a mistake, it's a 10-yard gain. If a defensive back makes a mistake, it's a touchdown. And that's the bottom line. It's like playing goalie in hockey. If you make a mistake, the scoreboard lights up."

Says Woodson, "A quarterback can go out there and complete 7 of 10 passes and he's had a good day. When a defensive back lets one ball get deep, he's gotten burned. He's had a bad day. He might pick one off and get even, but everyone remembers the one he got beat on."

One of the many characters on Bill Parcells' 1986 Giants team, which won Super Bowl XXI, was defensive back Elvis Patterson. Parcells called him "Toast" because he was burned so often. It was, believe it or not, a term of endearment. No wonder defensive backs are such a skittish bunch.

"You have to be halfway kind of cuckoo, cuckoo, cuckoo," says former Denver Broncos corner Tim McKyer. "Teammates are telling me all the time, 'Hey, I'm glad I don't have your job.'"

There are two ways to deal with the insane pressure a cornerback faces on every play: confidence and amnesia, usually in that order.

Ignore the hype: Deion Sanders is one of the best pure corners in the game today.

"The ball in the air is not for him—it's for me," Sanders says. "It was meant to come to me. I want to see you do what I do: bump-and-run every play with no help. That puts it on the line. I don't want to see no safety over the top of you and you hollering about how good you are."

"I'd rather play a guy one-on-one," says Green. "I mean, that's how I got to be Darrell Green in the NFL."

Aeneas Williams of the Arizona Cardinals is one of today's best cover corners. He says that veteran corner Gil Byrd taught him to change his mentality. "Stop thinking, 'I can't get beat,'" Williams says. "Start thinking, 'He has to beat me.'"

Of course, all this hubris crumbles when the defensive back is beaten for a big gain. The solution? Forget it. It never happened.

"You put it behind you," says McKyer, who calls himself "the Blanket" because of the suffocating coverage he provides. "It's just one play. On the field, you just kind of go clear. Never happened. Trust me, if you sit there, dwelling on a play, thinking, 'Shoot, I got beat,' then you'll get beat again. If that happens often enough, you'll get beat right out of the league."

Sanders takes the same approach. "I have a short memory," he says. "If you catch a ball on me, I don't remember that. It's time for the next play. Let's move on."

Says Green, laughing, "I've probably never gotten burned, at least in terms of where I have an excuse every time I get beat."

"The cornerback," Williams says, "has to have something similar to amnesia. You have to be able to forget, and forget real fast. It's really your most important skill.

"When adversity strikes, you find out what you're made of. I remember a game in Philadelphia when Fred Barnett got behind me a lot. I learned a lot from that situation because late in the game you still have to face that guy. He can make some plays early, but who's going to be there at the end? That's why you have to block

coaches and general managers who have an interest in the arcane subtleties of the game, a sense of history, and—for defensive backs, anyway—a sense of cruelty.

For two decades, in an attempt to increase scoring—and, by a leap of logic, fan interest—the Competition Committee has slowly robbed defensive backs of their few weapons. In 1982, the season after Raiders cornerback Lester Hayes intercepted an amazing 18 passes in the regular season and the postseason, the league outlawed the stickum (Kwik Grip Hold Tite Paste) he spread all over his hands and arms. In the last six seasons of his career, Hayes man-

Despite his defensive posture, Todd Lyght of the St. Louis Rams has always found a way to get to the ball.

the bad plays out. Your knees are shaking out there, but you have to make the play."

Woodson has the last word on selective amnesia: "You can't say it didn't happen because, obviously, it did. The most important thing is to learn from that mistake so it doesn't happen again."

Exceptions to the Rule

Everybody conspires to make the defensive back's life more miserable, even the NFL. The league's complex on-field rules are overseen by the Competition Committee, an august group made up of

aged only 14 interceptions total. In some ways, the defensive back's only consistent friend, his only source of relief and comfort beyond the sideline, is his teammates' pass rush.

And, as the stakes have grown higher for touchdowns, wide receivers have grown taller and stronger in recent years. The average cornerback tops out at something close to five feet ten inches (178cm), while the typical wideout may have a three- or four-inch (7.5 or 10cm) advantage, not to mention longer arms for better reach. This is a problem, particularly in the end zone, where winning a jump ball is worth 6 points. Defensive backs, who rely on

When he played for Pittsburgh, Rod Woodson was a state-of-the-art cornerback.

agility and balance in order to successfully do their jobs, are usually more compact.

The defender is allowed to lock up (that is, physically engage) with the receiver only within 5 yards of the line of scrimmage, which makes for some interesting skirmishes at the snap of the ball. In recent years, defensive backs were sometimes allowed to stretch this hands-on zone an extra 5 yards, but in 1993 the Competition Committee cracked down and instructed officials to strictly enforce the rule.

After the receiver has shaken loose, all a defensive back can do is try to stay close enough to make a play on the ball when it arrives. If the defensive back is turned to the ball and is following its journey into the receiver's hands, he is allowed a modicum of contact. If he happens to be slightly off balance and caught with his back to the ball, and he touches the receiver even slightly, the penalty flag for pass interference flies in his direction.

And while it may look like the defensive back is just blindly following in the wake of the wide receiver, there is an art and science to playing the position.

Study, according to Aeneas Williams, is a prerequisite. Believe him. Williams was a third-round draft choice of the Arizona Cardinals in 1991, from Southern Baptist College. He is sized typically by cornerback standards, at five feet ten inches (178cm) and 190 pounds (86kg). He had 6 interceptions as a rookie, but that was

like sending up a flare gun. After that, the NFL's offenses avoided Williams like the plague, which underlines the deceptive nature of interception totals.

Deion Sanders had all of 2 interceptions in 1995, meaning sixty-six players had more than he did. Does that mean Sanders is number sixty-seven on the defensive depth chart? Of course not. It means that teams merely refuse to throw to his side. He is so effective—what's the point?

Williams had only 3 interceptions in 1992 and 2 in 1993. Then, in 1994, he rediscovered his theory of thefts. His 9 interceptions—the players call them picks—got him tied for the NFL lead with Cleveland safety Eric Turner. Williams had 6 interceptions in 1995, a total surpassed by only four players.

"I want to know what a team's tendencies are in advance, so I study a lot of film during the week before a game," Williams says. "Teams' tendencies change, depending on what part of the field they're in and what the down and distance is. You can pick up things watching film that come in handy.

"Say I'm playing against the Cardinals. Their tendency is to run the slant pattern, so when I'm lining up against the receiver, I'm checking out his relationship with the [yardage] numbers [on the field]. If he's 2 yards outside the numbers, then I'm looking at the quarterback to see if it's going to be a three- or five-step drop. That's going to determine the distance of the route. If it's three steps, it's going to be something really quick and short. If it's five steps, it's something intermediate.

"When I'm lining up, I already have in my mind what I want to do with the receiver. If I'm going to try to take away the inside slant, I'm going to jam him hard and force him out. The only response he can have is to take it upfield and try to come back over the top.

"Most defenders kind of ride their hand on a receiver. It's not legal, but you can give a little push here and there to knock a guy off stride. You have to get close so the refs won't see it. Now, when the ball is delivered it's never a completely perfect pass. This gives you some options. This is where your peripheral vision comes in, because you have to somehow be watching the ball and the receiv-

er as they come together. As a defensive back you try to play an angle on the ball that doesn't allow the receiver to get to it cleanly. I try to keep pressure on the receiver the whole time, not letting him adjust the way he wants. If the ball is thrown perfectly, I'll just play the hands and try to knock it out of there.

"The whole thing is to dictate to the receiver. I may get in his face for a quick jam, or fake it and back off. I just want to give him something to think about. I want him more worried about trying to get off the line—worried about what I'm going to do to him—rather than getting into his pass route. That's all I'm trying to do. That's all any defensive back is trying to do."

Today's Best

Woodson, now playing in San Francisco, is one of the best defensive backs in the history of the game. Sanders gets a few votes, but football people wish he actually tackled opponents. Woodson sometimes lets receivers catch the ball so he can punish them.

When the NFL named its seventy-fifth anniversary team in 1994, Dick "Night Train" Lane, Mel Blount, Mike Haynes, and Rod Woodson were the corners. Woodson was one of only four active players so honored.

He entered the NFL in 1987, one of the most talented athletes since the days of Jim Brown, as a first-round pick from Purdue. He was six feet (183cm) and 200 pounds (91kg) even. He ran a 4.3-second 40-yard dash, with a vertical leap of thirty-six inches (91cm) and a standing broad jump of ten feet four inches (3.2m). He was a three-time football All-American and, in his spare time, a world-class hurdler. Early in his career, a local magazine posed him in a Superman suit; it wasn't a stretch by any means. Woodson changed the way people viewed defensive backs.

"It went from the days of the inside linebackers like Dick Butkus, to outside guys like Lawrence Taylor, then a few backfield guys like Ronnie Lott," Woodson says. "Now, the corners are the ones getting a lot of attention. It's harder to find someone to fill the corner position than any of the others. There are plenty of guys with the talent, but someone who can concentrate week after week for sixteen weeks? That's a tough order."

Before his seventh season, in 1993, the Pittsburgh Steelers gave Woodson an unprecedented contract for a corner: $13 million over three years. Woodson responded by intercepting 8 passes, one of the league's best totals, forcing 2 fumbles, collecting 2 sacks, and blocking a field goal. And he returned kickoffs and punts too. More important, in big games Woodson was huge. He was the best player on the league's best defense.

Before the 1995 season, Woodson tore knee ligaments. Only Woodson envisioned a late-season comeback following one of

Since 1994, the Cardinals' Aeneas Williams has been one of the NFL's leading interceptors.

football's most serious injuries. Working in the bowels of Three Rivers Stadium every day, Woodson brought back his knee by subjecting it to torturous exercises in the weight room and relentless pounding on the treadmill. Against all odds, he played in Super Bowl XXX, where the Steelers very nearly upset the Dallas Cowboys.

"You have to have pride at corner," Woodson says. "I mean, I hate it when they help me on the football field. I always want them to double someone else. I can't say I'm better than any corner in the league, but I can't have people out there saying that everybody else is better than me. That's just about having respect and confidence in yourself."

Deion Sanders, of course, has all the trappings of success: a seven-year, $35 million contract, a string of slick television commercials, and two Super Bowl rings. He won them for the two best teams of the 1990s, the San Francisco 49ers and the Dallas Cowboys. Only Deion could have pulled off that double.

After the 49ers won Super Bowl XXIX over the San Diego Chargers, Dallas owner Jerry Jones wooed Sanders with that record-setting contract, which included a $13 million signing bonus. And while Sanders had a relatively uneventful season, the Cowboys did indeed win Super Bowl XXX over the Steelers. Sanders has always been a bottom-line guy.

After a glorious career at Florida State, he balanced track and football; he once played the first game of a baseball tournament, left to run the anchor of the sprint relay in his baseball pants, then returned to a second baseball game and hit the winning home run. He played for the Atlanta Braves (baseball) and the Atlanta Falcons (football), not to mention the Cincinnati Reds. And although he wore more than a handful of different uniforms, there was always a consistency of effort.

Though Sanders, at six feet (183cm) and 187 pounds (85kg), is not an exceptionally physical player, the pro personnel men say he has the best "catch-up" speed in the business, maybe history. "When the ball is in the air," says the Bucs' Angelo, "he adjusts to it better than anyone. Part of it is speed, sure, but it's also athletic ability, incredible athletic ability."

In addition to playing wide receiver on a number of occasions (including a 47-yard catch in Super Bowl XXX), Sanders has made a name for himself by finishing his interceptions in the end zone.

"I am always looking to score," Sanders says. "I'm not content with picking a ball off and falling down. I feel like the ball was meant for me anyway, so let's take it to the house and celebrate once we get there."

Enduring Standards

Celebrating history's best defensive backs is a subjective business at best. To make interceptions, you have to have opportunities; the best don't get as many as the vulnerable corner that a defense can't

hide. That said, you can find some of the best in the record book: they truly have a nose for the ball.

Paul Krause, who played four seasons in Washington and another twelve in Minnesota, finished his career with 81 interceptions, an average of more than 5 per season. Emlen Tunnell, of the Giants and Packers, had 79, and Dick "Night Train" Lane is third with 68, compiled over fourteen seasons with the Los Angeles Rams, Chicago Cardinals, and Detroit Lions. Lane might have been the best of that lot.

Dick Lane did not enter the NFL in the customary way. In fact, he was fresh out of the U.S. Army by way of Scottsbluff Junior College (Nebraska) when the Rams invited him to training camp in 1952. His nickname came from the Buddy Morrow recording of "Night Train," a tune that was a favorite of Rams receiver Tom Fears, whom Lane was in the habit of visiting for late-night pep talks.

Lane was six feet two inches (188cm) and 210 pounds (95kg), which prompted the Rams to try him at defensive end. But when coach Joe Stydahar saw Lane make a spectacular play in training camp, Lane was placed at cornerback. In his rookie season, Lane had 14 interceptions—in only twelve games. To put that figure in perspective, consider that no player, rookie or veteran, before or since has managed that many.

That Lane was placed in the defensive backfield was almost a fluke, and it seems that a number of players with that kind of rangy size found themselves playing linebacker in the formative days of football. As a result, most of the accomplished defensive backs are relatively modern players.

Take Willie Brown, the father of the aggressive bump-and-run technique. He had been a tight end at Grambling. At six feet one inch (185cm) and 217 pounds (99kg), he was primarily a blocker. He wasn't even drafted in 1963, but Houston Oilers coach Frank "Pop" Ivy decided, for some reason, that he was a defensive back.

"I was kind of surprised," Brown says, "but I said, 'Why not?'"

After a few weeks of assimilating the position's skills, Brown wondered why defensive backs played 8 to 10 yards off the line of scrimmage. "It didn't make sense," he says. "If I was on the line of scrimmage, right in a guy's face, I was big enough so I could get my hands on him and fast enough so no one could outrun me."

Brown never stuck with the Oilers—they thought he was crazy—but the Denver Broncos took a chance with his avant-garde technique. Soon, teams from around the league were calling to find out how Brown did it. Over the years, Brown's bump-and-run style became the accepted way to shut down the most dangerous receivers—in effect, nip them in the bud before they can blossom and hurt you.

Brown's last twelve seasons were in a Raiders uniform and he finished with 54 career interceptions in his sixteen seasons. Brown did not see many opportunities, either. In 1971, for instance,

The receiver's nightmare: Detroit's Dick "Night Train" Lane stops the Rams' Jon Arnett with a lethal headlock.

Raiders coaches logged only 10 passes thrown in his area of responsibility, well under 1 per game.

Brown was a trailblazer with his numbers, too. In sixteen seasons, he had at least one interception in each, something no other defensive back has ever done. And on November 15, 1964, Brown intercepted an unbelievable total of 4 passes against the New York Jets, a record equaled by fifteen other players but never surpassed to this day.

Mel Renfro of the Dallas Cowboys is the most recent defensive back enshrined in the Pro Football Hall of Fame. He joined the Cowboys in 1964 as a second-round pick from the University of Oregon, and played with them for the next fourteen seasons, longer than any other Cowboys player besides Ed "Too Tall" Jones, who played for fifteen.

Renfro, a six-foot (183cm), 192-pound (87kg) sprinter, was an offensive halfback in college and spent his first six NFL seasons at free safety before switching to cornerback. Coach Tom Landry, who had a handful of talented receivers, didn't want Renfro to sit on the bench and decided to play him on defense. Perhaps Landry, who played defensive back himself, sensed that

The Raiders' Lester Hayes is best remembered for the stickum he slathered all over his hands and arms, but he was a pretty fair corner, too.

Renfro was a kindred spirit. In any case, Tom Landry promised Renfro that he would work him into the offensive lineup when an opening occurred. It never happened.

"I guess I made one big, fat mistake," Renfro says. "I played defense too well."

He was selected to play in ten straight Pro Bowls, but missed one due to injury. He also played in four Super Bowls. His dazzling career numbers: 52 interceptions, which he returned for 626 yards and 3 touchdowns.

George Allen, the head coach of the Washington Redskins from 1971 to 1977, also knew the value of a great defensive back. He had always admired safety Ken Houston from afar, but in 1973 he finally had the opportunity to trade for him. Houston, appropriately enough, had played for the Houston Oilers for six seasons and was coming off five consecutive Pro Bowl appearances. His success was something of a surprise, considering he had been a lowly ninth-round choice in the 1967 draft out of Texas' Prairie View A&M. In 1971, he led the American Football Conference with 9 interceptions; incredibly, 4 of them were returned for touchdowns.

The price for Houston was steep—five players: Mack Alston, Mike Fanucci, Clifton McNeil, Jeff Severson, and Jim Snowden—but Allen was willing to pay. All he got was a player who never missed practice, who counseled younger players, and, most importantly, who always made the plays within his reach—and even some that weren't.

Houston rewarded Allen's support with six straight Pro Bowl visits; only a broken arm in 1979 could end his streak. That injury also ended his run of 183 consecutive games played. He retired after the 1980 season with a total of 49 interceptions and 898 return yards. His record of 9 interceptions returned for touchdowns, Deion Sanders notwithstanding, is still the NFL standard.

Every generation, every sport, has a few players who change the way the game is played. Mel Blount was the prototypical cornerback in virtually every way imaginable. At a lanky six feet three inches (191cm) and 205 pounds (93kg), he had the size and reach to master the position and the speed and reflexes to excel.

The Pittsburgh Steelers, in the process of building a nucleus that would win four Super Bowl championships, selected him in the third round of the 1970 draft, out of Southern University

Mike Haynes, who played for the Patriots and Raiders, was named to nine Pro Bowl teams.

(Louisiana). But Blount was hardly an instant success. In a game during his second season, Miami wide receiver Paul Warfield, himself a future Hall of Famer, beat Blount for 3 touchdowns. A year later, in 1972, Blount wasn't responsible for a single score.

Borrowing his bruising bump-and-run style from Willie Brown, Blount manhandled receivers to such an extent that the NFL changed its rules to protect them. The Competition Committee decreed in 1974 that defensive backs could bump receivers only once, at the line of scrimmage. In 1975, Blount proved he could adjust by posting 11 interceptions, a team record. He was also the NFL's Defensive Player of the Year and earned the second of four Super Bowl rings. In 1978, the rule was amended to include only a 5-yard zone where bumping was permitted, and Blount made a seamless transition. In 200 regular-season games, over fourteen seasons, Blount produced a total of 57 interceptions.

The Raiders, with their perpetual chips on their shoulders, have always been a sanctuary for players with an attitude. It all stemmed from owner Al Davis, who played football while he attended Wittenberg College. And while the position he played wasn't recorded for posterity, how could Davis have been anything but a defensive back? That kind of in-your-face thinking comes standard with most successful cornerbacks.

Lester Hayes, who had 13 interceptions in 1980, was a Raiders corner. His partner on the other side for four seasons was Mike Haynes. Haynes came to the Raiders under duress.

Haynes, who entered the league as the fifth overall draft choice in 1976, had learned to play defensive back at Arizona State under

coach Frank Kush. With talented receiver John Jefferson already on campus, Haynes began the conversion from running forward and catching the ball to backpedaling and knocking it away.

The New England Patriots made him one of their highest picks ever, and Haynes was a Pro Bowl player for six of his first seven seasons. Then, in 1983, the free agent held out for a contract better than the one the Patriots were offering. Haynes might have missed the entire season if Davis hadn't intervened and put principal ahead of principle. At midseason, Davis gave the Patriots first- and second-round draft choices and Haynes an enormous contract. Naturally, Haynes was brilliant as the Raiders reached the Super Bowl. In fact, Haynes had an interception in the Raiders' 38–9 razing of the Washington Redskins in Super Bowl XVIII.

His 46 career interceptions do not do his fourteen seasons justice; opposing quarterbacks knew better than to test Haynes.

Once you get past all the technical jargon, the size-and-speed "measurables" that pro personnel men like to see, a defensive back either has an intuitive sense for the ball or he doesn't. Everson Walls had that knack; he is the only man in NFL history to lead the league three times in interceptions. He did it in a Dallas uniform in 1981, 1982, and 1985.

In fact, Giants coach Bill Parcells was so tired of seeing Walls intercepting his quarterback, Phil Simms, that he traded for Walls in 1990. Walls played three seasons and, already past the age of thirty, led the Giants in pickoffs for two of them.

When you ask football people today about role models at safety, they all offer the same name: Ronnie Lott. He started out as a

cornerback, but the six-foot-one-inch (185cm) athlete belonged at safety. The truth is that he had the mentality of a linebacker.

"You want to be the best. You want to be tough," says Lott, who has a keen sense of history and his place in it. "You want to be a guy that's like [Dick] Butkus. You want to be a guy that brought what Kenny Houston brought to the field. You want to be a guy who plays as hard as he possibly can.

"That ingredient alone is what usually separates you from being almost good to good, almost great to great. It's because of that attitude, being able to turn on the switch. I think I make myself perform at that level, particularly that violent level. You really ask yourself how tough you can be? It's always that badge of courage that everyone is searching for. Whether it's Chuck Yeager, trying to search for it flying in an F-14 or an F-16, trying to hit Mach-One, or a defensive back trying to make the Hall of Fame. I think I was able to understand at an early age that I could find the violence that I needed to have to be great."

Lott, who made nine trips to the Pro Bowl, led the league in interceptions twice—in 1986 with the 49ers and in 1991 with the Raiders. He finished his career in 1995 with 63 interceptions, fifth on the all-time list.

90

The Defensive Line

Green Bay Packers defensive end Reggie White, an ordained Baptist minister, sees no contradiction between his current Sunday occupation, laying out opposing quarterbacks on the field, and his future Sunday calling, laying out the word of God from the pulpit.

"The transformation is not hard at all," White says. "People know what kind of person I am off the field. I try to be as gentle and humble as I can. Off the field. On the field, I try to be aggressive in a physical manner. A lot of people say the game is violent, but I don't think they know what violence is unless they grew up on the mean streets. Our game is what I'd call aggressive.

"If somebody said, 'Reggie, look, we're playing tomorrow.' Or 'We've got a game this afternoon. We need you to get ready.' I can change real quick, because I want to win. I'm a football player. That's my job. When it's time to play ball I can change. When it's time to do what God called me to do, I can change it back."

White is quite possibly the best defensive lineman who has ever played the game. At six feet five inches (196cm) and 300 pounds (136kg), he is massive and powerful, and has the reflexes of a cat. Heading into the 1998 season, no player in history—at any posi-

After changing his mind several times, Green Bay defensive end Reggie White (No. 92), the NFL's all-time leading sacker, decided to unretire and play one more season in 1998.

tion—had more than the 176.5 sacks he has accumulated since joining the NFL in 1985. That works out to nearly 13 sacks for each of his eleven NFL seasons. If you factor in the 23 1/2 sacks he recorded for the Memphis Showboats of the United States Football League in 1984 and 1985, his professional total is an unapproachable 200.

Buffalo's Bruce Smith, with 154, is the next most active player behind White on the all-time sack list.

In 1997, at the age of thirty-six, White recorded 11 sacks during the regular season and, fighting leg and back injuries, powered the Packers into their second consecutive Super Bowl. It was White who carried Green Bay defensively in Super Bowl XXXI, with 3 sacks. He was a factor, too, in the Packers' surprising loss to the Denver Broncos in Super Bowl XXXII.

"Reggie is every bit as effective now as when he first came into the league," says Green Bay defensive coordinator Fritz Shurmur. "He takes excellent care of his body and, as a result, prepares well for the season. During the season, he stays in excellent condition. He's the leader of our defensive team. He is obsessed with taking this team to the final game, the Super Bowl. He leads by example better than any player I've ever been around."

Reginald Howard White was born in Chattanooga, Tennessee, and distinguished himself playing for the University of Tennessee. He signed with the USFL's Memphis franchise before the Philadelphia Eagles made him the fourth player chosen in the NFL's 1984 supplemental draft of USFL players. "The Minister of Defense" quickly made his mark in Philadelphia, producing 13 sacks in thirteen games. In the strike-shortened 1987 season, White produced 21 sacks, one short of the record set by the Jets' Mark Gastineau in 1984. White, however, appeared in only twelve games, while Gastineau appeared in sixteen, making it one of the most effective seasons ever by a defender. Still, beyond the flashy style of sacks, there is substance to White's game.

He is considered one of the league's great run-stoppers, as his gaudy unassisted tackle totals suggest. The other factor worth noting is the double- and triple-teams that White sees on almost every play.

"I envision my opponent as more nervous than I am," White says, in a massive understatement.

As well they should. Consider some of White's overlooked achievements:

- He has made twelve consecutive Pro Bowl appearances; he had a record 4 sacks in the 1986 game in Hawaii.
- His athletic ability allowed him to return 2 fumbles for long touchdowns—70 yards against Washington in 1987 and 37 yards against Phoenix in 1992.
- He has posted 2 safeties and blocked 3 kicks.
- Playing with his injured left arm in a brace in the 1994

Thanksgiving game between the Eagles and Dallas, White lifted 325-pound (148kg) offensive tackle Larry Allen off the ground repeatedly as he fought upfield to reach quarterback Troy Aikman.

Exploits like these prompted the Packers to make White the highest-paid lineman in NFL history in 1993. When free agency dawned that year, White was the player in greatest demand. After considering a dozen viable offers in what amounted to a bidding frenzy, he accepted a four-year, $17 million deal from Green Bay. White registered 13 sacks in his next season, an NFC high, and helped the Packers into the playoffs. The defense, ranked twenty-third among twenty-eight teams in 1993, moved up the charts in 1994 to second overall.

More than anything, White remains a solid citizen: the NFL Players Association honored him with the prestigious Byron "Whizzer" White Humanitarian Award in 1992 for his service to the community.

Getting It Done

White is, admittedly, a unique specimen—as an athlete and a person as well. But his physical attributes of strength and speed are crucial to his success as a defensive lineman. His desire to succeed, his mental toughness, is another factor in his great record. There is also the overlooked matter of finesse.

White is strong and swift, certainly, but how does he routinely defeat two opposing blockers who are of comparable size? In real estate, the key is location, location, location. Players and coaches will tell you that the defensive line is all about technique, technique, technique.

"It's not all smashing into people, despite what some people might think," says no less an authority than Buffalo's Bruce Smith. "Seriously, you have to know what you're doing out there. We all have little wrinkles, little things we do to get the job done."

On a very basic level, there are only a few ways to start from a three-point stance, defeat a blocker or two (or three) across the line of scrimmage, and get to the quarterback. You can go left, right, or over the blocker. Smith knows this and the blockers know this. So how does Smith ever win?

First of all, at six feet four inches (193cm) and 273 pounds (124kg), he has exceptional athletic ability. Sometimes, that's enough. Most of the time, he uses the element of surprise. Often, with two closely matched athletes like a defensive end and offensive tackle, the winner is determined by a split-second. This is the science applied in sumo wrestling, where two behemoths posture, move, and countermove toward the end of gaining that momentary upper hand.

Even at the age of thirty-four, Smith managed to produce 14 sacks for Buffalo in 1997, the highest total in the AFC. Speed is still his most effective weapon, and he uses it to take an outside rush on

THE COLLEGE DRAFT

In recent years, the National Football League college draft has become a true phenomenon. Football fanatics descend on a New York City hotel in April and watch the future unfold before their eyes. There are seven rounds for the thirty teams—more draftees than ESPN's Chris Berman can provide nicknames for.

Before the free agency rules were liberalized in the early 1990s, the draft was the most important factor in a team's success. Scouts labored in the field through the fall, following the nation's best college players in places like Tuscaloosa, Alabama, and Columbus, Ohio. Personnel directors fed the information into computers and produced elaborate lists, position by position, of the best prospects. From their war rooms, teams operated with the precision of a military operation.

All of that still happens, but free agency means that teams have only a few seasons to develop a player before he is eligible for the open market. In today's game, the abilities to secure veteran talent and to mesh personalities have become vital to building championship teams.

The draft has never been a sure thing. In 1995, the Cincinnati Bengals used the first overall pick for Penn State running back Ki-Jana Carter. He did not carry the ball even once that season after suffering a serious knee injury. The Jacksonville Jaguars used the second choice on Southern California offensive tackle Tony Boselli; he, too, was lost with a knee injury. And Houston's third overall choice, Alcorn State quarterback Steve McNair? He actually threw 80 passes, completing 41 of them.

In 1996, the New York Jets made a splash, signing free agent quarterback Neil O'Donnell, who led the Pittsburgh Steelers to the Super Bowl. To complement their passer, they used the draft's first pick for USC wide receiver Keyshawn Johnson, a six-foot-three-inch (191cm) playmaker. This was their dubious reward as the NFL's only team to win three games in 1995—this in a year with two expansion teams.

The Jets had actually made their decision months before, in a darkened room at Weeb Ewbank Hall in Hempstead, New York. Personnel director Dick Haley watched each of the 168 passes Johnson caught in two seasons at USC.

Coach Rich Kotite said he was thrilled about the choice of Johnson. "He's an animated player," Kotite said. "As a big man, he can do all the things a little man can do. He's a game-breaker. He really is the total package as far as we're concerned. I think he's the guy for New York, to be honest with you. He's been looking forward to coming to New York for months and months."

Was Johnson reluctant to come to a team that hadn't had a winning record in seven seasons?

"I don't look at this franchise as having to be saved," Johnson said. "Every NFL club struggles at times. Hopefully one day things will change around here like that."

After he was drafted first by the New York Jets, Keyshawn Johnson caught a respectable 63 passes for 844 yards and 8 touchdowns.

OPPOSITE: Buffalo's Bruce Smith has perhaps the best combination of acceleration and power ever seen in a defensive lineman.

opposing left tackles, that is, he works to their left side and attempts to beat them outside so that he can reach the quarterback with a short sprint. If the tackle pushes him far enough outside, he will never reach the passer before the ball is thrown. If the tackle overcommits to the outside, Smith goes to Plan B by spinning 360 degrees back inside to his right. And so, as the tackle spins out of the play, Smith is free on an inside lane to the passer—unless, of course, the guard is helping the tackle; if so, Smith must use another move. Perhaps he fakes right and goes left, using his hands to break the blocker's hold on his shoulders, arms, and uniform. The other option is the bull rush, a straight-ahead burst of power that can leave a blocker on his back.

Just as offenses use blockers in combination, defenses do the same. In 1995 Smith's teammate Bryce Paup, a six-foot-five-inch (196cm), 247-pound (112kg) linebacker, led the NFL with 17 1/2 sacks. A number of them were partly attributable to Smith because his presence caused opponents to pay less attention to Paup. There were also times when the Bills took their two best weapons and aligned them together in plays called stunts. Imagine the quandary if Paup lined up outside Smith and then, at the snap of the ball, crossed over and went inside with Smith bending outside. If an offense isn't prepared, a stunt can permanently stunt the growth of its quarterback.

Just as tackles are the best athletes on the offensive line, ends represent the glamour position along the defensive line. They play at the corners of the trench, where the action is far more unpredictable. Defensive tackles, like Green Bay's six-foot,-two-inch, 385-pound Gilbert Brown, tend to be heavier and less mobile. Some teams use a three-man front, which means the two ends flank a nose tackle.

"It takes a special kind of player to play the D-line," Smith says. "There's a lot of ugly stuff that goes on in there. You have to have the right mind-set."

Lett It Be

Leon Lett was minding his own business, having the game of his life in Super Bowl XXVII, when fortune, well, spit on him.

The Dallas Cowboys' defensive tackle, an anonymous seventh-round draft choice from Emporia State (Kansas), had come off the bench and slammed around the Buffalo Bills for a few quarters. In part-time action Lett managed 3 tackles and forced 2 fumbles and a sack. Then the marvelous opportunity of a lifetime bounced into view in the fourth quarter: Dallas teammate Jim Jeffcoat drilled Buffalo quarterback Frank Reich and the ball came loose at the

Cowboys' 35-yard line. All Lett had to do was grab the ball and run for what looked like a certain touchdown.

And that's just what seemed to be happening when Lett gathered in the ball and began sprinting, all six feet six inches (198cm) and 288 pounds (131kg) of him, down the sideline toward history and celebrity. As he approached the goal line, Lett could not resist a minor celebration, a little hotdogging. Lett heard the rising cheers of the fans at the Rose Bowl in Pasadena, thinking that they were for him. Actually, they were shrieks of terror, for Buffalo wide receiver Don Beebe—the epitome of perseverance—was still chasing Lett. He caught him and stripped the ball loose, preventing the expected score. Tens of millions watching at home on television gasped. Lett was mortified.

"It was the Super Bowl," Lett says. "We were having fun. We were up by almost 40 points. I was out there just smiling and giggling. I was disappointed, but I've blown it off now. It doesn't even matter anymore. But I'll probably be reminded of it the rest of my career."

The Cowboys won going away, 52–17, but the image of Lett and Beebe from that January 1993 game is the one that lingers.

And then it happened again. The following season, the Cowboys faced the Miami Dolphins in their traditional Thanksgiving game. When Dallas defensive tackle Jimmie Jones blocked Miami's 41-yard field goal attempt with fifteen seconds left, the Cowboys seemed to have the 14–13 victory in hand. The ball rolled harmlessly toward the Miami goal line, but the Cowboys knew when the ball came to a stop or was touched by Miami that it would belong to them. Lett, however, tried to recover the ball and knocked it closer to the end zone. Miami recovered, convert-

RIGHT: Unfairly, Leon Lett will always be remembered for a Super Bowl play he didn't make.

BELOW: Once he was moved to defensive tackle, Dallas' Bob Lilly quickly grasped the ferocious game of the trenches.

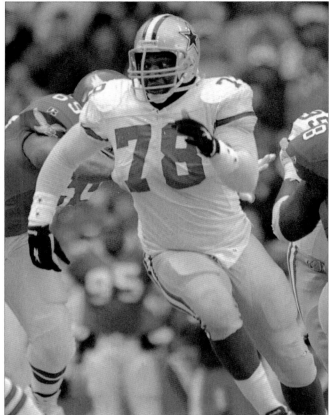

ABOVE: The Dallas Cowboys' Leon Lett slices through the Philadelphia offensive line.

ed a 19-yard field goal, and won, astonishingly, 16–14.

"I was trying to cover up the ball," Lett explained later. "But I slipped and it hit my foot. I felt terrible. I was thinking, 'Why does this have to happen to me on national TV?'"

In 1994 Lett, whom teammates call "Big Cat," was finally recognized for a job well done. His peers, who had always understood his vast ability, voted him to start in the Pro Bowl. He had helped the Cowboys lead the league in defense with 68 tackles, more than he had totaled in his three previous seasons.

"Those mistakes made me push to become better," Lett says. "I made a promise to myself that no matter what happened to me in the past, I was going to go all out and play hard all the time."

History's Best

After fighting in the Battle of the Bulge as an eighteen-year-old in the United States Army, how daunting were the NFL's combative trenches for Gino Marchetti?

Marchetti returned to Modesto Junior College (California) after World War II and earned a scholarship to the University of San Francisco. He was a hulking six feet four inches (193cm) and 245 pounds (111kg), a perfect fit for the New York Yanks in 1952. The troubled franchise became the Dallas Texans for a season before moving to Baltimore in 1953. Marchetti was originally seen as an offensive tackle, but he was soon switched to the other side of the ball to take advantage of his explosion off the line; he was a natural pass rusher.

In fourteen glorious seasons, Marchetti played in ten Pro Bowls. It might have been a record eleven consecutive appearances if not for teammate Gene "Big Daddy" Lipscomb. Marchetti had just made a critical stop of the Giants' Frank Gifford in the 1958 championship game when Lipscomb, all 300 pounds' (136kg) worth, landed on top of him by way of congratulation. Marchetti's ankle broke. And while the Colts prevailed in one of history's most stirring games, 23–17 in overtime, Marchetti had to miss the Pro Bowl a week later.

Broken ankle aside, Marchetti always came to play. He was a factor in the Colts' last 4 games in 1955, despite a painful dislocated shoulder. He announced his retirement after the 1963 season, but the Colts asked him to reconsider and he played again in 1964. When injuries cropped up the next two seasons, Marchetti, ever the good soldier, stepped in and performed.

The record shows that Reggie White has officially recorded more sacks than any other man in NFL history. The key word is "officially," because the league didn't start tracking sacks until 1982. Ask veteran football men if any old-timers could give White a run for his money and they offer the same name: David "Deacon" Jones.

The Rams spotted him first, in 1961, as an offensive lineman at Mississippi Vocational. Still, they didn't know he was future Hall of Fame material; they drafted him way down in the fourteenth round. Soon, his skills became evident and the Rams played him on defense.

It was Jones, at six feet four inches (193cm) and 260 pounds (118kg), who actually coined the word "sack." And it was Jones who perfected—if that is the word—the head-slap technique that left offensive linemen with ringing ears and wandering concentration. He even invented his nickname because nobody would ever remember a player named David Jones.

Whether or not he produced more sacks than White or Lawrence Taylor or Bruce Smith is open to question. This much is known: in 1967, a year in which Rams quarterbacks were sacked 25 times, the team's coaches had Jones down for 26 solo sacks in 14 games. That's nearly 2 per game. Jones was a Pro Bowl fixture, with eight appearances, and was one-quarter of Los Angeles' "Fearsome Foursome," the defensive line also featuring Merlin Olsen, Roosevelt Grier, and Lamar Lundy that struck terror into the hearts of opposing quarterbacks. Jones was voted the NFL's Defensive Player of the Year in 1967. The next year, Los Angeles set a record for fewest yards allowed in a 14-game season.

Jones played eleven seasons for the Rams, then moved down the West Coast for two seasons in San Diego. He was reunited with coach George Allen in 1974 for one more campaign in

Washington. Allen called Jones the best practice player he had ever seen, an observation that attitude—"want-to," as football coaches like to call it—is just as important as talent.

While Jones was viewed as an innovator and a spectacular talent, Merlin Olsen sometimes played in his considerable shadow.

The public persona that Olsen cultivated in later years was that of the Phi Beta Kappa from Utah State, a cerebral television analyst and actor who was the national spokesman for a florists' group. But make no mistake—Olsen loved to play the game, even with all its ragged edges.

He stood six feet five inches (196cm), weighed 270 pounds (123kg), and never lifted a single weight. The Rams outbid the Denver Broncos for Olsen's services in 1962, and by the end of the preseason Olsen was in the starting lineup alongside Jones. Because Jones was quicker, Olsen maintained responsibility for the area Jones often vacated when he pursued the passer. The result was an end-tackle combination for the ages.

Olsen was selected by his peers for fourteen consecutive Pro Bowls and helped the Rams win six division titles. Jones was enshrined in the Hall of Fame in 1980. Olsen followed two years later.

Today's Dallas Cowboys are known for their potent offense, the unit led by quarterback Troy Aikman, running back Emmitt Smith, and wide receiver Michael Irvin. But for many, Dallas will always be about Bob Lilly, an almost technically perfect defensive tackle.

He was, appropriately, the young franchise's first draft choice in 1960. He was a Texas native and a local star at Texas Christian University. At six feet five inches (196cm) and 260 pounds (118kg), Lilly was actually a rangy player who could function on the outside. The Cowboys placed him at end and he was voted Rookie of the Year and the first Dallas player in the Pro Bowl. After his second season, however, Dallas coaches wondered if he would be even more effective inside—the better to take advantage of his unnatural strength, they reasoned.

Lilly, who despite interference of tackles, guards, and centers always managed to keep his eye on the ball, thrived in the crucible of the NFL's trenches. Freed from the constraints of outside containment responsibilities, Lilly could focus solely on the quarterback or ball carrier.

Dallas' "Doomsday Defense" became a league standard and helped the Cowboys win Super Bowl VI. Lilly, who played in each of the Cowboys' 196 scheduled games in his fourteen professional seasons, was responsible for one more Cowboys first. In 1980, he was the first Dallas player enshrined in the Hall of Fame.

Back at North Texas State, he was known by the name "Mean Greene." When he arrived in Pittsburgh as the fourth overall player taken in the 1969 draft, his first name became part of the equation: "Mean" Joe Greene. He was ejected from two games in his rookie season; on one of those occasions, he angrily flung the ball

Colts' running back Don Nottingham is surrounded by Steelers L.C. Greenwood (68) and the legendary Jack Ham (59). "Mean" Joe Greene (75) closes in.

into the stands when officials refused to call holding on the Philadelphia Eagles.

The nickname was well taken, for Greene, who was six feet four inches (193cm) and 260 pounds (118kg), was a classic defensive tackle and the middle of the famed "Steel Curtain." Pittsburgh officials will tell you that Greene, not Terry Bradshaw or Franco Harris or Lynn Swann, was the most important player in the franchise's march to four Super Bowl victories.

In 1974, Greene collected his second NFL Defensive Player of the Year Award in three seasons. That same year, Greene began the practice of lining up between the guard and center at an angle. He believed it gave him a leverage advantage, and who could argue? Greene was selected to play in ten Pro Bowls over his thirteen-year career. He was inducted into the Hall of Fame in 1987, but continues his influence in the league as an assistant coach.

The Punter

Sean Landeta smiles and acknowledges that kicking footballs is a little easier than smashing headfirst into 300-pound (136kg) tackles.

"We get a lot of grief; people are always giving us a hard time about not being real football players," says Landeta. "But we work hard, we take pride in what we do."

Those 300-pound (136kg) tackles may not agree that punting is an essential service in the NFL, but as long as offenses fail on third downs, there will be athletes like Landeta hoisting the ball five or six times a game.

Landeta, a solid six-foot (183cm), 210-pound (95kg) athlete, is one of the more decorated and prolific punters in recent NFL history. In 1995, at the age of thirty-three, he finished third in punting with an average of 44.3 yards per kick. In fact, his all-important

OPPOSITE: The Raiders' Ray Guy was quite simply the only choice as punter for the NFL's seventy-fifth anniversary team.

net average (36.7) was actually better than Seattle's Rick Tuten and San Diego's Darren Bennett, who finished ahead of him. In 1997, Landeta was still punting, this time in Tampa Bay, after a stint in St. Louis.

Punting is a subtle art that goes beyond bare yards. Scan the punting statistics each year and scrutinize the "Inside the 20" column. The punter is, in some ways, a weapon for the defense because he has the power to pin an offense deep in its own territory.

"Some guys just kick it as far as they can," Landeta says. "How many times have you seen the ball sail downfield and then skip into and through the end zone? Well, you get credit for all those yards, but the ball comes out to the 20. If you can get it to run out of bounds on the 10, you might lose that off your average, but you're more valuable to your team."

In 1995, 23 of Landeta's 83 punts for the Rams were downed inside the opponent's 20-yard line, third in the league.

Landeta made his mark kicking for the New York Giants. He played college ball at Towson State (Maryland) and joined the United States Football League in 1983. He was a two-time All-USFL player as the Philadelphia Stars won league titles in 1984 and 1985. A coincidence? Landeta averaged 52.5 yards on 6 punts against the Michigan Panthers in a losing effort in the 1983 championship game. He led the USFL with a 38.1-yard net average in 1984 and produced a 41.8-yard gross in 1985.

The Giants, who had been building a championship contender of their own, signed him as a free agent in 1985. That year Landeta dropped a career-high 24 punts inside the 20 and led the NFC with a 44.1-yard average. He played in the Pro Bowl a week after the Giants won Super Bowl XXI.

In 1989, Landeta led the league with a net of 37.8 yards and was named to the NFL's all-1980s team by a Hall of Fame committee. Landeta returned to the Pro Bowl in 1990 with an NFC-high 44-yard average. The Giants also won their second Super Bowl. In fact, years after the Giants won their two titles, former coach Bill Parcells always insisted that, after linebacker Lawrence Taylor and quarterback Phil Simms, Landeta had a profound impact on the team's success.

More than half a century ago, the Washington Redskins' Sammy Baugh made an impact on football that is still remembered.

In 1943, Baugh led the NFL in passing, interceptions, and punting. It was the fourth consecutive season that Baugh, a quarterback by trade, led the league in punting, a mark only Jerrel Wilson of Kansas City managed to equal. You will also find Baugh at the head of the list for best career average (45.1) and single-season average (51.4 in 1940).

For the record, Dave Jennings of the New York Giants and Jets lofted the most punts in league history (1,154), a tribute to his lively leg and the weak nature of his teams' respective offenses. Jennings once kicked 623 consecutive balls without a block, a record

approached only by the Raiders' Ray Guy, who punted 619 in a row cleanly.

Guy, who played from 1973 to 1986, was the league's single choice for the seventy-fifth anniversary team. He was an expert in the arcane area of "hang time," the precious time the ball was in the air, allowing the coverage to assemble around the returner. If you accept the idea in physics that there is only so much energy to propel a kick, Guy was willing to sacrifice distance for height.

The Raiders went against conventional wisdom and used a first-round choice to draft Guy out of Southern Mississippi. Coach John Madden had seen the highlight film, the one where Guy kicked a ball out of his own end zone that carried 80 yards in the air and bounced into the other end zone.

Guy led the league three times in punting average and was named to appear in six Pro Bowls. Not coincidentally, the Raiders won three Super Bowl games during Guy's tenure.

Punter Sean Landeta was named to the NFL's all-1980s team.

THE COACHES

Don Shula won the first game of his NFL career on September 22, 1963, when the Baltimore Colts scored 10 fourth-quarter points to defeat the San Francisco 49ers, 20–16.

At the time, Dan Reeves was a junior quarterback at the University of South Carolina. Marty Schottenheimer was a junior linebacker at the University of Pittsburgh. Mike Holmgren was a high school sophomore in San Francisco. Dennis Green was a freshman in Harrisburg, Pennsylvania. Ray Rhodes was a seventh grader in Mexia, Texas. Bill Cowher was a second grader in Beechwood, Pennsylvania. Oh, and David Shula was four years old.

All of those boys and/or men eventually followed Shula to the NFL as head coaches. None of them, realistically, will ever come remotely close to the standard Shula left after he retired from the Miami Dolphins following the 1995 season. He was the head coach of the Baltimore Colts and Miami Dolphins for thirty-three seasons and 525 games. He won 347 of them, the all-time record for NFL victories. Shula's coaching record of 347–172–6 was good (very good), for a winning percentage of .669.

To put those victories in some sort of context, consider these facts:
- Some seventeen NFL teams haven't won that many games in their franchises' histories.
- During Shula's glorious career, the New York Jets went through ten coaches and the United States had eight presidents.
- It would take a rookie coach about eighteen perfect seasons to catch Shula. As it turns out, Shula is the only coach on record

---

OPPOSITE: Most people know John Madden as the outrageous Fox football analyst. Long ago and far away, he was one of the best NFL coaches ever, for the Raiders.

to pull off an undefeated season: 17–0 with the Miami Dolphins in 1972.

No less an authority than Bill Walsh, who has been famously credited with genius status, calls Shula "the greatest coach ever." Shula won his 325th game and broke the record of Chicago's George "Papa Bear" Halas on November 14, 1993, when the Dolphins defeated the Philadelphia Eagles at hostile Veterans Stadium. It was a typically resourceful win for the man who says coaching and teaching are synonymous.

A month earlier Shula's Hall of Fame–bound quarterback, Dan Marino, had suffered a torn Achilles tendon. Backup Scott Mitchell won the next two games, but in the third quarter of the next game,

In characteristic fashion, Shula used the record as a platform to thank his players over the years. "I'm proud of that record because it primarily represents team success over a long period of time," Shula said in 1995. "I've always felt if you prepared as hard as you possibly can each and every week and then played well on Sunday, the numbers would take care of themselves. That philosophy has been reflected by the fact that in my thirty-two years as a head coach my teams have averaged 10 regular-season wins a year."

And when the season was over and the Dolphins were sitting at home during the playoffs with a 9–7 record, Shula preferred not to talk about that disappointment. His career was marked by an unflinching resolve: look ahead, never back.

Before his last season, at the age of sixty-five, Shula was eager to see his Dolphins improve. "My goal is the same every year—to win the Super Bowl," he said. "And we will do everything we can to do just that. I felt we made progress in that direction last year, and I hope we can use those accomplishments as a base to build on to make it back to the Super Bowl and then win it this season."

For every season, all thirty-three of them, winning it all was his single-minded goal.

Birth of a Legend

Donald Francis Shula was born on the fourth day of 1930 in Grand River, Ohio, and he didn't leave the football-happy state for twenty-three years. He grew up in Painesville and played ball at John Carroll University in Cleveland. He was a running back, but Cleveland Browns coach Paul Brown saw him as a defensive back. Shula was the only rookie to make the roster of the defending NFL champions. In 1953 he was part of a fifteen-player trade, the biggest deal in modern NFL history, and was sent to Baltimore. He played four seasons there and another in Washington. In seven NFL seasons he had an impressive total of 21 career interceptions.

Shula had been a cagey player and his intuitive feel for the game led him to coaching. After a year each at the U. of Virginia and U. of Kentucky, Shula was hired by Detroit Lions head coach George Wilson in 1960. With the thirty-year-old Shula as defensive coordinator, Detroit won twice as many games as it lost.

The Baltimore Colts were not so lucky in 1962. They were a so-so 7–7 under Weeb Ewbank, and thus Shula was signed as the head coach. He was all of thirty-three years old. His first season produced an 8–6 record; a foundation was being laid.

"The important thing is not what Don Shula knows or what any of my assistant coaches knows," Shula says. "The important thing is what we can transmit to the people we're responsible for. They're going to be tested on Sunday afternoon, and the fact that we win on Sunday afternoon indicates we're getting through to them. That's what coaching is: the ability to transmit information."

The Colts got the message in 1964, winning twelve of fourteen regular-season games and the NFL's Western Conference. They

against the Eagles, he was forced from the game with a separated shoulder. Miami was trailing, 14–13, when Doug Pederson entered the game in the third quarter. Somehow, Pederson guided the Dolphins to a pair of successful field goals, the defense shut out Philadelphia the entire second half, and Shula had the record. He did it in 482 games, as opposed to Halas' 506 games.

Like all great coaches, Shula managed to massage egos both large (hello there, Dan Marino) and small.

lost in the league's championship, 27–0, to Cleveland. Baltimore came back in 1968 with a 13–1 regular-season record, but lost to the New York Jets in Super Bowl III. In seven seasons in Baltimore, Shula's teams posted a record of 73–26–4, a winning percentage of .728. He was, the Miami Dolphins owners concluded, the one man who could take a young franchise to the next level.

Shula replaced George Wilson, the man who brought him into the NFL, in 1970. Under Wilson, the Dolphins had been a typically scattershot expansion team, with a record of 15–39–2. "Squish the fish," opposing fans would yell, and most of the time, it happened that way. Shula brought discipline and intensity to a team that desperately needed it. There were four practices a day during training camp, double the usual number. Ice and water, even in the sultry Miami heat, were not allowed on the field. Focus was his mantra, even before it became a buzzword of the 1990s. The Dolphins, probably out of self-defense, won ten games in each of Shula's first two seasons.

This is, after all, the man who proposed to his future wife, Dorothy, in the second page of a letter. The first page? It was filled with football fodder. It was Shula who, curious about how athletic their children might be, asked her to backpedal on their honeymoon. She must have been agile, for both sons, Mike and David, went on to outstanding college football careers.

This is the man who, when introduced to *Miami Vice* actor Don Johnson at the height of Johnson's popularity, wasn't exactly sure who the actor was. This is the man who missed exactly two and a half days of work in his entire coaching career—one was when Dorothy had a cancer operation, another when he had surgery on his Achilles heel injury. And then there was the day the team doctor wanted to perform arthroscopic knee surgery during the morning practice at training camp. Shula, with his trademark scowl intact, oversaw the afternoon practice from a golf cart.

Attaining Perfection

It is the goal of every player and every coach in every sport. Win every game. Perfection. It never happens—well, almost never.

In 1972, the Dolphins fielded an offense for the ages. Bob Griese was the quarterback. He handed off to running back Larry Csonka. Guard Larry Little and center Jim Langer opened holes for him. Paul Warfield was the receiver. All five of them would one day be enshrined in the Hall of Fame. The "No-Name Defense" was anchored by Nick Buoniconti.

If coaching is chemistry, Shula was the chief scientist.

"It was a once-in-a-lifetime situation," says Buoniconti. "You put forty-five men together who all got along, and had talent, a great chemistry, and a great coach."

In truth, 1972 did not start out well. In retrospect, maybe that was what fueled the fire for Shula and his Miami team. The 1971 version of the Dolphins reached Super Bowl VI, but was humbled by the Dallas Cowboys, 24–3. Even with a 5–0 start in 1972, the Dolphins appeared to be in trouble when Griese suffered a broken leg and a dislocated ankle against the San Diego Chargers. Earl Morrall, the thirty-eight-year-old quarterback Shula had picked up on waivers, stepped in and kept the unbeaten streak alive through the fourteen-game regular season. He was also the starter in Miami's 20–14 playoff victory over Cleveland.

Griese came off the bench in the AFC championship game in the third quarter, when the score was 7–7, to rally the Dolphins to a 21–17 victory over the Pittsburgh Steelers. In their second straight Super Bowl, the Dolphins were simply superb. They defeated Washington, 14–7, in Super Bowl VII. Griese's 28-yard touchdown pass to Howard Twilley and interceptions by Buoniconti and safety Jake Scott made the difference. Seventeen games, seventeen victories. History.

And then Miami did it all over again in 1973. This time the record was a mere 15–2. The Minnesota Vikings provided the token opposition in Super Bowl VIII, losing, 24–7, to the Dolphins. He didn't know it then, but those two Super Bowl victories would produce Shula's only two championship rings.

Shula entered the NFL at a time when players still respected authority. As the 1970s blurred into the 1980s, the game and its players changed. When salaries began to increase dramatically, the power of the head coach started to wane. Shula, who once released a player after he had argued with an assistant coach on the team plane, managed to adapt.

From 1981 to 1985, the Dolphins were AFC East champions. The anchor of the offense for the next decade and beyond arrived in 1983. His name was Dan Marino, and while teams that were wor-

The Dolphins' Larry Csonka ran through the Minnesota Vikings early and often in Super Bowl VIII.

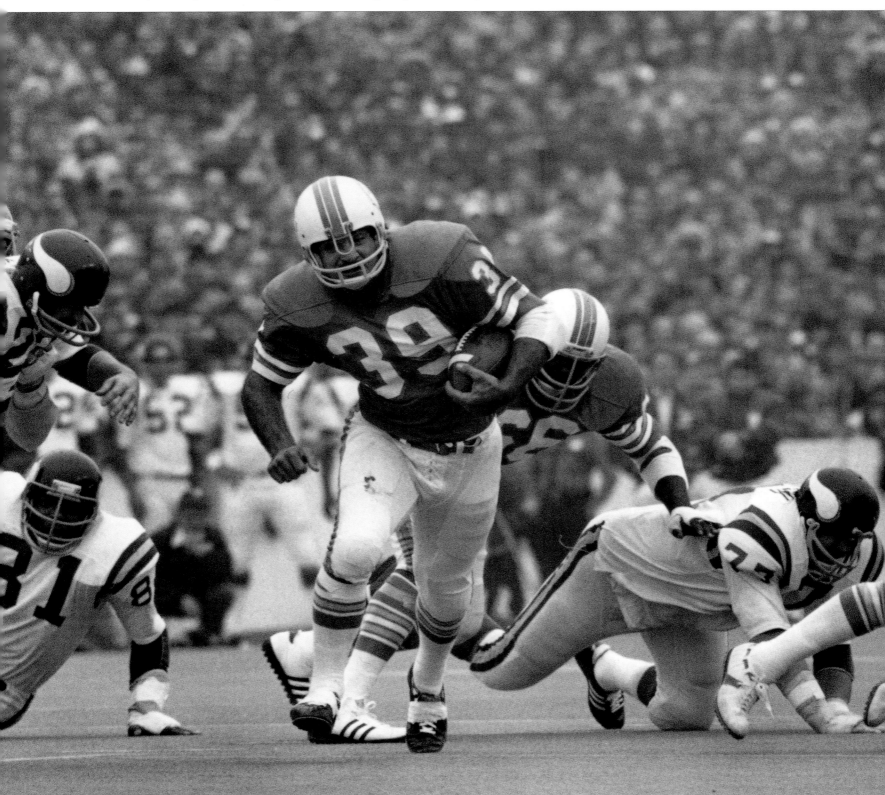

ried about off-the-field rumors shunned the strong-armed quarterback in the first round of the draft, Shula took him with the twenty-seventh overall pick. Miami chose second to last only because it had reached the Super Bowl the year before, losing to Washington at the end of a strike-shortened season. A year later, in 1984, the Dolphins were back in the Super Bowl. And although they lost to the San Francisco 49ers, 38–16, who could imagine that Shula and Marino would never return together to the championship?

On paper, the 1990s were kind to Shula and the Dolphins. They averaged exactly ten victories over the decade's first five years. But in 1995 there was a new sense of urgency. H. Wayne Huizenga, the owner of Blockbuster Video, became the full owner before the 1994 season. Sizing up the aging and increasingly injured Marino and some of his talented teammates, Huizenga and Shula did some salary-cap maneuvering reminiscent of the 49ers. No fewer than eight of twenty-two starters had contracts that expired after the 1995 season. Translation: win, or else.

Shula, now sixty-five, felt the pressure. Four years earlier, with the financial stakes rising, nine NFL teams (of a total twenty-eight) elected to change head coaches. Jimmy Johnson, unemployed and highly visible while cruising in his boat *Three Rings* (for his two NFL championship rings and the NCAA title ring he won at the University of Miami), was only sixty miles (96.5km) south of Miami.

The Dolphins, almost predictably, disappointed. They were 9–7, third in the AFC East. The Buffalo Bills sent them home in the first round of the playoffs with a muscular 37–22 victory. Officially, Shula retired after the season but there was speculation that Huizenga asked him to step down. In any case, it wasn't long before Johnson was hired. And so, an era of football was over. It is quite likely that no coach, in any professional sport, will ever be more closely identified with his team than Shula was with the Dolphins.

"I'm about as subtle as a punch in the mouth," Shula said late in his career. "I'm just a guy who rolls up his sleeves and goes to work."

What It Takes

Art Modell, longtime owner of the Cleveland Browns, who today are known as the Baltimore Ravens, explains Shula's contribution to the game this way:

"Vince Lombardi wrote the book on coaching. Don Shula edited it."

Lombardi, like Shula, was loyal to his early roots. He was born in Brooklyn, New York, played on the line at Fordham, and was an assistant coach for the New York Giants from 1954 to 1958.

Green Bay just happened to be in the market for a coach because Ray "Scooter" McLean had presided over the worst season in Packers history, 1–10–1, in 1958. Lombardi was hired as head coach and general manager, and his first speech to the players was brutally direct: "Anybody who doesn't want to play winning football," he said, "get the hell out of here right now."

Lombardi was old-fashioned, even in the 1950s. He believed in the quaint notion that players should subjugate their individual desires for the good of the team. He was particularly keen on physical conditioning and fundamentals, the small, routine elements of play at each position. He repeated drills again and again until the moves became automatic. The end result was something coaches call execution. Under Lombardi, that's what usually happened to opponents. On the field, Lombardi had an uncomplicated strategy: muscle the other team; wear them down with the power sweep and a relentless defense.

The Packers, not surprisingly, were 7–5 for Lombardi, who was voted Coach of the Year in his rookie season. The NFL's Western Division title came the following year, foreshadowing one of the best runs in football history. The Packers won the league championship five times in seven years. His record in nine seasons with Green Bay was 98–30–4, giving him a winning percentage of .758. Most impressive was Lombardi's record in the crucible of the playoffs, when a loss means the end of the season. Under him, the Packers won nine of ten postseason games—a record that no other NFL coach has rivaled.

So what skills must a coach bring to the table? The great ones have two singular abilities that, on the surface, appear incongruous. He must have devoted much of his life to the study of the game's subtleties and nuances. At the same time, he must be a student of human nature. Coaching, after all, is all about managing people. And it remains an art. The coach must have a vision of what he wants to accomplish. His success depends less on the quality of his vision than the ability to translate it to assistant coaches and players.

Ten NFL coaches got together in 1995 and wrote the book *Game Plans for Success*. It offers the insight of Bill Walsh, Mike Ditka, Bud Grant, and Dennis Green in a diverse, sprawling debate that is intended to be applied to business.

Walsh's specialty was Xs-and-Os strategy. Based on scrupulous preparation, he scripted the offense's first twenty-odd plays. They were creative and effective. "More than creating, innovation involves anticipating," Walsh wrote. "It is having a broad base of knowledge on your subject and an ability to see where the game is headed."

A Different Game

Football, as coaches will tell you, is a lot like life. Today's coaches are in a difficult position. They stand squarely between the owner, who controls the purse strings, and the increasingly militant players. Maybe that's one reason Mike Ditka was on the sidelines for several yeras, analyzing football games instead of coaching them. He and the Chicago Bears won Super Bowl XX in one of the most dominant seasons in history. Ditka later accepted a job with NBC after the 1992 season, but returned to coaching, with the New Orleans Saints in 1997.

109

After winning two Super Bowls in Dallas, coach Jimmy Johnson moved to Miami, where he succeeded a legend named Don Shula.

"In the old days, the owners would hire a coach who was responsible for putting the team together," Ditka wrote in a revealing article published in *Inside Sports* magazine. "He had a tremendous amount to do with the draft and was involved in all trades. What we have now is a changing of the guard with the new breed of NFL owner. Some of them made their money in business and some of them inherited their money, but it's an ego thing that I see now.

"If George Halas were alive today I think he'd call a lot of today's owners sons of bitches. He'd say they've lost their minds, and he'd say it right to their faces. He'd say they've forgotten about the integrity of the game and they worry too much about themselves. It's becoming an owner thing now. For example, you would never see Kansas City Chiefs owner Lamar Hunt or New York Giants owner Wellington Mara ever getting involved hands-on like some of these owners do today. They simply had too much class. They're not showboats. Today it's pure showmanship because it's big business, and there's no question that it really started with Jerry Jones.

"A lot of people thought the Jones–Jimmy Johnson association was the relationship of the century, but it wasn't. The problem there was that both egos were too dynamic—but the guy who owns the ball and bat calls the shots. I learned that when I was a kid.

Jones got rid of a good coach and, he's probably going to cause that organization to sink pretty quickly."

Ditka wrote that before the 1994 season and, sure enough, the San Francisco 49ers ended Dallas' reign as two-time Super Bowl champions. But then the Cowboys, under the leadership of head coach Barry Switzer, came back and won Super Bowl XXX, their third in four years. Switzer was given very little credit for the Cowboys' championship. It was more a tribute to the quality of the Cowboys themselves, many of them procured by Johnson.

Johnson was hired after the 1988 season, after a phenomenal stint at the University of Miami. Johnson, who had an eye for talent, had recruited terrific players and convinced them that they were the best. The Cowboys, who finished 3–13 in coach Tom Landry's final season, would be a tougher job. Johnson wasted no time in gutting the team and building for the future. He traded running back Herschel Walker, the team's best player, but he got a handful of players and draft choices in return from Minnesota.

In Johnson's mind, 1989 was going to be a washout, so why not focus on 1990? Instead of using veterans with mediocre talent as a stopgap measure like many new coaches do, Johnson threw young players into difficult situations. They learned on the job; most of the time, players had to sneak looks to see who was playing next to them. Johnson walked the fine line of being considered a players'

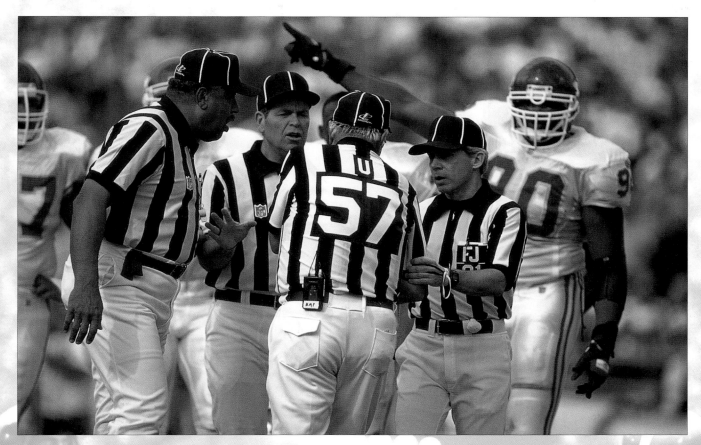

Being an NFL official is perhaps the most difficult part-time job in the world.

THE OFFICIALS

During the week they are merely ordinary people. On weekends, however, the National Football League's 112 officials are pillars of authority in their part-time jobs. Poof! Ed Hochuli, the Texas–El Paso trial attorney, becomes Ed Hochuli, NFL referee, chief of a seven-man crew.

"Believe me," Hochuli says, "there's a lot more stress and pressure on me in connection with my officiating job than there is with my trial lawyer job. How many of us have jobs where we're tape-recorded throughout the job and then the boss analyzes it after the fact to decide if they liked everything you did?

"Once that play starts, you don't hear the noise, you don't think about anything. These athletes are so good and everything happens so fast that if you're not concen-trating and ready for it when it happens, you miss it."

The NFL briefly flirted with instant replay in recent years, but ultimately, the seven-man officiating crew proved more accurate and efficient. Think about the daunting proposition the officials face: fourteen eyes responsible for more than fifty thousand square feet (4,650 sq m) of field—more than half a million cubic feet (14,000 cu m), including airspace—and enforcing 127 pages of complex rules.

Officials are graded on every single play by the supervisors at league head-quarters in New York City. There is also a demanding written test each week. Crews arrive for games on Saturdays, review videotape, and take another quiz.

And while the NFL's offensive and defensive squads are eleven-man teams with a single purpose, so too is the officiating crew. When a complicated play unfolds, the officials who saw it often form a huddle. When this happens, the assumption is ". . . that we're confused," says back judge Jim Poole, "when in real-ity, what we're really doing is reconstruct-ing the play. If we've got a very unusual play, we're putting it back together. We're saying, 'Mike, what did you see?' And, 'What did you see, Neil?' And then we'll say, 'Here's what I saw.'"

Ron Spitler, a field judge on Hochuli's crew, says, "You go out there to be per-fect. And we know we're not perfect, but we still want to be perfect. We take the 'I think' out of our vocabulary. How many times do you say, 'I think' during the day? We have to either know, or we don't know."

coach and a tough disciplinarian. He released a player for merely fumbling at an inopportune time. Fear of losing a lucrative job is a motivating tool most good coaches know how to use.

Johnson's 1989 Cowboys were hideous—1–15, if you must know—but the kids were learning the value of humility. Quarterback Troy Aikman, the first pick in the 1989 draft, was starting to come around. With another high draft choice in 1990, the Cowboys took running back Emmitt Smith. Aikman and Smith would lead Dallas to greatness; they were the Most Valuable Players in Johnson's two Super Bowl victories.

The Cowboys were 7–9 in 1990, a six-game improvement. Their record in 1991 was 11–5—astonishing, considering where they came from. They won a playoff game, and by 1992 they were the best team in football. The Cowboys won Super Bowls XXVII and XXVIII over Buffalo, but as Ditka points out, there was a huge cost for those victories. Less than two months after the second championship, Johnson and Jones parted in dramatic fashion. Jones, who acted as the team's general manager, and Johnson could no longer bear each other's company.

They haven't spoken since.

"I was all set to be cordial and civil, but as time went on he continually degraded what I did for the Cowboys," Johnson says. "I became very irritated and bitter about that. I obviously gained a lot, but I also gave a lot for five years. I worked every day and night to make Jerry Jones a very rich man and a very powerful man in the NFL. I thought it was wrong for him to try to tear me down."

Johnson may have the last laugh. When Jones signed cornerback Deion Sanders to a seven-year, $35 million contract in 1995, Jones' son Steve, a Cowboys vice president, wanted to punch him. The team's salary cap was stretched to the breaking point and it may be years before Dallas recovers. Johnson, meanwhile, should eventually prosper in Miami.

As he said when he took the job in early 1996, "Let's do it all over again."

Out of the Shadow

No one envied George Seifert when he became the San Francisco 49ers' twelfth head coach in 1989. That was because the eleventh

ABOVE: Bill Walsh, being carried off the field after the 49ers won Super Bowl XIX, was the first coach to receive the "genius" label from the nation's sporting media.

was Bill Walsh. All Walsh did was revolutionize the way offenses attack defenses. All he did was produce a sterling record of 102–63–1 in ten seasons. All he did was win three Super Bowls, the last a magnificent send-off into retirement. These were difficult footsteps to follow.

Seifert, who had spent nine seasons under Walsh as an assistant, the last six as defensive coordinator, knew the history. Phil Bengston, trying to follow Vince Lombardi in Green Bay, lasted only three seasons and produced a 20–21–1 record. When George Halas retired for the last time after the 1967 season, Jim Dooley took the Bears to a 20–36 mark in four seasons.

Instead of trying too hard to put his own stamp on the team, Seifert bided his time. He wrestled with trying to maintain continuity and making the changes he felt necessary. As an assistant he had appreciated it when Walsh let him make pivotal decisions; Seifert the head coach delegated authority well. "I present ideas, not mandates," he says.

In Seifert's first season, the 49ers won fourteen games and outscored three opponents, 126–26. The pièce de résistance was Super Bowl XXIV, a resounding 55–10 victory over Denver. Critics suggest that Seifert's success is attributable to the 49ers' organization, probably the finest in the modern game. And while it may have been true for that first season, how do they explain 1990 and 1992, when the 49ers also went 14–2? How do they explain 1994, when Seifert won his second Super Bowl, a 49–26 destruction of the San Diego Chargers? In those years, the 49ers were a team that he put together.

Seifert is on a short list of coaches who have won two or more Super Bowls: Lombardi, Walsh, Johnson, Shula, Landry, Noll, Joe Gibbs, Parcells, and Tom Flores. That said, it may be hard to believe what you are about to read. Seifert—not any of the above

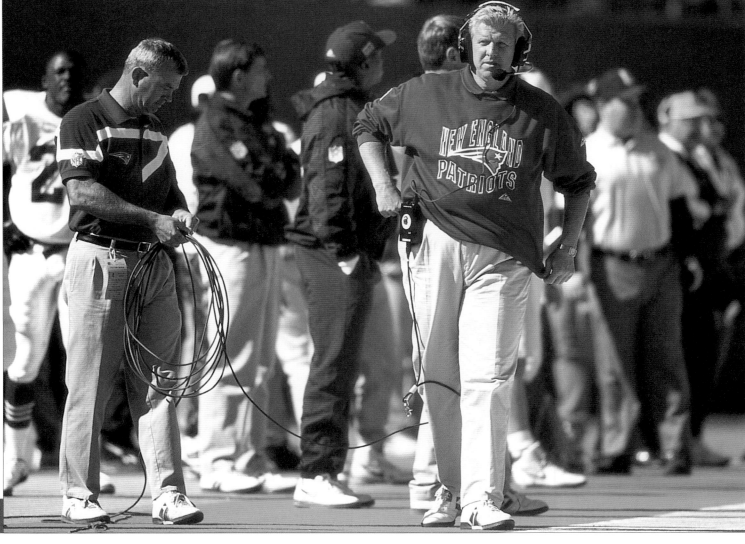

Bill Parcells, a.k.a. "The Tuna," won two Super Bowls with the Giants and reached a third with the Patriots.

coaches—has the best winning percentage in NFL history. His seven-season record of 95–29 works out to .766. Vince Lombardi (.740) and John Madden (.731) are the only other coaches to surpass the .700 mark.

One of Seifert's best decisions was actually a nondecision concerning Deion Sanders, the brash cornerback. Seifert, a thoughtful and conservative coach, worried that Sanders might be a disruptive force when he was signed as a free agent in 1994. Still, he did not ask Sanders to tone down his hotdogging dances in the end zone. In the end, Sanders' enthusiasm was infectious and helped carry the team to new heights.

"I honestly felt that if I tried to impose too much of myself on that team and be too restrictive, the whole thing would have crumbled," says Seifert.

Even Seifert was not immune to the pressures placed on NFL coaches, and he eventually stepped down (some say at the request of San Francisco management) after the 1996 season. Seifert had compiled an astounding 108–35 record, the highest winning percentage (.755) of any coach in history.

In the grand scheme of things, Deion Sanders and Buddy Ryan are a lot alike. They are colorful and controversial; in short, their reputations generally precede them. Another thing: despite appearances to the contrary, they are both students of the game.

Ryan made his reputation as the defensive coordinator for Ditka's Chicago Bears. He created the "46" Defense, out of a need to put pressure on the quarterback, and today it is a scheme most teams employ to some degree. In five seasons in Philadelphia he was 43–38–1, and the Eagles made the playoffs his last three years. Eventually, his personality clashed with owner Norman Braman and Ryan departed. After a tour of duty in Houston, Ryan surfaced as the head coach of the Arizona Cardinals, who were 8–8 in his first season.

Ryan's philosophy, to hear him tell it, is pretty basic.

"The main thing I try to do is win," Ryan says. "I try to hire good people—people who understand how things work. Like my dad used to say, 'If you get to your job before the boss and leave after him, you've got a good chance at keeping it.' I work hard at my end of it, and I expect the same thing out of them. I think I probably let coaches coach. I never worry about who's boss because I've always thought I was the boss.

"No coach can win without good players, but a lot of coaches can't win with them. Coaching in the pros is the ability to get the most out of your players. That's the biggest asset you can have. I don't holler at players and grab them by the face mask. But I get them to play for me."

Good coaches have that ability to know just when to say what to whom. Bill Parcells displayed that knack in winning two Super Bowls in eight seasons with the New York Giants. His record: 85–52–1, and that includes the absolutely horrific 3–12–1 of 1983, his rookie season.

Parcells almost didn't survive that stumble from the gate, but he recovered quickly and produced playoff teams in 1984 and 1985 before the Giants went 14–2 and won Super Bowl XXI over Denver, 39–20. Parcells made a point of speaking to each of his fifty-odd players each day. Sometimes it was just a hello, sometimes a stinging barb designed to motivate. Parcells cared less about being liked than respected, and the players responded on the field.

The 1990 Giants season was Parcells' finest effort; the Giants were probably the third-best team in football that year. And yet they managed to beat San Francisco in the NFC championship game despite scoring no touchdowns, and squeezed past Buffalo, 20–19, in Super Bowl XXV when the Bills missed a last-second field goal.

A combination of coaching burnout and an ailing heart sent Parcells into retirement. He worked as an analyst for NBC for two seasons before the New England Patriots talked him into returning to football. The Patriots, 2–14 under jovial Dick MacPherson, were desperate for discipline. New England won five games in 1993, including the last four, but Parcells scoffed when it was suggested that all the Patriots needed to do was continue their momentum.

"People walk up and say, 'If you can just pick up where you left off,'" Parcells said before the 1994 season. "I tell them, 'Get that idea out of your head.' Picking up where you left off never, ever works. You go back to where you started last time. The idea is to keep everything the same, then accelerate through it faster than you did the time before, like we didn't at the start of last season."

Much to Parcells' dismay, the Patriots started slowly again, los-

Coach Marv Levy, the man with a degree from Harvard, stepped down in Buffalo after the 1997 season.

ing six of their first nine games. But then they won their last seven and made the playoffs. New England was 6–10 in 1995, a sour season that prompted Parcells to reconsider his future. He asked owner Robert Kraft to reduce his contract by a year, meaning 1996 would probably be his last. And what a final year it was. The Patriots went all the way to Super Bowl XXXI in New Orleans, where they lost to the Green Bay Packers. Parcells broke with Kraft, and after much posturing took a job with the New York Jets.

Parcells showed the strength of his leadership with the Jets in 1997, taking a team that had won just a single game in the 1996 season to a record of 9–7, only one game short of a playoff berth.

Steady Hands

Football coaches come in all guises and shapes. Take the Buffalo Bills' Marv Levy, who after Shula retired in 1995 became the leading active coach in the NFL. Levy, 154–120 when he retired after the 1997 season, coached the Kansas City Chiefs from 1978 to 1982 and the Buffalo Bills from 1986 to 1997.

People choose to dwell on the incredibly sad fact that Levy's Bills lost four consecutive Super Bowls, but give him credit for getting his team there four straight times. No coach has ever done that. The silver-haired Levy is an affable and urbane coach with a Phi Beta Kappa degree from Coe College and a master's degree in English from Harvard. And while his players sometimes joke about his war analogies and off-the-chart vocabulary words, they nonetheless played hard for him.

The same can be said of Atlanta Falcons coach Dan Reeves, who is first on the active list with a mark of 156–122–1. Like Levy, he is a coach who is remembered for losing Super Bowls—three, in fact—with the Denver Broncos. But Reeves averaged nearly ten victories a season before running afoul of quarterback John Elway and owner Pat Bowlen.

Reeves was the third choice of Giants general manager George Young, but after his 11–5 debut in 1993 he was named Coach of the Year. Reeves is a quick study. He played for Tom Landry in Dallas and coached with him as an assistant before going to Denver in

There is no better broadcast tandem, in any sport, than Pat Summerall, left, and John Madden.

JOHN MADDEN AND PAT SUMMERALL

The last broadcast was the 1993 NFC championship game, when Dallas throttled San Francisco, 38–21.

Pat Summerall and John Madden had been calling games for CBS Television for thirteen seasons, but media master Rupert Murdoch changed all that. The Fox Network chairman had spent $1.58 billion to secure the rights to NFC broadcasts for four years. And so, Summerall and Madden's long run seemed over.

"The time came [to close] and I looked at him, and I guess it hit us," Summerall says. "We just said what we were feeling at that moment. We probably both appeared to be groping. It was a very emotional day. It was such a great partnership, the NFL and CBS, and such a big part of my life, that it was a shock to stand there and say, 'Well, it's over.'"

As it turned out, football's best broadcast pair wasn't finished. Murdoch and Fox hired the two and their gifted support crew, producer Bob Stenner and director Sandy Grossman. And a nation of couch potatoes gave silent thanks to the sports broadcasting gods.

A Summerall-Madden broadcast is the standard by which all football announcers are judged. Summerall, with his minimalist, matter-of-fact approach is complemented perfectly by the colorful and emotional bam-pow-zap yet insightful observations of Madden.

Both men know their football. Summerall is so smooth that people forget he was a player once—a good one. He played a decade in the NFL, as a receiver and a placekicker with the Giants, Lions, and Cardinals. Madden coached the Oakland Raiders for a decade as well, producing a 112–39–7 record and a Super Bowl victory.

The first time the two were paired was in 1981 in a midseason game between the Dallas Cowboys and St. Louis Cardinals. Actually, Summerall had been working with former player Tom Brookshier, an analyst whose breezy style was similar to Madden's. When Brookshier took a week of vacation, Madden was assigned to work with Summerall.

"I knew after two series that John would be very good," Summerall says. "With Tom and me it was like two players talking. With John and me, it was like a player and a coach talking. He was enthusiastic, I was low-key, but it worked."

Did it ever. They became the best team in network television. They would arrive each week at the game's site and interview players and coaches for background information that served to elevate their telecasts. When Summerall and Madden call a playoff game or the traditional Thanksgiving contest, fans know they will be treated to a little inside football, not to mention a trip around the parking lot to see what the tailgaters were eating that week.

"We see things differently," Summerall says. "Not everything John says makes sense, even to me, but we're able to play off that."

1981. Reeves swiftly eliminated the Giants' biggest potential problem: a quarterback controversy. Both Phil Simms and Jeff Hostetler had led the team to Super Bowls, but their presence together had divided the players. Reeves opted for Simms while Hostetler was signed by the Los Angeles Raiders. Both players and both teams prospered because of Reeves' decisive action.

Marty Schottenheimer, second on the active list with a record of 144–87–1, hasn't been afraid to make important decisions in his twelve seasons as a head coach in the NFL. His winning percentage of .624 compares favorably to history's best coaches. Being consistent and true to yourself, he says, is vital to success—in or on any field. When he joined the Kansas City Chiefs in 1989, after five seasons with the Cleveland Browns, he didn't try to reinvent himself.

"What the new group is looking for, essentially, is what you delivered before," Schottenheimer says. "It would be a mistake for an executive to make a lateral move, one company to another, and suddenly decide to blaze a new trail."

The vertical move, from college coaching to professional, is not attempted often. Jimmy Johnson pulled it off, of course, but there aren't many success stories. In fact, of the top ten coaches of all time with respect to victories, none of them split time between college and the NFL. Rich Brooks ignored that history and jumped at the chance to coach in the NFL after eighteen seasons at the University of Oregon. Brooks joined the St. Louis Rams in 1995 after leading the Oregon Ducks to their first Rose Bowl berth in thirty-seven years.

"I have no delusions," Brooks said before his rookie season. "We have a lot of work ahead of us. But I believe that an NFL team can be made competitive faster than a college team. It was a long process. It can be quicker here. I fully realize I don't have eighteen years to make the Rams a winner."

Brooks, whose record at Oregon was 91–109–4, inherited a team that was 4–12 in 1994. "You have to have confidence in what you're doing, and this team didn't," Brooks said. "The first thing we'll need to establish is confidence."

The team's first season in St. Louis was a relative success, however; the Rams were 7–9 under Brooks, who was a Rams assistant for two seasons in the early 1970s.

Some coaches argue that coaching in college, where there are about twice as many players and authorities to answer to, is more difficult than the professional ranks. Johnson, who coached at Oklahoma State for five seasons and another five at Miami, is one of them.

"You put in more hours coaching in the pros because of the longer season, but coaching in college is more demanding, and there's more tension," Johnson says. "Coaching at a high-profile school has become an extremely difficult job because you have to answer to so many different groups: administrators, alumni, fans,

the media. There are so many different things to deal with that you have little time to actually coach.

"When I was a freshman at Arkansas, there were sixty-six players entering school, and only twelve graduated. But I don't recall the media jumping on [coach] Frank Broyles, asking, 'What ever happened to those other fifty-four? Why didn't they graduate? It's your fault.' It was survival of the fittest, and nobody ever said a word. Nowadays, if you don't graduate every one of your players, or if a kid has too many beers one night, well, you obviously didn't counsel him very well."

History's Best

The record book says Don Shula is the winningest coach in NFL history, but George Halas was first in a very real sense. He was actually in the 1920 meeting in which the NFL was created. In 1921, he bought the Decatur Staleys and moved them to Chicago where they later became the Bears. Halas played for the Staleys, coached them, and served as the general manager, trainer, equipment man, business manager, and public relations man, too.

He served professional football for sixty-four years until his death in 1983. He coached the Chicago Bears for four different tours of duty and the result was a 324–151–31 record, a total only Shula approached over the NFL's seventy-six years of play. The Pro Football Hall of Fame in Canton, Ohio, is a tribute to Halas' contribution: the Hall is located at 2121 George Halas Drive Northwest.

Tom Landry, the first coach of the Dallas Cowboys—and the team's only coach for twenty-nine seasons—is third on the all-time list with a 270–178–6 record.

He was born in Mission, Texas, played at the University of Texas, joined the New York Giants in 1950, and played six seasons, the last two as a player-coach. The Dallas Cowboys, an expansion team in 1960, made him their head coach. Landry was an innovative coach credited with designing the Flex Defense and the Shotgun Offense. He coached a handful of Hall of Fame players and guided the Cowboys to a pair of Super Bowl victories, but his greatest achievement was this: for twenty consecutive seasons he coached the Cowboys to a winning record.

Of the sixteen coaches enshrined in the Pro Football Hall of Fame, only one has managed to come away with the ultimate prize, a Super Bowl trophy, four different times. Think about it. In San Francisco, Bill Walsh (three) and George Seifert (two) split five trophies. In Dallas, Landry and Johnson won two each.

Only Pittsburgh Steelers coach Chuck Noll has four gleaming Super Bowl trophies he can point to—displayed attractively in the Steelers lobby underneath Three Rivers Stadium.

Like Halas and Landry, Noll was a one-team coach. For twenty-three seasons, from 1969 to 1991, he was the Steelers. His final record was 209–156–1.

Many football fans, particularly younger ones, watch John Madden analyze games for the Fox television network and wonder where he got his insight. Long ago, he was a coach. Madden only coached the Oakland Raiders for ten seasons, from 1969 to 1978, but what a marvelous decade it was. The Raiders under his reign were 112–39–7, and one of those victories was in Super Bowl XI, over Minnesota. Madden made up for a lack of quantity in victories with quality; his winning percentage of .731 is surpassed only by George Seifert and Vince Lombardi.

There are twenty-five coaches who have reached the century mark for victories in NFL coaching. Bill Walsh, the revered coach of the San Francisco 49ers, is twenty-fifth on the list with a mark of 102–63–1. He, too, coached a fleeting ten years. Yet his impact can still be seen on the NFL.

Almost half the league's teams use at least some of the plays from the offense that made Walsh's reputation with the 49ers. Six head coaches in the NFL in 1995 once worked for Walsh with the 49ers, and two others worked in San Francisco after Walsh left.

It was Walsh who drafted Joe Montana and Jerry Rice. Walsh who gave them marvelous plays to run. Walsh who masterminded three Super Bowl victories and, probably, most of a fourth won by Seifert.

In January 1996, seven years after he had left the 49ers, Walsh was back. His second-floor office at the 49ers complex in Santa Clara used to be a storage room, but there is nothing old or musty about Walsh's enthusiasm for the game. At the age of sixty-four, Walsh returned to the 49ers as a consultant.

"My guess is I'll be associated with the 49ers in varying roles for another ten years," Walsh says. "I may have that powder-blue shirt on with a badge on it, checking people into the facility, but there will always be an association. The ties are very strong."

The most recent coaching addition to the Hall of Fame, appropriately, is Joe Gibbs of the Washington Redskins. He was enshrined in 1996 after compiling a record of 140–65 and a lofty winning percentage of .683.

Gibbs was so focused on his job that he regularly slept on a cot in his Redskins Park office. He sometimes forgot where he parked his car, and there was the time he had to ask someone exactly who pop star Madonna was. Still, in Gibbs' twelve seasons, the Redskins had only one losing effort, and made four Super Bowls, winning three of them. Gibbs' postseason record of 16–5 (.762) is surpassed only by Lombardi (.900) and Weeb Ewbank (.800).

Seen here in later years, legendary Bears coach George Halas had been present at the NFL's moment of creation.

QUARTERBACKS COACHES

The quarterback position is the most complicated in today's world of professional sports. Why, then, is it also the most undercoached?

"Sometimes you almost take it for granted that a quarterback—say of a Marino, an Elway, or a Kelly status—already knows everything," says Jim Kelly of the Buffalo Bills. "We don't. We can still learn."

In 1993, San Francisco 49ers quarterback Steve Young was the National Football League's best quarterback. But in 1994, his game rose to a new level; Young's passer rating of 112.8 was history's best. The difference? Quarterbacks coach Gary Kubiak, a man who started all of five games in his NFL career.

"I would definitely point to Gary as an important factor in taking my game to the next notch," Young says. "A lot of times you can just watch a quarterback's footwork, balance, and how he finishes throws, whether he's jumping around or not. A quarterbacks coach now has the time to sit there and go through that five times a day watching all that."

Says Kubiak, "A lot of times the quarterback, the sharp guy, the guy who can handle everything, maybe we take things for granted with him sometimes. If anything, he needs more attention than anybody."

In 1990, only nine of the NFL teams employed quarterbacks coaches whose sole responsibility was supervising the

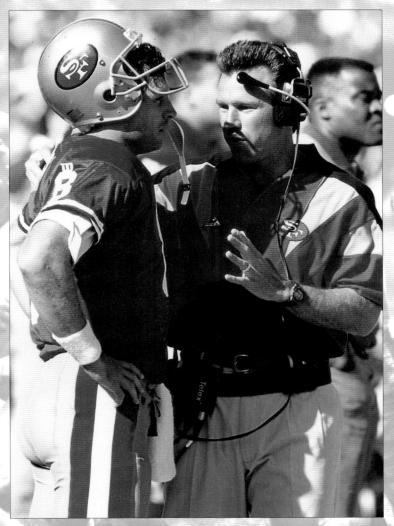

San Francisco quarterback Steve Young listens to then-49ers assistant coach Gary Kubiak.

quarterback. In 1995, there were fourteen in the NFL. Still, there were sixteen teams without one. Those teams—many of them having a tight ends coach for those two or three players—generally left the quarterbacks to the offensive coordinator.

"Often the man that is the coordinator is the best qualified to coach the position," says 49ers former head coach Bill Walsh. "But he's so darn busy with other things that he can't give it the time he should."

In 1995, the Giants brought in former NFL starter Steve DeBerg to tutor their young quarterback, Dave Brown. "DeBerg comes in and he says, 'Well, there's one thing I've noticed, that your head moves when you throw the ball,'" Brown says. "My head moves? Like I don't know what he's talking about, and he says my head is moving a half inch [12mm] to the left, sometimes, or an inch [2.5cm] to the right. It's not stationary. He says, 'Try to read a book with your head moving. It's impossible to do.'

"One of the things I did poorly [in 1994] was my five-step drop, because my head was only pointed at one-third of the field. This year, he brought films of Dan Marino out, films of John Elway—the guys who open up their shoulder and see the entire field. And I thought I'd never be able to do it. But Steve Young does it, Troy Aikman does it.

"Something as little and simple as that . . . helped me to play a lot better."

THE POSTSEASON

The Super Bowl

On the surface, anyway, the Super Bowl is all about flash and excess and hyperbole. So what better man to dominate the landscape at Super Bowl XXX in Tempe, Arizona, than bombastic Dallas Cowboys owner Jerry Jones?

It was Jones who first hired coach Jimmy Johnson before the 1989 season. It was Jones who fired him after two Super Bowl championship seasons, in 1992 and 1993. It was Jones who hired Barry Switzer to replace Johnson. And, yes, it was Jones who clutched the Super Bowl XXX trophy after the Cowboys held off the Pittsburgh Steelers team, 27–17, on January 28, 1996.

How did the Cowboys do it? In a word: talent.

Quarterback Troy Aikman completed 15 of 23 passes for 209 yards and 1 touchdown. Running back Emmitt Smith, wide receiver Michael Irvin, and an offensive line for the ages kept the Steelers off balance. The defense, led by cornerback Larry Brown's 2 second-half interceptions, controlled Pittsburgh when it had to. Brown, the Most Valuable Player, set up touchdowns with each of his interceptions off Neil O'Donnell. The second, with four minutes and nine seconds left, stopped what might have been a winning drive by Pittsburgh. A subsequent 4-yard run by Smith, with 3:43 left, put a game open to suggestion out of reach.

The Dallas defense, despite spending most of the second half on the field, kept O'Donnell (28-of-49 and 239 yards) scrambling, sacking him four times and forcing a number of misfires.

OPPOSITE: John Riggins of the Washington Redskins enjoyed himself all week long in Pasadena, California, then ran all over the Miami Dolphins in Super Bowl XVII.

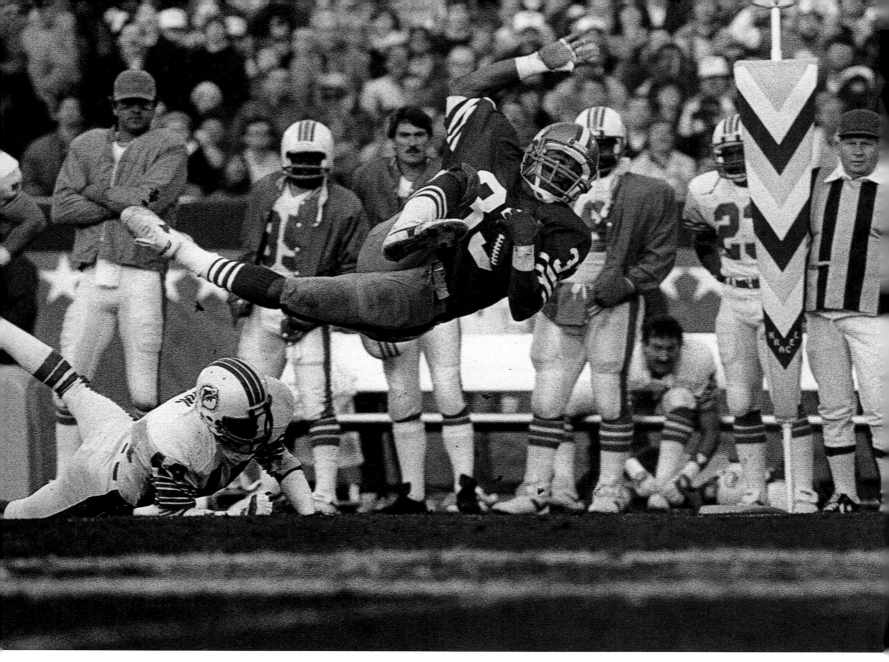

Roger Craig hurtles through the air for a first down in this play from Super Bowl XIX.

Dallas thus joined San Francisco as the only National Football League franchise to win five Super Bowls, and became the first to win three in four seasons.

First in Our Hearts

In thirty-two short years, the Super Bowl has gone from nothing at all to the biggest item on the social calendar.

In a survey of Americans, researchers recently discovered that Super Bowl parties were more popular than Halloween or New Year's celebrations. For three or four hours on a Sunday in late January, the country focuses on a football game that decides the NFL championship. Television viewership consistently surges past 100 million. Ratings show that more than 40 percent of the nation's televisions are tuned to the ballyhooed game.

Unlike baseball's World Series and the National Basketball Association's Finals, football's title is always decided by a single all-or-nothing game, which brings with it a certain sense of urgency. And as the NFL mines markets far afield, the global audience is expanding. In 1989, for instance, Super Bowl XXIII was seen in sixty foreign countries, including China, with an estimated 300 million viewers.

In theory, the Super Bowl pits the league's two best teams against each other. In actual practice, it rarely works out that way. The NFC championship game, in recent years, has offered the best pure matchup.

How to explain the NFC's dominance over the AFC, which, after the 1998 game, featured fourteen victories in fifteen games?

The bottom line here is probably defense. AFC teams over those years typically were built around quarterbacks; nine of those losses came to quarterbacks from the glittery class of '83. The NFC has fielded more balanced teams.

Consider turnovers, the barometer of success in playoff games. AFC teams have turned the ball over four times as much as NFC teams in the ultimate game.

Also in that streak, NFC teams have more than twice the yardage of the AFC, despite the Steelers' edge over the Cowboys, 103 yards to 56.

There is also the bitter rivalry between San Francisco and Dallas. Seven of the twelve victories in the NFC streak belong to those teams.

Some in football believe that the Dallas Cowboys mortgaged their long-term future by signing free agent cornerback Deion

Sanders before the 1995 season. Others aren't so sure. Still, judging by San Francisco's brisk off-season free agent activity, the 49ers aren't prepared to watch the Cowboys set a new record for Super Bowl victories.

Not without a fight.

Super Bowl I

To begin with, it wasn't even officially called Super Bowl I. Nor was it particularly superb. In retrospect the history books now describe the drama and splendor of the first game between the American Football League and the National Football League. But, really, it was just another day at the office for the Green Bay Packers. The Kansas City Chiefs never had a chance.

Here, believe it or not, is what happened to the Chiefs: the Packers' star of the game was an aging wide receiver, who had been out the night before—the entire night and a good deal of the morning—investigating the social circles of Los Angeles. Max McGee, forced to play when teammate Boyd Dowler was injured, caught 7 passes in that game, 2 of them for touchdowns, worth a total of 138 yards. This was something of an upset, because McGee had caught exactly 4 passes for 91 yards in 14 regular-season games

The game was mandated into being on June 8, 1966, when the two leagues agreed to merge with a common schedule, beginning in 1970. Before that, there would be four world championship games, starting in January 1967. Credit Kansas City owner Lamar

Hunt's daughter and her bouncy Super Ball with the superlative tag. Hunt liked the name and the media ran with it. Oddly enough, Hunt's Chiefs found their way into the first Super Bowl against Vince Lombardi's heavily favored Packers.

America's fascination with the Super Bowl had not yet surfaced; the first Super Bowl did not have official Roman numerals, and there were only 61,946 paying spectators in the cavernous 100,000-seat Los Angeles Memorial Coliseum. With CBS and NBC both showing the January 15, 1967, game, there were estimates that 60 million watched the game on television.

The Packers led 14–10 at the half and scored 3 unanswered touchdowns in the second half to win a 35–10 game. Green Bay quarterback Bart Starr, who completed 16 of 23 passes for 250 yards and 2 touchdowns to McGee, was the Most Valuable Player. Safety Willie Wood made a critical interception and returned it 50 yards to the Chiefs' 5-yard line to set up the first score in the second half. The Packers took home $15,000 per man (the Chiefs settled for $7,500 each), the largest single-team share in professional sports history.

Super Bowl II

The plot line already established, Green Bay bulldozed the AFL champion Oakland Raiders, 33–14, in the second Super Bowl. Vince Lombardi's Packers were favored by 14 points and they delivered on that faith with a few points to spare on January 14, 1968.

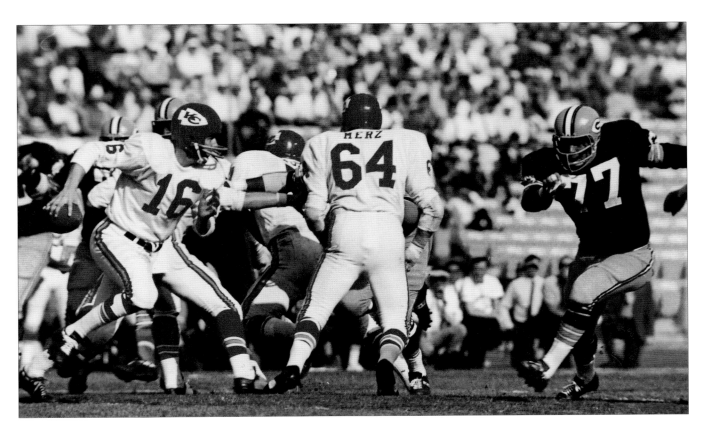

Kansas City quarterback Len Dawson heads around right guard Curt Merz in Super Bowl I.

Quarterback Bart Starr was again the Most Valuable Player, completing 13 of 24 passes for 202 yards and a touchdown. Placekicker Don Chandler kicked 4 field goals, and as usual the defense never rested. The crowd of 75,546 at the Orange Bowl in Miami made history, producing the first $3 million gate in football history.

It was actually the third consecutive NFL championship for Lombardi's Packers, and their fifth in seven years. It was also their last, together or apart. Lombardi stepped down after the season and predicted hopefully that the future of the Packers would be just as bright as the past. Though as of yet Green Bay hasn't won the NFL title again, football's future was bright, in part, thanks to Lombardi and his dominant Packers.

After the game, NFL commissioner Pete Rozelle awarded the elegant championship trophy to Lombardi. Today, that gleaming piece of silver hardware is known as the Vince Lombardi Trophy.

Super Bowl III

Before January 12, 1969, the American Football League was nothing more than a passing curiosity on the national sporting landscape. The real football teams were in the National Football League—you could ask George Halas and Tom Landry and Vince Lombardi. But on that marvelous day in the Orange Bowl, the AFL gained enormous credibility when a brash quarterback named Joe Willie Namath and the New York Jets met the Baltimore Colts and conquered them.

The Jets were, predictably, 18- to 23-point underdogs, depending on your choice of oddsmaker. This did not prevent Namath, he of the gaudy white shoes, from predicting that the Jets would, in fact, beat the Colts. "The Jets will win on Sunday," he told the Miami Touchdown Club three days before the game. "I guarantee it."

This was verbal suicide because of the way the Kansas City Chiefs and Oakland Raiders had been manhandled in the previous two Super Bowls, not to mention the Colts' compelling record. Baltimore's only regular-season loss, to Cleveland, was avenged by a resounding NFL championship victory over the Browns by the improbable score of 34–0. Whatever possessed Namath to put his foot in his mouth and then repeat it several times within hearing-distance of reporters? Maybe it was just the truth.

Namath was the best player on the field against the Colts, completing 17 of 28 passes for 206 yards, but he had a lot of help from excellent players. His offensive line was magnificent, opening holes for Matt Snell, worth 121 yards and a touchdown. Snell's 4-yard touchdown was the only score of the first half and Jets placekicker Jim Turner kicked 3 second-half field goals to make it 16–0. The majority of the 75,389 fans seemed stunned. The Colts managed a single fourth-quarter touchdown, but the Jets dominated the 16–7 game. They produced 337 yards of offense and the defense intercepted Baltimore quarterback Earl Morrall three times in the first

Super Bowl V's moment of truth: Colts placekicker Jim O'Brien follows through on the winning 32-yard field goal.

half and roughed up Johnny Unitas, who replaced Morrall in the second half.

"This is a new era in football," declared Jets head coach Weeb Ewbank. He wasn't kidding. The Jets' win gave the Super Bowl a new cachet. Now, discussions of great sporting events like the Kentucky Derby and World Series included the Super Bowl.

Super Bowl IV

You would think the old guard of the NFL would have learned by January 11, 1970. The formal merger with the AFL was about to become a reality, but the senior league's Super Bowl IV entry, the Minnesota Vikings, were 13-point favorites over the Kansas City Chiefs. Maybe it was because they had a catchier nickname: the Purple People Eaters.

The Chiefs looked a little vulnerable; they placed second in their own division over the regular season and their quarterback,

Len Dawson, was reeling from a series of misfortunes. He suffered a knee injury in the second game of the season and missed six games. Later, his father died. Finally, the week before the Super Bowl, Dawson was named in a federal investigation into sports gambling. The Vikings were so confident that they forgot to cover Kansas City's wide receivers.

All day long at Tulane Stadium in New Orleans, Dawson threw underneath Minnesota's loose coverage. Kansas City scored the game's first 16 points. Nine of Dawson's 12 completions were to the wide men, including a 47-yard touchdown to Otis Taylor to make the final score 23–7. Overlooked was the Chiefs defense that forced 5 turnovers and limited the Vikings to 67 yards rushing.

The crowd of 80,562 was a Super Bowl record; the gate of $3.8 million was a record for all sports. The AFL finished its four-game set with the NFL dead even at two games apiece. From now on, it would be the AFC and the NFC under the umbrella of the NFL.

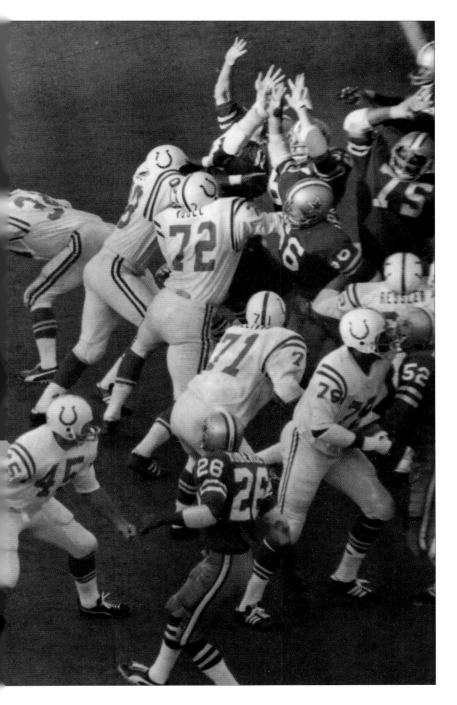

up the middle by Norm Bulaich, the Colts called time-out. Rookie placekicker Jim O'Brien entered the game to try a 32-yard field goal. With five seconds left, his kick was true and the Colts were 16–13 winners. The 79,204 witnesses would agree they had seen the most thrilling Super Bowl to date.

Super Bowl VI

Losers have two choices: they can dwell on the past at the expense of the future, or they can move on and try to change that future. The Dallas Cowboys chose the second approach in their return to the Super Bowl on January 16, 1972. The record crowd of 81,023 at Tulane Stadium in New Orleans saw the Cowboys vindicate themselves in brutal fashion with a 24–3 victory over Don Shula's Miami Dolphins.

Dallas running back Dwayne Thomas, who rushed for 95 yards, should have been the Most Valuable Player, but it was most likely his controversial off-field behavior that led to the award being delivered to quarterback Roger Staubach, who completed 12 of 19 passes for touchdowns to Mike Ditka and Lance Alworth. The Cowboys defense shut down the Dolphins, producing the first no-touchdown effort in the game's young history.

"It's unfortunate that our season had to end this way," said a dejected Shula, the first coach to lose two Super Bowls. "We have a very fine football team, but we never really got untracked."

Super Bowl VII

Just as the Cowboys did before them, the Miami Dolphins learned from their mistakes a year later in a second consecutive Super Bowl. The date was January 14, 1973, and the venue was Memorial Coliseum in Los Angeles. This time, 90,182 fans appeared and a record 75 million watched at home on television to see if Shula's Dolphins could complete the NFL's first-ever perfect season.

By halftime it was clear the Dolphins were playing for history. They led 14–0, and the Washington Redskins didn't score until there were just over two minutes left in the game. The final score, 14–7, gave the Dolphins their cherished 17–0 record. Miami safety Jake Scott, with 2 critical interceptions, was named Most Valuable Player.

For the record, Miami became the fourth straight team to win the Super Bowl after losing in its first appearance.

Super Bowl VIII

The Super Bowl changed venues on January 13, 1974, to Houston's Rice Stadium, but the result was precisely the same. Miami won its second Super Bowl in as many tries; Minnesota lost its second of two. The final score before 71,882 spectators: a lopsided 24–7.

The game was essentially over after the Dolphins' first 2 possessions, both of which resulted in touchdowns. Fullback Larry

Super Bowl V

There was a curious feel to the fifth Super Bowl on January 17, 1971. It was on the very same Orange Bowl field in Miami two years earlier that the Baltimore Colts had been stunned by the upstart New York Jets of the old American Football League. Well, now the shoe was on the other foot; the Colts, along with longtime NFL clubs the Cleveland Browns and Pittsburgh Steelers (spurred by a cash incentive of $3 million), had joined the AFC.

And so it was that Baltimore reached Super Bowl V opposite the Dallas Cowboys.

The Cowboys led, 13–6, at the half, but after a scoreless third quarter Baltimore rallied to tie when Tom Nowatzke scored from 2 yards out. With less than two minutes remaining in the game, Dallas quarterback Craig Morton tried to hit halfback Dan Reeves with a swing pass. Baltimore linebacker Mike Curtis intercepted and returned the ball to the Dallas 28-yard line. After two plunges

127

Roger "The Dodger" Staubach was the ultimate choice for Most Valuable Player of Super Bowl VI.

Csonka scored from 5 yards out less than five and a half minutes into the game, and halfback Jim Kiick scored a 1-yard touchdown eight minutes later to give Miami an insurmountable 14–0 lead. Quarterback Bob Griese handed the ball off a staggering 53 times, attempting only 7 passes. Csonka, the Most Valuable Player, carried 33 times for 145 yards and 2 touchdowns.

It was the first time a team had repeated as back-to-back Super Bowl champions since Green Bay won the first two ultimate games. And, like the Packers, the first two Super Bowl titles would be Miami's last.

Super Bowl IX

The word for first-time Super Bowl teams was clear: "losers."

It happened to the Kansas City Chiefs, Oakland Raiders, Baltimore Colts, Dallas Cowboys, Miami Dolphins, and Washington Redskins. They all lost in their first Super Bowl appearance before winning the second time around.

In this context, the outcome of the January 12, 1975, Super Bowl seemed painfully obvious at the outset. The young, talented Pittsburgh Steelers played their way through the AFC and found themselves opposite a veteran Minnesota Vikings team that was making its third Super Bowl appearance. The Vikings were two-time losers, including the painful loss to Miami the year before. Surely they wouldn't exhibit the nerves of the rookies from Pittsburgh.

Of course, there was a little history working in the Steelers' favor. In short, they were due. Art Rooney had owned the team for forty-two years and never come home with an NFL championship. But when quarterback Terry Bradshaw produced 3 fourth-quarter touchdown drives to defeat the Raiders, 24–13, in the AFC championship game, anything seemed possible.

At halftime, however, the 80,997 spectators at Tulane Stadium in New Orleans might have wondered if they were watching a baseball game. The score at intermission was, incredibly, 2–0. Minnesota quarterback Fran Tarkenton and running back Dave Osborn botched a pitchout and Osborn was forced to fall on the ball in the end zone with 7:11 left in the half for a safety. Neither offense could generate any momentum.

Washington saw only flashes of daylight in Super Bowl VII as Miami prevailed in a grinding 14–7 classic.

129

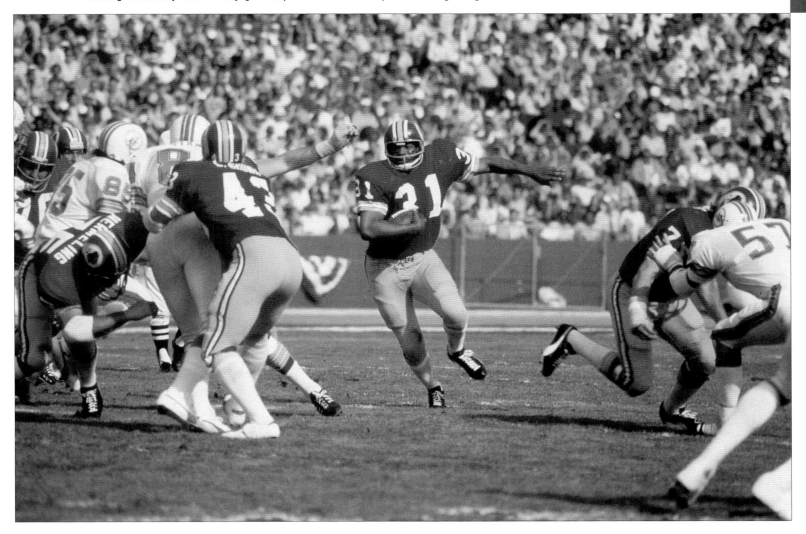

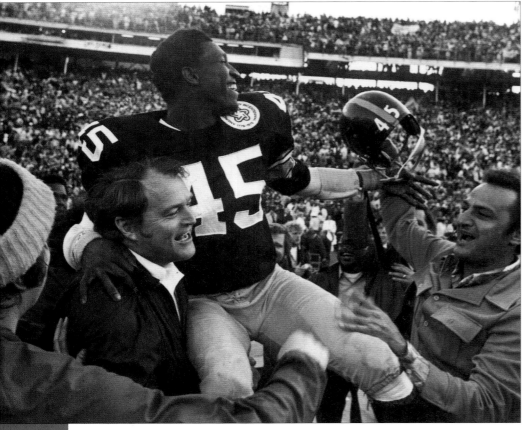

Pittsburgh coach Chuck Noll and defensive back Jim Allen were ecstatic after defeating Minnesota in Super Bowl IX.

to-Swann pass for a 64-yard score undid the Cowboys.

Eighty million people watched the game, the largest television audience in history.

The Steelers would win two more Super Bowls with many of the same players, but some people around the NFL will tell you that the 1975 Pittsburgh team might have been the best in league history.

Super Bowl XI

By January 9, 1977, the Minnesota Vikings, a magnificent team for a sustained period of seven years, were old and tired. They had lost three Super Bowls under coach Bud Grant, and those defeats had revealed a weakness on the ground. Minnesota had difficulty running and, more importantly, stopping the opponent's running game. The comparative totals in the three games were 596 yards to 156.

Super Bowl XI was more of the same. The Oakland Raiders ran the ball 52 times for 266 yards. The Vikings were 26–for–71.

It was that simple; the Raiders controlled the game and won, 32–14, much to the delight of the majority of the record 103,000 spectators at the Rose Bowl in Pasadena, California.

Clarence Davis gained 137 of those yards on the ground, but wide receiver Fred Biletnikoff, with 4 catches for 79 yards, was voted the game's Most Valuable Player.

Super Bowl XII

As the end of the 1977 season approached, there was talk that the balance of power had shifted to the AFC, the junior circuit. Five times in a row AFC teams had won the Super Bowl, and the way Oakland and Pittsburgh were playing, it didn't appear as if the reign were going to end anytime soon.

The Denver Broncos, however, put together the AFC's best regular-season record, 12–2. The Broncos, with their Orange Crush Defense, handled Pittsburgh, 34–21, in the playoffs and then squeezed past Oakland, 20–17, in the AFC championship game. Their opponents on January 15, 1978, were Tom Landry's Dallas Cowboys, likewise a 12–2 team that had rolled through the playoffs.

With 75,583 squeezed under the roof of the Louisiana Superdome in the first-ever indoor Super Bowl, the Cowboys punched the Broncos' lights out. It was 13–0 at the half, thanks to 2 interceptions by Dallas' defense, a Tony Dorsett 3-yard touchdown run, and a pair of Efren Herrera field goals. The final score, 27–10, did not tell the complete story of the Cowboys' dominance.

Another Minnesota mistake led to Pittsburgh's first touchdown. Running back Bill Brown fumbled a kickoff and Marv Kellum recovered on the Minnesota 30. Pittsburgh's Franco Harris ran three straight times, the last around the left end for 9 yards, to give Pittsburgh a 9–0 lead. Minnesota closed to 9–6, blocking a punt and recovering it in the end zone, but Pittsburgh did not quail. Bradshaw drove the Steelers 66 yards, hitting tight end Larry Brown with a 4-yard touchdown pass to make the final score 16–6.

The Vikings were 0–for–3 in Super Bowls; the Steelers, 1–for–1, were just getting started.

Super Bowl X

In retrospect, it was something of an upset that Lynn Swann played in the tenth Super Bowl at all. The wide receiver had spent two nights in the hospital following the AFC championship game against Oakland with a concussion, courtesy of Raiders safeties Jack Tatum and George Atkinson.

A week later the team was in Miami and Swann was listed as a doubtful starter against the Dallas Cowboys. On January 18, 1976, Swann not only played but was spectacular. He caught 4 passes from quarterback Terry Bradshaw that day for a game-record 161 yards and a touchdown. He was the Most Valuable Player in a 21–17 victory before a crowd of 80,187 at the Orange Bowl.

The Cowboys actually led 10–7 going into the fourth quarter, but a safety, two Roy Gerela field goals, and an amazing Bradshaw-

WHERE DYNASTIES COME FROM

What makes a dynasty? In basketball it can be as simple as two phenomenal players like Michael Jordan and Scottie Pippen. But in football, where there are two eleven-man units, even a handful of great players can't do it by themselves.

In football, it starts with a great coach. Hire that coach in the wake of a disaster and he'll have the draft choices to form a championship nucleus around a young quarterback. Basically, the formula is that simple. The Green Bay Packers, Pittsburgh Steelers, San Francisco 49ers, and Dallas Cowboys all used it to dominate their decades. You can look it up.

"I definitely think there's a pattern," says no less an authority than former San Francisco coach Bill Walsh. "Sometimes I think you have to hit rock bottom before things develop on a more positive note. Starr, Bradshaw, Montana, and Aikman all arrived precisely at the right time."

The Packers were a hideous 1–10–1 under Ray "Scooter" McLean in 1958, prompting Green Bay to hire Vince Lombardi as its head coach. Granted, four future Hall of Famers—quarterback Bart Starr, offensive tackle Forrest Gregg, running back Paul Hornung, and linebacker Ray Nitschke—were already on the roster, but they flourished under Lombardi.

With Starr starting for the first time in 1959, the Packers were 7–5. A year later they advanced to the NFL championship before losing to Philadelphia, 17–13.

And then the Packers won five league titles in seven seasons, including the first two Super Bowls, capping the 1966 and 1967 seasons. The cumulative record in those five championship seasons: 55–13–1.

Likewise, the Pittsburgh Steelers were a miserable last-place 2–11–1 under Bill Austin in 1968. Chuck Noll's rookie season as head coach was actually worse (1–13), but when quarterback Terry Bradshaw was drafted, the Steelers were destined for better things.

The Steelers won four Super Bowls in six seasons, between 1974 and 1979.

The 1978 San Francisco 49ers won only 2 of 16 games for coaches Pete McCulley and Fred O'Connor. Bill Walsh was an identical 2–14 a year later, but that finish put the 49ers in position to draft quarterback Joe Montana. Later, the 49ers added safety Ronnie Lott and wide receiver Jerry Rice as first-round draft picks.

San Francisco won four Super Bowls in nine seasons with that crew, from 1981 to 1989.

The Dallas Cowboys hit bottom in the most spectacular fashion, going 1–15 under Jimmy Johnson in 1989. But because Dallas had gone 3–13 the year before under departing legend Tom Landry, Johnson was able to draft promising young quarterback Troy Aikman. By 1992, the Cowboys had reached the Super Bowl. In a span of four seasons, they won three Super Bowls, including Super Bowl XXX over the Pittsburgh Steelers.

All NFL dynasties start with a great young quarterback. San Francisco's began with Joe Montana.

132

ABOVE: Roger Staubach hands off to Tony Dorsett in Super Bowl XIII, but it wasn't enough to keep the Pittsburgh Steelers in check. BELOW: The Dallas Cowboys flattened Denver in Super Bowl VII by a 27–10 score that didn't come close to revealing their dominance.

The defense intercepted Denver four times and recovered 4 fumbles. The co-MVPs were Harvey Martin and Randy White—the first (and last) time two teammates shared the award.

Super Bowl XIII

The memory that lingers is Dallas tight end Jackie Smith, his body completely extended in the end zone, his fists clenched in frustration after he bobbled a chance for a game-tying third-quarter touchdown. The ball fell harmlessly to earth and the Pittsburgh Steelers would prevail, 35–31.

The Orange Bowl crowd of 79,484 on January 21, 1979, was expecting big things from the Steelers and Cowboys, and they got them. There were 5 touchdowns in the first half, 3 of them touchdown passes by Pittsburgh quarterback Terry Bradshaw. He hit wide receiver John Stallworth for two touchdowns, first for 28 yards and then for 75 yards. His third touchdown pass was to running back Rocky Bleier, who scored from 7 yards out.

Pittsburgh's Jack Lambert drops in on beleaguered Rams quarterback Vince Ferragamo. The Steelers prevailed, 31–19, in a rousing Super Bowl XIV.

133

After Dallas narrowed the count to 21–17, the Steelers won the game with a pair of touchdowns in a nineteen-second span of the fourth quarter. Franco Harris ran 22 yards for a score, to give Pittsburgh a 28–17 lead with 7:10 left. Then, when Randy White fumbled the ensuing kickoff, Dennis Winston recovered for the Steelers. On the next play, Bradshaw threw his record fourth touchdown pass to Lynn Swann, good for 18 yards and a 35–17 lead with 6:51 to play.

Roger Staubach rallied the Cowboys, throwing 2 touchdown passes, but Dallas ran out of time. Bradshaw, who completed 17 of 30 passes for 318 yards (a personal high), was the Most Valuable Player.

Super Bowl XIV

While Super Bowl XIII was a well-played game with elements of drama, Super Bowl XIV was wildly entertaining—perhaps more than any other played before it.

The lead changed hands seven times before the Pittsburgh Steelers won, 31–19, on January 20, 1980, in front of another record crowd (103,985) at the Rose Bowl in Pasadena, California. In truth, it didn't figure to be much of a game.

The Steelers were looking for their fourth Super Bowl title in six years; the Los Angeles Rams had never been to the Super Bowl and were working with a backup quarterback. Vince Ferragamo had led the Rams to a 9–7 regular-season record, the worst of any team to ever reach the Super Bowl.

Yet at halftime the Rams were up, 13–10. Pittsburgh quarterback Terry Bradshaw hit Lynn Swann with a 47-yard touchdown pass early in the third quarter, but running back Lawrence McCutcheon flipped a 24-yard option pass to Ron Smith to reclaim the lead. On Pittsburgh's first possession of the final quarter, Terry Bradshaw lofted a perfect 73-yard scoring pass to John Stallworth to give the Steelers the lead for good. Franco Harris' 1-yard run closed out the scoring and Pittsburgh had completed back-to-back Super Bowl repeats for the second time.

After the game, Pittsburgh's "Mean" Joe Greene talked about winning a fifth Super Bowl, "one for the thumb," but the marvelous dynasty was already beginning to dissolve. The Steelers wouldn't even make the playoffs the next season.

Super Bowl XV

Super Bowls seem to belong to talented quarterbacks in the prime of their careers. So what can one make of Jim Plunkett as January 18, 1981, approached? The Oakland Raiders' signal caller didn't play a single down in 1978 as a backup; in 1979 he threw all of 15 passes. When the 1980 season began he was nearly thirty-three, watching Dan Pastorini take all the snaps.

Then Pastorini fractured his leg in the season's fifth game and Plunkett was all the Raiders had. He had won the Heisman Trophy and been named the AFC Rookie of the Year in 1971 with the New England Patriots, but that was all ancient history. The San Francisco 49ers had released him before the Raiders took pity.

THOMAS COUNTY, GEORGIA

Thomas County, Georgia, about an hour north on Route 319 from Tallahassee, Florida, has a modest population of thirty-nine thousand, but there is clearly something special in the water. No fewer than five Miss Georgias hail from the City of Roses. And, incredibly, ten National Football League players were spawned in the tree-lined town of Thomasville and the surrounding areas.

And these aren't just football players—these are stars. Heisman Trophy winner Charlie Ward, quarterback for the national champion Florida State team, came from Thomas County. So did eight Pro Bowls and five Super Bowl rings' worth of players, not to mention two other collegiate national champions, Eric Curry and Shawn Jones. Incredible.

Ward, Curry, and Jones all met on a field in Thomasville in 1987, when Central High School played Thomasville High School in the AAA state playoffs. Ward

was a captain for Central, while Jones (Ward's best friend) and Curry captained Thomasville. Three years later, Jones quarterbacked Georgia Tech to the national championship. Two years after that, Curry's Alabama team won the national title. Ward won it the year after that, but he went on to play guard for the New York Knicks of the National Basketball Association.

It all started with Henry Childs, who attended Magnolia High School before integration visited Thomas County. Childs played tight end for four NFL teams over eleven seasons. Then came running back William Andrews, whose 1974 Thomasville team won the national championship. Andrews later played for the home-state Falcons and was voted into four Pro Bowls.

"I put them on the map, in terms of knowing who and what Thomasville was," Andrews says. "But now, it's a drop in the

bucket. All these guys that are coming out of Thomasville now—it's unreal. I can't believe it."

Guy McIntyre watched Andrews play in high school. "After that, I saw him play with the Falcons," McIntyre says of Andrews. "So, when you thought about William Andrews, you thought about, hopefully, being the next one."

McIntyre, a prototypical guard for the San Francisco 49ers, won three Super Bowl rings and, like Andrews, was voted into four Pro Bowls. In 1984, the year McIntyre was a San Francisco rookie, the defense at Central lined up three future NFL players: Danny Copeland, Jesse Small, and Myron Guyton.

"We all went to Eastern Kentucky University," Guyton explains. "And we thought it was kind of weird that three players from the same high school team ended up going to the same university. Then we all went on to play in the NFC East. And then we thought it was a little weirder."

Ward remembers watching those three Central players in high school. He ought to; one of them, Copeland, took his sister to the prom.

"Those guys proved to me that it could be done," Ward says. "So I had some inspirations. I wanted to be like those guys."

William Andrews was the second player to matriculate to the NFL after undergraduate work in Thomas County, Georgia, but he wasn't the last.

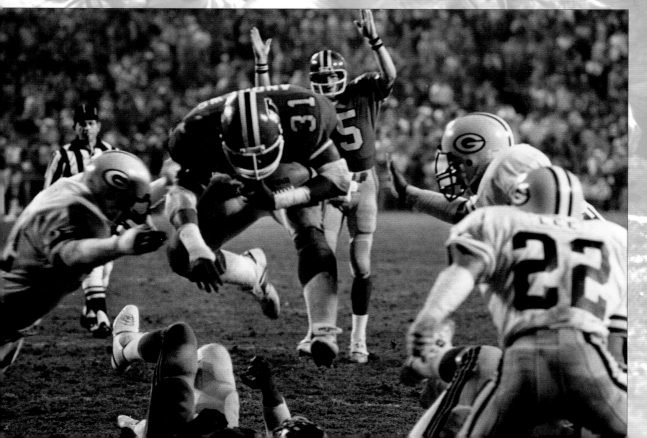

Quarterback Jim Plunkett carried the Raiders to victory in Super Bowl XV, a first for a wild-card team.

135

Under Plunkett, the Raiders somehow won nine of eleven games and made the playoffs as a wild-card entry. Their opponents at the Louisiana Superdome in New Orleans were the Philadelphia Eagles, an extremely hungry 14–4 team that hadn't played in a title game since 1960.

Early in the game, linebacker Rod Martin set up Oakland's first touchdown with an interception, his first of 3. Plunkett reached wide receiver Cliff Branch with a 2-yard score, and the Raiders were on their way. Plunkett connected with running back Kenny King for an 80-yard touchdown—the longest in Super Bowl history—to give Oakland a 14–0 first-quarter lead. The final, 27–10, before 76,135 fans, was a tribute to Oakland's resilience. Not only were the Raiders the first wild-card team to win the Super Bowl, but they overcame three road games to reach that final contest.

Super Bowl XVI

After fifteen Super Bowls in the warm climes of places like Miami and Los Angeles, for some reason the NFL organizers elected to move the big game to the Pontiac Silverdome, just outside Detroit. While the temperature, factoring in the wind chill, flirted with 0°F (-18°C), the 81,270 watching the January 24, 1982, game sat in climate-controlled comfort.

It was that kind of hot and cold game. What would you expect from two teams that had never been there?

The Cincinnati Bengals, born in 1968, committed 3 turnovers in the first half, costing them 17 points. The San Francisco 49ers capitalized at every turn and wound up with a record-setting 20 points in the first two periods.

The record shows that a young quarterback named Joe Montana scored the game's first points on a 1-yard plunge. In the second quarter, Cincinnati's Cris Collinsworth fumbled and Montana drove the 49ers to a Super Bowl–record 92 yards for a touchdown. Earl Cooper caught the 11-yard scoring pass. After two Ray Wersching field goals, it was 20–0 at the half.

Still, it was a third-quarter goal line stand that won the game for the 49ers. Four times the Bengals tried to score from the 49ers' 1-yard line. Four times they failed. The final score was 26–21 and Montana, who completed 14 of 22 passes for 157 yards, was the Most Valuable Player. It wasn't the last time—or even the second-to-last time—that he would be.

Super Bowl XVII

There was an air of déjà vu as the Washington Redskins prepared for the Miami Dolphins. Ten years earlier, in a California Super Bowl game with one fewer "X" in the title, the Dolphins had dispatched the Redskins, 14–7. Now, here they were again, just up the road from Los Angeles at the Rose Bowl in Pasadena.

Other than the presence of Bob Kuechenberg starting at left guard for the Dolphins, the two games were a study in contrasts.

This was the year of the Super Bowl tournament, when a labor dispute cut the 1982 regular season to a paltry nine games and the NFL opened the playoff field to sixteen teams, including two teams, Cleveland and Detroit, with 4–5 records. The Redskins took an 11–1 record into the January 30, 1983, game; the Dolphins were 10–2.

The story of the game was Washington's 230-pound (104kg) fullback, the iconoclastic John Riggins. He partied the Friday before the game in white tie and tails and two days later danced all over the Dolphins. Running behind a huge, skilled offensive line, Riggins carried 38 times for 166 yards—both game records. With an additional 15 yards he gained on a pass from Joe Theismann, Riggins outgained the entire Miami offense.

Yes, it was that bad, 27–17, before 103,667 fans.

The Dolphins led, 17–13, heading into the third quarter, but Riggins made a signature run, smashing into and then shaking off Dolphins cornerback Don McNeal and going 43 yards for the go-ahead touchdown. With a little less than two minutes left, the Redskins iced it when Theismann hit wide receiver Charlie Brown with a 6-yard scoring pass.

Super Bowl XVIII

A team is a delicate thing, almost like a snowflake; no two are ever exactly alike. This is especially true in football, where the personalities of fifty-odd players and a dozen coaches come together in a diverse blend of weird science. Just ask the Washington Redskins what a difference a year can make.

The season before, the Redskins had won twelve of thirteen games, including Super Bowl XVII, and had been dominant under second-year coach Joe Gibbs. Washington ripped through the 1983 regular season, winning sixteen of eighteen games to reach the January 22, 1984, Super Bowl. The two losses were by a single point each in nationally televised Monday night games.

The Raiders, who now called Los Angeles home, were 14–4, but one of those four losses was to Washington. The defending champions were installed as 3-point favorites, and some people thought the point spread was a tad low.

The game, predictably, was over at halftime; the stunner was that Los Angeles, not Washington, was in control.

It happened this way at Tampa Stadium before 72,920: Derrick Jensen blocked a Redskins punt and recovered it in the end zone for a 7–0 Raiders lead about five minutes into the game. Midway through the second quarter, aging quarterback Jim Plunkett threw a 12-yard touchdown pass to wide receiver Cliff Branch. The Redskins narrowed the score to 14–3 before Jack Squirek made the play of the game.

With seven seconds left, the Redskins' Joe Theismann inexplicably threw a screen pass to Joe Washington. Squirek, a linebacker, read the play perfectly, made the interception, and walked into the end zone for a devastating score and a 21–3 halftime lead. The final, 38–9, was the most one-sided in Super Bowl history.

Raiders running back Marcus Allen, who carried twenty times for a game-record 191 yards and 2 touchdowns, was the Most Valuable Player. The highlight after Squirek's play was Allen's spectacular 74-yard touchdown run (another record) that featured a conventional sweep to the left, a quick reversal back toward the right side, and a sharp cut up the middle.

The Raiders, representing both Oakland and Los Angeles, had now won three Super Bowls in an eight-year span. Not only was it the last time that the Raiders would appear in the ultimate game, it was the end of the AFC's dominance over the NFC. To that point, the AFC had prevailed in twelve of eighteen Super Bowls. After the Dallas Cowboys' victory over the Pittsburgh Steelers in Super Bowl XXX, the NFC had won an amazing twelve straight.

Super Bowl XIX

The first time, when Bill Walsh and Joe Montana were relatively new to the NFL, the San Francisco 49ers snuck up on people. By the time January 20, 1985, arrived, football fans knew the 49ers. They were familiar with the dazzling plays Walsh drew up, the gorgeous passes that Montana lofted to Dwight Clark and Freddie Solomon, and the tough defense.

The game was billed as a matchup of the league's best two teams, featuring the best two quarterbacks. Miami's Dan Marino, in his second season, set NFL regular-season records with 5,084 yards passing and 362 completions. He shattered the old standard for touchdown passes (36) with a surreal 48. The Dolphins entered the game averaging 4 touchdowns per game.

The 49ers, playing very close to home at Stanford Stadium before 84,059 largely partial spectators, were not impressed. In fact, all the attention generated by Marino left San Francisco in an ill humor come game time.

When it was over, San Francisco had won, 38–16. The Dolphins' scoring machine had produced a mere 314 yards and a single touchdown. The Walsh-Montana collaboration yielded a robust 537 net yards: the highest total in Super Bowl history. Montana, the runaway Most Valuable Player, was incandescent, completing 24 of 35 passes for 331 yards and 3 touchdowns.

Super Bowl XX

Some things are destined to happen. Somewhere in the middle of the Chicago Bears' brutal run through the 1985 regular season it became obvious that they were, far and away, the best team in football. It wasn't a matter of whether they would win the Super Bowl; it was really only a question of whom the victim would be and whether

Marcus Allen, in a sublime performance, carried twenty times for 191 yards in the Raiders' 38–9 victory over Washington in Super Bowl XVIII.

OPPOSITE: Chicago quarterback Jim McMahon and the Bears soared over the New England Patriots, 46–10, in Super Bowl XX, the most one-sided championship game to that point.

the point spread would be 3 touchdowns or 4. Or how about 5?

This was, after all, a Chicago team with character—and characters—to spare. Snarling Mike Ditka was the coach; Jim McMahon was the quarterback who loved to cross swords with convention in general and Ditka in particular. The engine was Walter Payton, destined to become the most prolific running back in league history. There was also defensive tackle William "the Refrigerator" Perry. The defense? The "46" Defense, designed by Buddy Ryan, was as frightening as it was innovative.

For the record, the score on January 26, 1986, before 73,818 at the Louisiana Superdome was, appropriately, 46–10. The victims were the New England Patriots, who, believe it or not, acquitted themselves well. The Patriots actually led, 3–0, and had another chance to score before Chicago got on the board. But linebacker Don Blackmon couldn't hold an interception, and Chicago went off on a 44-point run.

The Most Valuable Player was Chicago defensive end Richard Dent, who harried New England quarterbacks Tony Eason and Steve Grogan all day. Still, it was Perry who stole fans' hearts with a 1-yard touchdown run. Some 127 million watched on television, breaking the record set by the final *M*A*S*H* episode as the most-watched television program in history.

Thirty-six points was the largest margin in Super Bowl history and there was nothing to suggest that the Bears would not follow Green Bay, Miami, and Pittsburgh as back-to-back winners.

Super Bowl XXI

Very quietly, the New York Giants were becoming a presence under coach Bill Parcells. Even as the Bears were trashing the rest of the league, the Giants were only a few plays away from being competitive in their 21–0 playoff loss at Chicago in 1985. In 1986,

No quarterback, before or since, has been as perfect as the Giants' Phil Simms was in Super Bowl XXI.

the Giants followed the 49ers and Bears as football's most dominant team for a single season.

There were just two losses—to Dallas on a Monday night opener and on the road in Seattle—and then the Giants roared into the playoffs. They stunned the 49ers by an on-the-money score of 49–3, then muscled the Washington Redskins, 17–0, in the NFC championship game. What kind of resistance would the AFC champion Denver Broncos offer?

Plenty—at least for the first half of the January 25, 1987, game at the Rose Bowl in Pasadena. The Broncos, led by quarterback John Elway, were up, 10–9, at the half, but there was a pervading sense in the crowd of 101,063 that the Giants, anchored by linebacker Lawrence Taylor and quarterback Phil Simms, would soon awaken.

And that's just what happened in the third quarter. The Giants defense held Denver to exactly 2 yards in the third quarter while Simms produced 17 points. The Giants scored on their first 5 possessions of the second half. When it was over, linebacker Harry Carson, disguised in a yellow security jacket, snuck up and dumped the trademark victory vat of Gatorade on Parcells; the Giants had won, 39–20. Simms had been very nearly perfect. He completed 22 of 25 passes for a record completion percentage of 88. He also posted 268 yards and touchdowns in an MVP performance.

In three playoff games, the Giants had outscored their opponents by a record total of 82 points. Not even the Chicago Bears did that.

Super Bowl XXII

How fast can you say goodbye? It took the Washington Redskins exactly fifteen minutes to write off the Denver Broncos in the twenty-second Super Bowl.

THE HEISMAN TROPHY

In theory, anyway, the Heisman Trophy annually goes to the best college football player in the nation. The problem is, the National Football League never seems to agree with the choice.

The 1994 winner, Rashaan Salaam of the University of Colorado, was the twenty-first overall choice in the 1995 draft. The Chicago Bears made him the fifth running back taken, following Ki-Jana Carter, Tyrone Wheatley, Napoleon Kaufman, and James Stewart. Salaam had the last laugh, however. He outgained all the others with a sporty 1,074 yards as a rookie. Of course, the New England Patriots' Curtis Martin, the 74th overall choice, finished with 1,487 yards, third in the league.

Winning the Heisman Trophy looks great on the résumé, but in truth, it is not necessarily a career enhancer. Consider the two winners before Salaam: quarterbacks Charlie Ward and Gino Torretta. Ward, who played for Florida State, was not drafted by the NFL and went on to play guard for the New York Knicks. Torretta, of the University of Miami, was drafted in the seventh round by Minnesota. A year later, he was looking for an invitation to another training camp.

In 1995, Ohio State running back Eddie George tried to change the trend. He gained 1,927 as a senior and scored 24 touchdowns. He also caught 44 passes for 399 yards. At 6-feet, 2-inches (188cm), 238 pounds (108kg), he had the size and speed to succeed in the professional game. True to form, George was selected fourteenth overall in the 1996 draft, after Nebraska running back Lawrence Phillips and Michigan running back Tim Biakabutuka, by the Houston Oilers.

Given these Heisman-winning players' experiences, maybe Jay Berwanger, the 1935 Heisman Trophy winner, had the right idea. He gave the impressive trophy to his mother. She was said to have used it as a doorstop.

In 1997, Michigan cornerback Charles Woodson became the first defensive player ever to win the Heisman Trophy.

Denver quarterback John Elway was constantly under pressure in Super Bowl XXII.

On January 31, 1988, before a crowd of 73,302 at San Diego's Jack Murphy Stadium, the Washington Redskins and quarterback Doug Williams made history of an amazing kind. The Denver Broncos led, 10–0, after the first quarter before Williams went, certifiably, crazy.

In 18 plays, Washington piled up 357 yards and 5 touchdowns. The previous record for postseason touchdowns in a quarter was 3. Williams threw 4 scoring passes (in order) to Ricky Sanders (80 yards), Gary Clark (27 yards), Sanders again (50 yards), and tight end Clint Didier (8 yards). Snuck in there was a 52-yard run by rookie Timmy Smith, who carried 22 times for 204 yards, another Super Bowl record. Final score: 42–10.

Williams, the first black quarterback to start in the Super Bowl, was the Most Valuable Player, and the Redskins finished with a record 602 offensive yards and 6 touchdowns.

Four different NFC teams had now defeated the AFC teams by the cumulative score of 165–56. Super Bowls were starting to get out of hand.

Super Bowl XXIII

Just when it looked like the NFC would turn the Super Bowl into a joke, the AFC's Cincinnati Bengals returned some credibility to the contest.

As a franchise, the Bengals have been to the Super Bowl twice and it is their misfortune to have faced the San Francisco 49ers both times. On January 22, 1989, at Joe Robbie Stadium in Miami, the Bengals gave it their best shot. Only the heroics of Joe Montana and his wide receivers saved the 49ers in the end.

The first half was a wash; the Bengals and 49ers traded field goals. It happened again in the third quarter and the score was 6–all

when Stanford Jennings returned a kickoff 93 yards for a touchdown. Cincinnati, a big underdog, led, 13–6, and the crowd of 75,129 began to grow restless.

San Francisco drove 85 yards in 4 plays on its next possession, with Montana hitting Jerry Rice with a 14-yard touchdown pass to even the score fifty-seven seconds into the fourth quarter. With 3:20 left, Cincinnati's Jim Breech kicked his third field goal of the day, from 40 yards, to give the Bengals a 16–13 lead.

The 49ers got the ball back on their 8-yard line with 3:10 left on the clock. What happened next is the stuff of legend. Montana, exhausted and hyperventilating, rallied the 49ers down the field, completing 8 of 9 passes; the only incompletion was intentional to buy the dizzy Montana a little time. Finally, with 34 seconds left, Montana found John Taylor slanting across the middle of the end zone for a 10-yard score.

The 49ers won, 20–16, and Rice, with 11 catches for 215 yards, was the Most Valuable Player. San Francisco put itself in elite company with its third Super Bowl victory in three tries. The 49ers became the first NFC team to win three times. Only the AFC's Pittsburgh Steelers, with four victories, had more. That would soon change.

Super Bowl XXIV

After San Francisco won its third Super Bowl of the 1980s, coach Bill Walsh promptly retired. How would the departure of their offensive wizard affect the 49ers? In a way, it actually motivated the players, some of whom felt that Walsh got too much credit for their success.

With George Seifert, a defensive specialist, running the team, Mike Holmgren followed Walsh on the offensive side. Quarterback Joe Montana had a dazzling array of weapons: wide

In Super Bowl XXIV, Jerry Rice caught 7 passes for 148 yards and 3 touchdowns.

receivers Jerry Rice and John Taylor, tight end Brent Jones, half-back Roger Craig, and fullback Tom Rathman. Believe it or not, those five players combined for 8 touchdowns on January 28, 1990, at the Louisiana Superdome in New Orleans.

The final score against the outmanned Denver Broncos was 55–10, a Super Bowl record that seemed to surprise the 72,919 in attendance. The 49ers scored touchdowns on 4 of their 6 first-half possessions and led 27–3 at the half.

Montana was virtually flawless, completing 22 of 29 passes for 297 yards and a record 5 touchdowns. He won his third Most Valuable Player award as the 49ers became the fourth franchise to repeat as Super Bowl champion. Rice caught 7 passes for 148 yards and 3 touchdowns.

It was San Francisco's fourth Super Bowl victory in the 1980s, and it put the 49ers in the same class with the dominant team of the 1960s (Green Bay) and the 1970s (Pittsburgh).

Super Bowl XXV

To begin with, the New York Giants were probably the third-best team in football during the 1990 season. San Francisco and Buffalo both had more talent, but that doesn't diminish the Giants' accomplishments. Rather, it elevates them.

The team was personified by running back Ottis Anderson, a lumbering thirty-three-year-old who succeeded with grit and power as opposed to niftiness and speed. Under coach Bill Parcells the Giants were a ball-control team with a narrow margin of error.

They somehow beat San Francisco in the NFC championship game, 15–13, without the benefit of a touchdown. And then, on January 27, 1991, before 73,813 spectators at Tampa Stadium, the Giants wore down the Buffalo Bills with a muscular display of concentration.

The Giants held the ball for forty minutes and thirty-three seconds, a Super Bowl record, keeping the ball out of the hands of Buffalo quarterback Jim Kelly. The Bills, who had scored 95 points in two previous playoff games, had the ball for less than eight minutes in the second half.

Giants quarterback Jeff Hostetler, playing for injured Phil Simms, was efficient, completing 20 of 32 passes for 222 yards. Anderson, the Most Valuable Player, carried 21 times for 102 yards. Placekicker Matt Bahr kicked a 21-yard field goal to give the Giants a 20–19 lead.

Scott Norwood, the Buffalo placekicker, had a chance to win the game with eight seconds left, but his 47-yard field goal attempt sailed, hauntingly, wide right. It was the Bills' first of four straight disappointing appearances in the Super Bowl. One wonders how that dismal history might have changed if Norwood's field goal had been good.

Super Bowl XXVI

In 1991, the Washington Redskins overcame their NFC East rivals, the Giants, and rolled into the playoffs with a 16–2 record, the best in football. The Buffalo Bills were again the AFC's best, but this time they couldn't give the NFC a competitive game in the Super Bowl.

1995 EXPANSION SUCCESS

Scan the final standings of the National Football League's 1995 season. Down at the bottom of the NFC Western Division, you will find the Carolina Panthers with a 7–9 record, tied with the St. Louis Rams and New Orleans Saints. On paper, that record isn't much to look at. But consider where those Panthers were coming from. That losing record happens to be the best expansion record in the history of the NFL.

The Dallas Cowboys, the team of the 1990s, started out a humbling 0–11–1 in 1960. The 1976 Tampa Bay Buccaneers were worse—a horrific 0–14. The Seattle Seahawks were 2–12 that same year. The Minnesota Vikings, Atlanta Falcons, Miami Dolphins, New Orleans Saints, and Cincinnati Bengals? They all started out 3–11. How did the Panthers do it?

When former NFL player Jerry Richardson was awarded the franchise in the fall of 1993, he said, "I want to create an attitude and spirit. Professional football requires passion to do well and win, and I think that's the number one thing to do. The way we do that is to attract people who share our values and appreciate how important an attitude is to winning."

Richardson, who made Flagstar Companies, Inc., into one of the nation's leading food service companies, was as good as his word. He hired Mike McCormack, a Hall of Fame tackle, as his president. Richardson also signed Bill Polian, architect of the great Buffalo Bills teams, as his general manager. Polian, in turn, hired Pittsburgh defensive wizard Dom Capers as head coach.

With that brain trust, the Panthers took advantage of the extra draft choices allowed expansion teams; in a seven-round draft, the Panthers had fourteen selections. All three first-round choices— quarterback Kerry Collins, cornerback Tyrone Poole, and tackle Blake Brockermeyer—were starters at season's end. Frank Garcia, a fourth-round pick, started the final thirteen games at guard.

One thing those other expansion teams never had going for them was the league's new liberal free agency system. The Panthers built a respectable defense, signing eight free agents who became starters. Pro Bowl linebacker Sam Mills, safeties Brett Maxie and Pat Terrell, defensive ends Mike Fox and Gerald Williams, and linebackers Lamar Lathon, Darion Conner, and Carlton Bailey grew into the league's seventh-rated unit. Mills, for instance, led the team with 130 tackles.

Three players from Polian's Bills— quarterback Frank Reich, wide receiver Don Beebe, and tight end Pete Metzelaars—brought experience and leadership to the young squad.

The Panthers began the season with a predictable 0–5, but then something wonderful happened. Actually, the Panthers happened. They won seven of their final eleven games; all seven victories came with Collins guiding the offense. The wake-up call for the NFL came on November 5. One week after defeating the New England Patriots in overtime, the Panthers stunned the world champion San Francisco 49ers, 13–7.

Amazingly, the Panthers reached the NFC championship game following the 1996 regular season and the Jacksonville Jaguars, who had also arrived in the league in 1995, made it to the AFC championship game. And while both teams lost their bids for the conference championships, it was a huge moment for expansion franchises. Never before had two new teams made it to the top so quickly.

Quarterback Kerry Collins was a starter for the Carolina Panthers as a rookie.

On January 26, 1992, the Redskins defeated the Bills, 37–24, at the Metrodome in Minneapolis before a crowd of 63,130. The statistics of the opposing quarterbacks told the story:

Washington's Mark Rypien completed 18 of 33 passes for 292 yards and 2 touchdowns and was named the game's Most Valuable Player. Buffalo's Jim Kelly hoisted a record 58 passes, completing 28 of them for 275 yards and 2 touchdowns. But the Redskins intercepted Kelly four times.

The Washington defense shut down versatile Buffalo running back Thurman Thomas, limiting him to 13 yards on 10 carries.

Thus, the Redskins won their third Super Bowl under Joe Gibbs in a decade. The fact that Gibbs did it with three different quarterbacks—Joe Theismann, Doug Williams, and Rypien—was a tribute to his offensive savvy.

The NFC had now won eight straight Super Bowls over the AFC. And it wasn't about to get any better for the younger conference.

Super Bowl XXVII

While the Redskins, 49ers, and Giants had won two Super Bowls each in a six-year span, "America's Team" was slowly returning to full strength. Under coach Jimmy Johnson, the Dallas Cowboys were a horrific 1–15 in 1989, an improved 7–9 a year later, and an even better 11–5 in 1991. Finally, in 1992, the Cowboys won the NFC East for the first time in seven seasons with a 13–3 record.

The Cowboys advanced past Philadelphia and San Francisco to reach Super Bowl XXVII at the Rose Bowl in Pasadena, California,

on January 31, 1993. The opponent? None other than the Buffalo Bills, who again were the heads of the class of the AFC.

The game was not close, to say the least. Dallas quarterback and Most Valuable Player Troy Aikman threw 4 touchdown passes, Emmitt Smith ran for 108 yards, and the Cowboys converted an extraordinary 9 turnovers into 35 points. The final score: 52–17, before 98,374.

The return of America's Team rekindled one of the great love 'em or hate' em relationships among professional sports fans. The game broke all the television records, drawing an amazing 133.4 million viewers.

Super Bowl XXVIII

The Cowboys-Bills sequel that punctuated the 1993 season was marginally better than the first and drew another record television audience, 133.8 million viewers.

On January 30, 1994, at the Georgia Dome in Atlanta, Emmitt Smith was the star, rushing for 132 yards and 2 touchdowns. A crowd of 72,817 witnessed the 30–13 game.

Buffalo quarterback Jim Kelly was again heroic, completing a Super Bowl record 31 of 50 passes for 260 yards. None of them, however, was for a touchdown.

Dallas joined San Francisco and Pittsburgh as the only NFL franchises with four Super Bowl titles. Buffalo, the first team to reach four consecutive Super Bowls, joined Denver and Minnesota as four-time losers in the ultimate game.

Buffalo quarterback Jim Kelly brought the Bills to four consecutive Super Bowls, all losses.

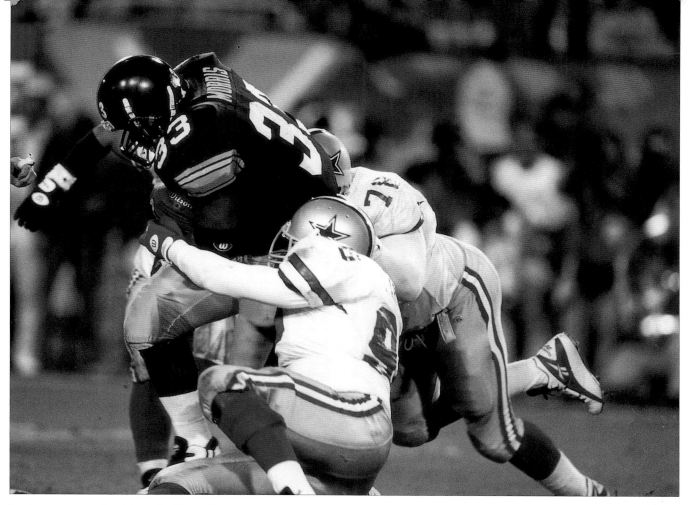

In a twenty-year reunion of Super Bowl X, the Dallas Cowboys repaid an old debt, bringing down the Pittsburgh Steelers, 27–17, in Super Bowl XXX.

Super Bowl XXIX

For two straight years, the NFL playoff game that featured the best two teams was the NFC championship game. The Dallas Cowboys prevailed over the San Francisco 49ers in the 1992 and 1993 seasons, but the tide turned in 1994 when the 49ers beat Dallas, 38–28.

Was there any doubt that the NFC would hammer the AFC for the eleventh straight time? No, not really.

The San Diego Chargers, making their first appearance in the Super Bowl, were overwhelmed by the San Francisco offense, which this time was led by quarterback Steve Young. Even Joe Montana never completed a record 6 touchdown passes, as Young did on January 29 with 74,107 fans on hand at Joe Robbie Stadium in Miami. Young, the Most Valuable Player, completed 24 of 36 passes for 325 yards.

Wide receiver Jerry Rice added 3 more touchdowns along with 10 catches and 149 yards—each a Super Bowl record.

The 49ers, meanwhile, became the first team in history to win five Super Bowls. A year later, the Dallas Cowboys would get even.

Super Bowl XXX

As Super Bowl games go, the thirtieth edition of the NFL's ultimate game was at least interesting.

The Dallas Cowboys prevailed over the Pittsburgh Steelers, 27–17, in Tempe, Arizona, on January 28, 1996. It was the closest Super Bowl in five years, but the NFC still won its twelfth straight game over the AFC. If not for Dallas cornerback Larry Brown, that streak might have ended.

In the end, it was not quarterback Troy Aikman or running back Emmitt Smith or wide receiver Michael Irvin who made the critical difference, it was that anonymous fifth-year cornerback named Brown. For while the Steelers were busy trying to climb back into the game in the second half, Brown intercepted 2 Neil O'Donnell passes that led to two Dallas touchdowns. That earned Brown the Pete Rozelle Trophy as the game's MVP.

The Cowboys took a 13–0 lead, scoring on each of their first three possessions, but the Steelers closed to within 6 points when O'Donnell hit Yancey Thigpen with a 6-yard touchdown thirteen seconds before halftime.

Brown's first interception ended a Pittsburgh drive near midfield and set up a 1-yard touchdown run by Smith. Once again Pittsburgh came back, scoring 10 unanswered points on a Norm Johnson field goal and a 1-yard Bam Morris touchdown run. That made it an unsettling 20–17 game with 6 minutes and 36 seconds left to play.

When the Steelers forced the Cowboys to punt, O'Donnell had 4 minutes and 15 seconds left on the clock and was looking to move Pittsburgh into field goal range and forge a tie. On second down, Brown intercepted O'Donnell's pass at the Steelers' 39-yard line and returned it to the 6-yard line. Two plays later, Smith scored from 4 yards out. O'Donnell, the NFL's career leader in fewest interceptions per pass attempt, had been picked off three times in all.

And so the Cowboys won their third Super Bowl title in four years, their first under Barry Switzer, and their record-tying fifth as a franchise.

Super Bowl XXXI

It had been twenty-nine seasons since the Green Bay Packers had won a Super Bowl, much less played in one. But through the 1996 season a variety of factors had led to the Packers being seen as the favorite to win the NFL's ultimate game.

OPPOSITE: In Super Bowl XXXII, veteran quarterback John Elway turned in a gutsy performance, finally winning a championship on behalf of the whole Class of '83.

CHAPTER 5: THE POSTSEASON

Green Bay quarterback Brett Favre was only one compelling reason the Patriots failed to prevail in Super Bowl XXXI.

Over the sixteen-game regular season, the Packers scored the most points and allowed the fewest. After whipping the San Francisco 49ers and the Carolina Panthers in the playoffs, Green Bay arrived in New Orleans as 14-point favorites.

The New England Patriots, overwhelming underdogs, had surprised people by emerging as the AFC champions, beating the Pittsburgh Steelers and then the Jacksonville Jaguars in the playoffs. The Jaguars previously had upset the front-running Denver Broncos.

The game in the Big Easy was billed as the battle of the Cheese Heads of Wisconsin versus the Chowder Heads of New England. The contest at the Louisiana Superdome on January 26, 1997 lived up to the hype—at least for three quarters.

The Packers ran out to a 10–0 lead in the first 6 minutes and 18 seconds, but the Patriots showed resilience by coming back with 2 quick touchdowns. Green Bay responded with 17 unanswered points in the second quarter. But just when the game appeared to be over, the Patriots made another comeback.

They narrowed the margin to a credible 27–21 on Curtis Martin's 18-yard touchdown run, and then came the play of the game.

With the momentum shifting to the Patriots, the Packers needed a big play—and they got it from the smallest player on the field. Desmond Howard, the five-foot ten-inch (178cm), 180-pound (82kg) kick returner, had won the Heisman Trophy in college but had been waived by two pro teams before the Packers rescued him from unemployment before the season began. He had produced a magnificent season and already had set a Super Bowl record for punt return yardage before the end of the first half.

He took Adam Vinatieri's kickoff at his own 1-yard line and sprinted through a crack in the Patriots' special teams defense. Only Hason Graham even touched him. It was a 99-yard return, a Super Bowl record. The Packers made a 2-point conversion to stretch their lead to 35–21. That was the final score and it precisely reflected the pre-game point-spread.

The difference in the game, beside Howard? Patriots quarterback Drew Bledsoe, without the support of a running game, threw 4 interceptions. Packers quarterback Brett Favre threw none.

Howard was the Most Valuable Player, just edging Favre, who threw touchdown passes of 81 and 54 yards to Antonio Freeman and Andre Rison, respectively. Defensive end Reggie White, who had 3 influential sacks in the second half, won his first championship at any level of football.

The Packers had returned to the top of the football world they had once dominated. Appropriately, head coach Mike Holmgren was handed the gleaming silver trophy that bears the name of legendary Packers coach Vince Lombardi.

"Coach Lombardi had a wonderful legacy for the rest of us," Holmgren said. "Now we're trying to do our part. I hope we can do it for a long time to come."

Super Bowl XXXII

In one of the most exciting, improbable Super Bowls ever, the Denver Broncos stunned the Green Bay Packers, 31–24, at Qualcomm Stadium in San Diego.

Behind the running of Most Valuable Player Terrell Davis (30 carries, 157 yards, 3 touchdowns), the Broncos ended the NFC's thirteen-game winning streak in dramatic fashion.

On January 25, 1998, Davis scored from 1 yard out with 1 minute and 45 seconds left in the game, culminating a 5-play drive.

Soon after, the heavily favored Packers had a chance to force the game into overtime, which would have been a Super Bowl first, but Brett Favre threw 3 straight incomplete passes as time ran out for Green Bay.

The win delighted many of the 133 million viewers because it gave Denver quarterback John Elway his first Super Bowl victory in four tries. The thirty-seven-year-old's contribution was a 1-yard touchdown run and a reckless, diving 10-yard effort that set up a second score.

147

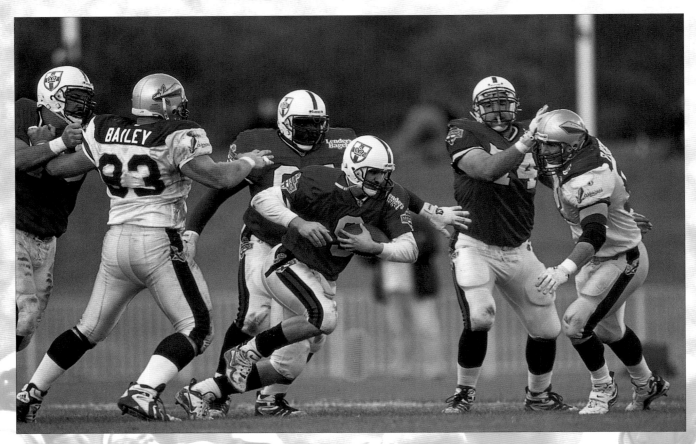

The London Monarchs were the class act of the World League's inaugural season.

THE WORLD LEAGUE

It was 1950 when the National Football League first cast its eye beyond America's borders, when the gleam of an inter-National Football League first appeared. That was when theNew York Giants played a preseason game against the Canadian League's Ottawa Rough-riders in Toronto. After staging five strategically placed American Bowls in such places as London, Tokyo, Berlin, and Montreal, the NFL went global in 1991.

They called it the World League, and it served two purposes. One, it helped familiarize the world with America's grid-iron game. Two, it was to provide devel-opmental opportunities for players not quite ready for the big league. From a financial standpoint, the former was the league's chief motivation.

"Eventually professional sports, including American football, are going to be played around the globe to large inter-national audiences," NFL commissioner Paul Tagliabue explained by way of intro-duction. "The NFL was built in this coun-try over the past seven decades by own-ers with vision and energy. I think our cur-rent owners will bring the same vision and energy to the development of American football overseas."

The ten-team league became the first major sports circuit to operate on two separate continents on a weekly basis. There were three European teams—the London Monarchs, the Barcelona Dragons, and the Frankfurt Galaxy—along with the Montreal Machine and seven teams from the United States: New York, Orlando, Raleigh, Durham, Birmingham, San Antonio, and Sacramento.

The four franchises outside the U.S. averaged more than thirty-three thousand fans per game, and the championship game, World Bowl '91, was played before 61,108 spectators at London's Wembley Stadium. The Monarchs prevailed, 21–0, over the Dragons.

Sacramento was the World Bowl '92 champion, before the league went into a three-year hiatus. World Bowl '95 crowned Frankfurt the new league cham-pion after a 26–22 win over Amsterdam. After that contest the NFL, which had stopped funding the league for financial reasons, offered a commitment for the 1996 season.

NFC quarterback Steve Young eludes the AFC's Cortez Kennedy in the 1993 Pro Bowl.

The Pro Bowl

The National Football League is a fairly closed shop. There are about fifteen hundred players who make their living at football's highest level. They all know who can play—and who can't.

Every December, teams receive the Pro Bowl ballots, and players vote for the players to be on each of the two teams that will appear at Aloha Stadium in Honolulu, Hawaii, the Sunday after the Super Bowl. There are biases, of course, and petty jealousies, but the best players usually go. More meaningful than the financial incentives many players collect for appearing is the pride that goes with being honored by peers.

Since the Pro Bowl was a consequence of the merger between the American Football League and the National Football League, it has been in existence only since 1971. For the record, the NFC leads the series, 15–11, including the February 4, 1996, game won by the NFC, 20–13.

Still, some of the greatest names in football history are at the top of the charts for Pro Bowl service. The best three defensive players of the 1980s, Giants linebacker Lawrence Taylor, San Francisco safety Ronnie Lott, and Chicago linebacker Mike Singletary, all played in ten games. For Taylor and Singletary, they were consecutive games. San Francisco wide receiver Jerry Rice has also played in ten games; in his second season he was a starter in the 1986 game, and has returned each year since in that role.

The roster of nine-game stars: Houston defensive back Ken Houston, Pittsburgh defensive tackle "Mean" Joe Greene, Pittsburgh linebacker Jack Lambert, Chicago running back Walter Payton, Giants linebacker Harry Carson, Pittsburgh center Mike Webster, Cincinnati tackle Anthony Munoz, and Green Bay defensive end Reggie White. Houston was selected for ten games, but did not play in one; Munoz was actually voted in a record eleven times, but missed two games with injuries.

Some fun Pro Bowl facts, suitable for trivia questions:

- Placekicker Morten Andersen, most recently of the Atlanta Falcons, leads all scorers with 45 points, including 8 in the 1996 game.
- Packers running back John Brockington holds the single-game scoring record with 3 touchdowns in the 1973 game.
- Chicago's Walter Payton, with 368 yards on 81 carries, leads all rushers in yards and attempts. O.J. Simpson is second in both categories with 356 yards on 68 carries.
- San Diego quarterback Dan Fouts—not Miami's Dan Marino—leads in attempts (120), completions (63), yards (890), and interceptions (8).
- The 49ers' Jerry Rice leads in catches (28) and yards (399).
- Dallas defensive back Everson Walls leads in interceptions with 4.

THE PRO FOOTBALL HALL OF FAME

The annual enshrinement ceremony at the Pro Football Hall of Fame in Canton, Ohio, is one of sport's great spectacles.

The first organizational meeting that evolved into the National Football League was held in Canton, Ohio, in 1920. Forty-one years later, the league recognized that city as the home of the Pro Football Hall of Fame, and two years after that, on September 7, 1963, the doors were officially opened.

It is tucked away quietly, some fifty-five miles (88.5km) south of Cleveland, off Interstate 77. An $8.6 million expansion project completed in 1995 increased the Hall's size to more than eighty-three thousand square feet (7,719 sq m), more than four times its original size.

One of the new additions is the GameDay Stadium, a theater utilizing Cinemascope, a film experience so real that Hall of Fame enshrinees like Joe Namath and Larry Csonka actually flinched in their seats when they attended

screenings. There are also new exhibits that allow fans to play videos of their favorite Super Bowls, plus interactive trivia games and contests that allow visitors to play the game against each other, using footage of real NFL games.

For the more traditional fan, there are the bronze busts of the 185 players enshrined within. You'll find the most recent class of 1996, featuring coach Joe Gibbs, wide receiver Charlie Joiner, defensive back Mel Renfro, and offensive tackles Dan Dierdorf and Lou Creekmur. Those players were chosen by a national panel of thirty-four sportswriters representing all the NFL's cities. Enshrinees must receive approximately 80 percent of the votes cast in a particular year.

There's also Bronko Nagurski's massive championship ring; a 300-pound (136kg) bronze statue of Jim Thorpe; the

world's tallest trophy (nearly twenty-three feet [7m] high), commemorating Harold Carmichael's streak of 127 consecutive games with at least one catch; Jim Otto's famous No. 00 Oakland Raiders jersey; a tribute to the 1972 Miami Dolphins and their undefeated season; and, most recently, the jersey and shoes of Denver's Glyn Milburn, who accumulated 404 all-purpose yards in a December 1995 game—130 rushing, 45 receiving, 95 on punt returns, and 134 on kickoff returns.

The Hall of Fame, which is open every day except Christmas, has steadily drawn an average of 220,000 people per year. Admission is a reasonable $9 for adults, $6 for seniors, and $4 for children ages six to fourteen.

The Class of 1996, including coach Joe Gibbs (LEFT), wide receiver Charlie Joiner (ABOVE), and offensive tackle Dan Dierdorf (BELOW), was a memorable one.

AFTER THE GAME

The football player steps into the arena for the last time. Never again will he experience this ultimate high. Never again will he command such a staggering salary. Never again will he feel the eyes of millions on him, hear the cheers of tens of thousands.

Dr. Len Burnham, a former player and director of the NFL's player programs, puts it this way: "I can't think of any other earthly experience that comes close to approaching the magnitude of being a professional athlete. Also, I can't think of many things that approach the level that you drop emotionally when you can't do that anymore."

Following his walk on the moon, astronaut Buzz Aldrin grappled with his return to Earth, literally and figuratively. Football players, we now know, face the same issues.

Dr. Beverley Pitts of Ball State University is co-author of an NFL Players Association study on life after football. She interviewed dozens of players.

"As long as they could remember, someone had told them where to be, told them how to eat, what to eat, when to practice," Pitts says. "And the goal for their lives had been very clearly directed. And even though they were educated and had planned for their futures, within just a couple of hours they were told, 'This is no longer your life.'"

Mike Wise, who played for the Raiders from 1986 to 1990, suffered after the cheering stopped and devised the ultimate solution to his pain.

He was a six-foot-seven-inch (201cm), 270-pound (123kg) defensive end with a tattoo of the Grim Reaper on his calf. But after five seasons with Los Angeles, Wise was released. He played briefly for Cleveland, but knee and back injuries sent him to the sidelines. At the age of twenty-eight, Wise was out of football.

"It becomes your life," says Bob Golic, a Raiders teammate. "It is your life. And so, all of a sudden, to have it taken away from you? Before you want it to be gone? Brutal."

A $600,000 house that Wise bought in Davis, California, was his dream home. It was also his curse. Money problems forced him to put the house on the market late in the summer of 1992. Two weeks later, alone and in the middle of the night, he took his life.

"Mike's an extreme, that's an extreme result," Golic said. "But to deny that guys leave the game and don't feel that pain that Mike felt, that hurt, that sense of loss? That's ridiculous. I mean, they do."

Mike Wise moved back to Oakland for financial reasons in 1995.

The playoffs are a different animal, when it comes to intensity. Sometimes, even the usually laid-back Pro Bowl produces jarring moments. Here, Buffalo cornerback Nate Odoms crushes Dallas receiver Michael Irvin.

In truth, the players do not take the game so seriously that they forget to soak up the Hawaiian sun with their friends and family. The Pro Bowl is seen by players as one of the perks of being at the top of their profession. This lack of focus has made for some interesting results.

In the inaugural Pro Bowl in 1971 at Memorial Coliseum in Los Angeles, Dallas defensive back Mel Renfro returned a pair of punts 82 and 56 yards for touchdowns in the fourth quarter to pad the NFC's 27–6 victory over the AFC.

The first game in Aloha Stadium, in 1980, featured running back Chuck Muncie, who ran for 2 touchdowns and passed for another— a 25-yard play to Tony Hill—in the NFC's 37–27 victory.

The biggest rout? The NFC's 45–3 win in 1984, when Joe Theismann completed 21 of 27 passes for 242 yards and 3 touchdowns.

Kansas City defensive end Art Still returned a fourth-quarter fumble 83 yards for a touchdown the following season to give the AFC a dramatic 22–14 victory.

The biggest comeback? In 1986, the Giants' Phil Simms rallied the NFC from a 24–7 halftime deficit to defeat the AFC, 28–24. Simms completed 15 of 27 passes for 212 yards and 3 touchdowns.

In 1995, Colts running back Marshall Faulk carried 13 times for 180 yards, a Pro Bowl record, as the NFC won, 41–13.

A week after Super Bowl XXX, the NFC beat the AFC by a touchdown. The game was decided in the second quarter when Rice took a 1-yard pass from Green Bay quarterback Brett Favre and Washington linebacker Ken Harvey intercepted a pass and returned it 36 yards for a touchdown. It was one of 4 NFC interceptions of AFC quarterbacks; the other 3 were off Jeff Blake, Jim Harbaugh, and Steve Bono.

Selected Statistics (current through end of 1997 season)

TOP 20 PASSERS

Player	Years	Att.	Comp.	Pct. Comp.	Yards	Avg. Gain	TD	Pct. TD	Int.	Pct. Int.	Rating
Steve Young	13	3,548	2,300	64.8	28,508	8.03	193	5.4	91	2.6	97.0
Joe Montana	15	5,391	3,400	63.2	40,551	7.52	273	5.1	139	2.6	92.3
Brett Favre	7	3,206	1,971	61.5	22,591	7.05	182	5.7	95	3.0	89.3
Dan Marino	15	7,452	4,453	59.8	55,416	7.44	389	5.2	220	3.0	87.8
Jim Kelly	11	4,779	2,874	60.1	35,467	7.42	207	5.0	175	3.7	84.4
R. Staubach	11	2,958	1,685	57.0	22,700	7.67	153	5.2	109	3.7	83.4
Neil Lomax	8	3,153	1,817	57.6	22,771	7.22	136	4.3	90	2.9	82.7
S. Jurgensen	18	4,262	2,433	57.1	32,224	7.56	255	6.0	189	4.4	82.6
Len Dawson	19	3,741	2,136	57.1	28,711	7.67	239	6.4	183	4.9	82.6
Troy Aikman	9	3,696	2,292	62.0	26,016	7.04	129	3.5	110	3.0	82.3
Ken Anderson	16	4,475	2,664	59.3	32,838	7.34	197	4.4	160	3.6	81.9
Bernie Kosar	12	3,365	1,994	59.3	23,301	6.92	124	3.7	87	2.6	81.8
Danny White	13	2,950	1,751	59.7	21,959	7.44	106	5.3	132	4.5	81.7
Dave Krieg	18	5,290	3,093	58.5	37,948	7.17	261	4.9	199	3.8	81.5
Warren Moon	14	6,628	3,827	58.6	47,465	7.27	279	4.3	224	3.4	81.2
Boomer Esiason	14	5,205	2,969	57.0	37,920	7.29	247	4.7	184	3.5	81.1
Jeff Hostletler	14	2,338	1,357	58.0	16,430	7.03	94	4.0	71	3.0	80.5
Neil O'Donnell	9	2,519	1,438	57.1	16,810	6.67	89	3.5	53	2.1	80.5
Bart Starr	16	3,149	1,808	57.4	24,718	7.85	152	4.8	138	4.4	80.5
Ken O'Brien	10	3,602	2,110	58.6	25,094	6.97	128	3.6	98	2.7	80.4

1,500 or more attempts. The passing ratings are based on performance standards established for completion percentage, interception percentage, touchdown percentage, and average gain.

TOP 20 PASS RECEIVERS

Player	Years	No.	Yards	Avg.	Long	TD
Jerry Rice	13	1,057	16,455	16.6	96	155
Art Monk	16	940	12,721	13.5	79	66
Andre Reed	13	826	11,764	14.2	83	80
Steve Largent	14	819	13,089	16.0	74	100
Henry Ellard	15	807	13,662	16.9	81	65
James Lofton	16	764	14,004	18.3	80	75
Cris Carter	11	756	9,436	12.5	80	89
Charlie Joiner	18	750	12,146	16.2	87	65
Irving Fryar	14	736	11,427	15.5	80	75
Gary Clark	11	699	10,856	15.5	84	65
Michael Irvin	10	666	10,680	16.0	87	61
Ozzie Newsome	13	662	7,980	12.1	74	47
Charley Taylor	13	649	9,110	14.0	88	79
Andre Rison	9	641	8,839	13.8	75	73
Drew Hill	14	634	9,831	15.5	81	60
Don Maynard	15	633	11,834	18.7	87	88
Raymond Berry	13	631	9,275	14.7	70	68
Tim Brown	10	599	8,588	14.3	80	60
Anthony Miller	10	595	9,148	15.4	76	63
Sterling Sharpe	7	595	8,134	13.7	79	65

TOP 20 INTERCEPTORS

Player	Years	No.	Yards	Avg.	Long	TD
Paul Krause	16	81	1,185	14.6	81	3
Emien Tunnell	14	79	1,282	16.2	55	4
Dick (Night Train) Lane	14	68	1,207	17.8	80	5
Ken Ritcy	15	65	596	9.2	66	5
Ronnie Lott	14	63	730	11.6	83	5
Dick LeBeau	13	62	762	12.3	70	3
Dave Brown	15	62	698	11.3	90	5
Emmitt Thomas	13	58	937	16.2	73	5
Bobby Boyd	9	57	994	17.4	74	4
Johnny Robinson	12	57	741	13.0	57	1
Mel Blount	14	57	736	12.9	52	2
Everson Walls	13	57	504	8.8	40	1
Lem Barney	11	56	1,077	19.2	71	7
Pat Fischer	17	56	941	16.8	69	4
Willie Brown	16	54	472	8.7	45	2
Bobby Dillon	8	52	976	18.8	61	5
Jack Butler	9	52	826	15.9	52	4
Larry Wilson	13	52	800	15.4	96	5
Jim Patton	12	52	712	13.7	51	2
Mel Renfro	14	52	626	12.0	90	3

TOP 20 SCORERS

Player	Years	TD	FG	PAT	TP
George Blanda	26	9	335	943	2,002
Nick Lowery	18	0	383	562	1,711
Jan Stenerud	19	0	373	580	1,699
Gary Anderson	16	0	385	526	1,681
Morten Andersen	16	0	378	507	1,641
Norm Johnson	16	0	322	592	1,558
Eddie Murray	19	0	337	521	1,532
Pat Leahy	18	0	304	558	1,470
Jim Turner	16	1	304	521	1,439
Matt Bahr	17	0	300	522	1,422
Mark Moseley	15	0	300	482	1,382
Jim Bakken	17	0	282	534	1,380
Fred Cox	15	0	282	519	1,365
Lou Groza	17	1	234	641	1,340
Jim Breech	14	0	243	517	1,246
Al Del Greco	14	0	263	435	1,224
Chris Bahr	14	0	241	490	1,213
Kevin Butler	13	0	265	413	1,208
Gino Cappelletti	11	42	176	342	1,130
Ray Wersching	15	0	222	456	1,122

Cappelletti's total includes 4 two-point conversions.

TOP 20 RUSHERS

Player	Years	Att.	Yards	Avg.	Long	TD
Walter Payton	13	3,838	16,726	4.4	76	110
Barry Sanders	9	2,719	13,776	5.1	85	95
Eric Dickerson	11	2,996	13,259	4.4	85	90
Tony Dorsett	12	2,936	12,739	4.3	99	77
Jim Brown	9	2,359	12,312	5.2	80	106
Marcus Allen	16	3,022	12,243	4.1	61	123
Franco Harris	13	2,948	12,120	4.1	75	91
Thurman Thomas	10	2,720	11,405	4.2	80	63
John Riggins	14	2,916	11,352	3.9	66	104
O.J. Simpson	11	2,404	11,236	4.7	94	61
Emmitt Smith	8	2,595	11,234	4.3	75	112
Ottis Anderson	14	2,562	10,273	4.0	76	81
Earl Campbell	8	2,187	9,407	4.3	81	74
Jim Taylor	10	1,941	8,597	4.4	84	83
Joe Perry	14	1,737	8,378	4.8	78	53
Earnest Byner	14	2,095	8,261	3.9	54	56
Herschel Walker	12	1,954	8,225	4.2	91	61
Roger Craig	11	1,991	8,189	4.1	71	56
Gerald Riggs	10	1,989	8,188	4.1	58	69
Larry Csonka	11	1,891	8,081	4.3	54	64

154

TOP 20 COMBINED YARDS GAINED

Player	Years	Tot.	Rush.	Rec.	Int. Ret.	Punt Ret.	Kickoff Ret.	Fumble Ret.
Walter Payton	13	21,803	16,726	4,538	0	0	539	0
Herschel Walker	12	18,168	8,225	4,859	0	0	5,084	0
Marcus Allen	16	17,648	12,243	5,411	0	0	0	-6
Jerry Rice	13	17,075	614	16,455	0	0	6	0
Barry Sanders	9	16,528	13,778	2,632	0	0	118	0
Tony Dorsett	12	16,326	12,739	3,554	0	0	0	33
Henry Ellard	15	15,603	50	13,662	0	1,527	364	0
Thurman Thomas	10	15,489	11,405	4,084	0	0	0	0
Jim Brown	9	15,459	12,312	2,499	0	0	648	0
Eric Dickerson	11	15,411	13,259	2,137	0	0	0	15
James Brooks	12	14,910	7,962	3,621	0	565	2,762	0
Franco Harris	13	14,622	12,120	2,287	0	0	233	-18
Eric Metcalf	9	14,443	2,365	5,096	0	2,509	4,473	0
O.J. Simpson	11	14,368	11,236	2,142	0	0	990	0
James Lofton	16	14,277	246	14,004	0	0	0	27
Irving Fryar	14	14,174	180	11,427	0	2,055	505	7
Bobby Mitchell	11	14,078	2,735	7,954	0	699	2,690	0
David Meggett	9	13,901	1,660	3,023	0	3,668	5,550	0
Emmitt Smith	8	13,668	11,234	2,434	0	0	0	0
Earnest Byner	14	13,497	8,261	4,605	0	0	576	55

TOP 20 LEADERS IN SACKS

Player	*Years	No.
Reggie White	13	176.5
Bruce Smith	13	154.0
Richard Dent	15	137.5
Kevin Greene	13	133.0
Lawrence Taylor	12	132.5
Rickey Jackson	14	128.0
Chris Doleman	13	127.5
Leslie O'Neal	11	122.5
Sean Jones	13	113.0
Greg Townsend	13	109.5
Clyde Simmons	12	109.0
Derrick Thomas	9	107.5
Pat Swilling	11	105.5
Jim Jeffcoat	15	102.5
Andre Tippett	11	100.0
Simon Fletcher	11	97.5
William Fuller	12	97.5
Jacob Green	11	97.5
Charles Haley	11	97.5
Dexter Manley	10	97.5

Since NFL began compiling statistics in 1982.

155

COACHES WITH 100 CAREER VICTORIES (Order based on career victories)

Coach	Team(s)	Yrs.	Regular Season				Postseason				Career			
			Won	Lost	Tied	Pct.	Won	Lost	Tied	Pct.	Won	Lost	Tied	Pct.
Don Shula	Baltimore Colts, Miami Dolphins	33	328	156	6	.676	19	17	0	.528	347	173	6	.665
George Halas	Chicago Bears	40	318	148	31	.671	6	3	0	.667	324	151	31	.671
Tom Landry	Dallas Cowboys	29	250	162	6	.605	20	16	0	.556	270	178	6	.601
Earl (Curly) Lambeau	Green Bay Packers, Chicago Cardinals, Washington Redskins	33	226	132	22	.624	3	2	0	.600	229	134	22	.623
Chuck Noll	Pittsburgh Steelers	23	193	148	1	.566	16	8	0	.667	209	156	1	.572
Chuck Knox	Los Angeles Rams, Buffalo Bills, Seattle Seahawks	22	186	147	1	.558	7	11	0	.389	193	158	1	.550
Paul Brown	Cleveland Browns, Cincinnati Bengals	21	166	100	6	.621	4	8	0	.333	170	108	6	.609
Bud Grant	Minnesota Vikings	18	158	96	5	.620	10	12	0	.455	168	108	5	.607
Dan Reeves	Denver Broncos, New York Giants, Atlanta Falcons	17	148	115	1	.563	8	7	0	.533	156	122	1	.561
Marv Levy	Kansas City Chiefs, Buffalo Bills	17	143	102	0	.584	11	8	0	.579	154	120	0	.562
Steve Owen	New York Giants	23	151	100	17	.595	2	8	0	.200	153	108	17	.581
Marty Schottenheimer	Cleveland Browns, Kansas City Chiefs	14	138	76	1	.644	5	11	0	.313	143	87	1	.621
Joe Gibbs	Washington Redskins	12	124	60	0	.674	16	5	0	.762	140	65	0	.683
Hank Stram	Kansas City Chiefs, New Orleans Saints	17	131	97	10	.571	5	3	0	.625	136	100	10	.573
Weeb Ewbank	Baltimore Colts, New York Jets	20	130	129	7	.502	4	1	0	.800	134	130	7	.507
Bill Parcells	New York Giants, New England Patriots, New York Jets	13	118	88	1	.573	10	5	0	.667	128	93	1	.579
Sid Gillman	Los Angeles Rams, Los Angeles-San Diego Chargers, Houston Oilers	18	122	99	7	.550	1	5	0	.167	123	104	7	.541
George Allen	Los Angeles Rams, Washington Redskins	12	116	47	5	.705	2	7	0	.222	118	54	5	.681
Mike Ditka	Chicago Bears, New Orleans Saints	12	112	72	0	.609	6	6	0	.500	118	78	0	.602
Don Coryell	St. Louis Cardinals, San Diego Chargers	14	111	83	1	.572	3	6	0	.333	114	89	1	.561
John Madden	Oakland Raiders	10	103	32	7	.750	9	7	0	.563	112	39	7	.731
George Seifert	San Francisco 49ers	8	98	30	0	.766	10	5	0	.667	108	35	0	.755
Ray (Buddy) Parker	Chicago Cardinals, Detroit Lions, Pittsburgh Steelers	15	104	75	9	.577	3	1	0	.750	107	76	9	.581
Vince Lombardi	Green Bay Packers, Washington Redskins	10	96	34	6	.728	9	1	0	.900	105	35	6	.740
Tom Flores	Oakland-Los Angeles Raiders, Seattle Seahawks	12	97	87	0	.527	8	3	0	.727	105	90	0	.538
Bill Walsh	San Fransisco 49ers	10	92	59	1	.609	10	4	0	.714	102	63	1	.617

Active coaches in bold.

SUPER BOWL SUMMARIES

Super Bowl	Date	Winner (Share)	Loser (Share)	Score	Site	Attendance	MVP*
XXXII	1-25-98	Denver ($48,000)	Green Bay ($29,000)	31-24	San Diego	68,912	RB Terrell Davis, Denver
XXXI	1-26-97	Green Bay ($48,000)	New England ($29,000)	35-21	New Orleans	72,301	KR-PR Desmond Howard, Green Bay
XXX	1-28-96	Dallas ($42,000)	Pittsburgh ($27,000)	27-17	Tempe	76,347	CB Larry Brown, Dallas
XXIX	1-29-95	San Francisco ($42,000)	San Diego ($26,000)	49-26	Miami	74,107	QB Steve Young, San Francisco
XXVIII	1-30-94	Dallas ($38,000)	Buffalo ($23,500)	30-13	Atlanta	72,817	RB Emmitt Smith, Dallas
XXVII	1-31-93	Dallas ($36,000)	Buffalo ($18,000)	52-17	Pasadena	98,374	QB Troy Aikman, Dallas
XXVI	1-26-92	Washington ($36,000)	Buffalo ($18,000)	37-24	Minneapolis	63,130	QB Mark Rypien, Washington
XXV	1-27-91	NY Giants ($36,000)	Buffalo ($18,000)	20-19	Tampa	73,813	RB Ottis Anderson, NY Giants
XXIV	1-28-90	San Francisco ($36,000)	Denver ($18,000)	55-10	New Orleans	72,919	QB Joe Montana, San Francisco
XXIII	1-22-89	San Francisco ($36,000)	Cincinnati ($18,000)	20-16	Miami	75,129	WR Jerry Rice, San Francisco
XXII	1-31-88	Washington ($36,000)	Denver ($18,000)	42-10	San Diego	73,302	QB Doug Williams, Washington
XXI	1-25-87	NY Giants ($36,000)	Denver ($18,000)	39-20	Pasadena	101,063	QB Phil Simms, NY Giants
XX	1-26-86	Chicago ($36,000)	New England ($18,000)	46-10	New Orleans	73,818	DE Richard Dent, Chicago
XIX	1-20-85	San Francisco ($36,000)	Miami ($18,000)	38-16	Stanford	84,059	QB Joe Montana, San Francisco
XVIII	1-22-84	LA Raiders ($36,000)	Washington ($18,000)	38-9	Tampa	72,920	RB Marcus Allen, LA Raiders
XVII	1-30-83	Washington ($36,000)	Miami ($18,000)	27-17	Pasadena	103,667	RB John Riggins, Washington
XVI	1-24-82	San Francisco ($18,000)	Cincinnati ($9,000)	26-21	Pontiac	81,270	QB Joe Montana, San Francisco
XV	1-25-81	Oakland ($18,000)	Philadelphia ($9,000)	27-10	New Orleans	76,135	QB Jim Plunkett, Oakland
XIV	1-20-80	Pittsburgh ($18,000)	Los Angeles ($9,000)	31-19	Pasadena	103,985	QB Terry Bradshaw, Pittsburgh
XIII	1-21-79	Pittsburgh ($18,000)	Dallas ($9,000)	35-31	Miami	79,484	QB Terry Bradshaw, Pittsburgh
XII	1-15-78	Dallas ($18,000)	Denver ($9,000)	27-10	New Orleans	75,583	DT Randy White and DE Harvey Martin, Dallas
XI	1-9-77	Oakland ($15,000)	Minnesota ($7,500)	32-14	Pasadena	103,438	WR Fred Bletnikoff, Oakland
X	1-18-76	Pittsburgh ($15,000)	Dallas ($7,500)	21-17	Miami	80,187	WR Lynn Swann, Pittsburgh
IX	1-12-75	Pittsburgh ($15,000)	Minnesota ($7,500)	16-6	New Orleans	80,997	RB Franco Harris, Pittsburgh
VIII	1-13-74	Miami ($15,000)	Minnesota ($7,500)	24-7	Houston	71,882	RB Larry Csonka, Miami
VII	1-14-73	Miami ($15,000)	Washington ($7,500)	14-7	Los Angeles	90,182	S Jake Scott, Miami
VI	1-16-72	Dallas ($15,000)	Miami ($7,500)	24-3	New Orleans	81,023	QB Roger Staubach, Dallas
V	1-17-71	Baltimore ($15,000)	Dallas ($7,500)	16-13	Miami	79,204	LB Chuck Howley, Dallas
IV	1-11-70	Kansas City ($15,000)	Minnesota ($7,500)	23-7	New Orleans	80,562	QB Len Dawson, Kansas City
III	1-12-69	NY Jets ($15,000)	Baltimore ($7,500)	16-7	Miami	75,389	QB Joe Namath, NY Jets
II	1-14-68	Green Bay ($15,000)	Oakland ($7,500)	33-14	Miami	75,546	QB Bart Starr, Green Bay
I	1-15-67	Green Bay ($15,000)	Kansas City ($7,500)	35-10	Los Angeles	61,946	QB Bart Starr, Green Bay

*Award named Pete Rozelle Trophy since Super Bowl XXV.

Bibliography

Garber, Greg. *Football Legends*. New York: MetroBooks, 1993, 1995

Garber, Greg. *Great Quarterbacks: Football's Legendary Leaders*. New York: MetroBooks, 1995

Hubbard, Steve. *Great Running Backs: Football's Fearless Foot Soldiers*. New York: MetroBooks, 1996

Hubbard, Steve. *Shark Among Dolphins: Jimmy Johnson's Transformation of the Miami Dolphins*. New York: Ballantine Books, 1997

King, Peter. *Inside the Helmet*. New York: Simon & Schuster, 1993

Majewski, Stephen. *Great Linebackers: Football's Defensive Dynamos*. New York: MetroBooks, 1997

Peary, Danny, ed. *Super Bowl: The Game of Their Lives*. New York: Macmillan, 1997

Various. *75 Seasons: The Complete Story of the National Football League*. Atlanta: Turner Publishing Inc., 1994

Various. *The National Football League Record and Fact Book*. New York: NFL Publications, 1998

Various. *Total Football: The Official Encyclopedia of the National Football League*. New York: HarperCollins Publishers, 1997

Photography Credits

Agence France Presse-Corbis Bettmann: p. 147

Allsport: ©Simon Bruty: p. 40; ©Rick Stewart: pp. 42, 146; ©Jed Jacobsohn: p. 48; ©Stephen Dunn: pp. 52, 62, 93; ©Al Bello: p. 57; ©Otto Creule: pp. 64, 74; ©Andy Lyons: p. 69; ©Jonathan Daniel: p. 140; ©Clive Brunskill: p. 148

AP/Wide World Photos: pp. 8, 11, 15, 18, 20, 38, 49, 50, 51, 56, 59, 68, 73 top, 76, 80, 83, 84, 89, 90-91, 95, 97 right, 101, 119, 123, 124-125, 126-127, 131, 133, 134, 149, 151 bottom, 153, 155; (all side-bar backgrounds: pp. 16, 21, 22, 31, 51, 63, 64, 69, 93, 111, 116, 119, 131, 134, 140, 143, 148, 150, 151, 152)

Archive Photos: pp. 13, 28-29, 108; ©American Stock: p. 14; ©Tadder: p. 17; ©Reuters/Jeff Mitchell: p. 36; ©Reuters/Gary Caskey: p. 116; ©Reuters/WIN McNamee: p. 144

Reuters/Corbis-Bettmann: pp. 23, 30, 142

Sports Chrome East/West: pp. 2, 82, 85, 152; ©Rich Kane: pp. 22, 65, 111, 114, 115, both endpapers; ©Rob Tringali, Jr.: pp. 47, 112, 145, 150; ©Vincent Manniello: p. 61

Sports Photo Masters: p. 27; ©Jonathan Eric: pp. 6-7, 41, 67, 70; ©Mitchell B. Reibel: pp. 16, 19, 26, 44-45, 54, 75, 88, 94, 100, 106, 110, 120, 139, 143, 151 top left, 151 top right; ©Jeff Carlick: p. 24; ©Jonathan Kirn: pp. 33, 58; ©Al Kooistra: p. 34; ©Craig Melvin/PBI: p. 39

UPI/Corbis-Bettmann: pp. 9, 10, 12, 21, 25, 37, 53, 63, 71, 73 bottom, 79, 87, 96-97 left, 99, 102, 103, 104-105, 107, 113, 118, 121, 122, 128, 129, 130, 132 top, 132 bottom, 135, 137, 138, 141

Index